EVEN IF IT COSTS ME MY LIFE

Systemic Constellations and Serious Illness

By Stephan Hausner

English translation by Colleen Beaumont

Routledge
Taylor & Francis Group

LONDON AND NEW YORK

First published 2011 by GestaltPress

Published 2015 by Routledge

2 Park Square, Milton Park, Abingdon, Oxon OX14 4RN
711 Third Avenue, New York, NY 10017 USA

Routledge is an imprint of the Taylor & Francis Group, an informa business

Library of Congress Cataloging-in-Publishing Data
    1. Family Systems; 2. Constellations; 3. Systemic approaches
    to serious illness; 4. Transitional healing; 5. Gestalt therapy;
    6. Stephan Hausner

ISBN: 978-0-415-89805-8
Cover artist: Elena Siderova

ISBN: 978-1-315-78270-6 (eISBN)

My dedication is to my wife Birgit.
She made this book possible by taking over
most of the care of our home and our children
during the process of collecting and writing.

My dedication is also to our wonderful six children:
Simon, Janika, Sophia, Joanna, Leonie and Gabriel,
who had to let go of precious time
with their father.

ACKNOWLEDGEMENTS

My heart is full of joy that this book is now available for the English speaking world. I wish to thank all who contributed to this book. Special acknowledgement I feel for Colleen Beaumont, for her accurate and sensitive translation, Sheila Saunders and Deborah Ullman for their careful editing and final overview of the book. A special connection and gratitude I feel to Nancy and Gordon Wheeler. According to their intention/wish to connect the Gestalt and Constellation fields I also dedicate the book to the great number of Gestalt therapists all over the world, especially the ones who became my teachers, healers and friends. May the book fulfill its intention and bring benefit to all readers and their families.

Stephan Hausner, March 2011

TABLE OF CONTENTS

Foreword

FOR ENGLISH LANGUAGE EDITION
BY DEBORAH ULLMAN

This is a book about a fairly new form of therapeutic work, a methodology engaging a process called Family Systems Constellations. This Constellations work supports a view that there are two forces playing on us all the time. One is the force of love, generativity, healing; the other is the force for regression, attachment or loyalty to old, often distorted, imbalanced relationships of the past. Many of these latter forces were set in motion by unresolved woundings or traumas to generations before our own.

What you have before you is the work of a particularly gifted therapist and a naturopathically trained healer. You will find here experiences, stories that rival the best theater, life dramas, that will engage you not because of the craft of embellishment, but because they are deeply compelling and true experiences, shared by a master constellations practitioner. They represent ways people exploring new perspectives on long held trans-generational family situations feel something change and can begin the long journey of healing.

If you read carefully you might also learn something about how change happens -- how hearts and souls can be touched and in that moment, melt our bodies, so that we can allow something new in. Stephan Hausner presents this work, work he does mostly with patients who are ill or suffering from chronic symptoms of many sorts. These stories help us to see the degree to which many of these problems carry a component of multi-generational influences, or transpersonal properties, including unassimilated traumatic events and other woundings, often unacknowledged in family histories – the family secrets whose effects play out in the emotional life of the family even while no one speaks of them. These effects last even for generations into the future.

Gestalt therapists know all this as ground – the ground of our experience that was, in part, developmentally imprinted at the earliest ages, affected by the attachments we established or failed to. Family Systems Constellation work when offered as an experimental inquiry into this ground, and as practiced by a growing number of second generation practitioners, concerns itself with the web of relationships, the context or field out of which we each emerge. As an approach to intervention strategies, this may be one perfect complement to Gestalt therapy which, in turn, is an integration of the field relational and embodied focus of much of today's psychotherapy as well as human science research. For a much deeper look at these two therapeutic practices, relational Gestalt and Family Systems Constellations, and how they have evolved, indeed how humans have evolved right up to our current world moment, the reader is referred to Gordon Wheeler's orienting insights in the Afterword: Constellations and Gestalt: a Closer Look for Gestalt Readers (although equally interesting for Family Systems practitioners who are not Gestalt trained).

In the introduction to this first English language edition of Even If It Costs Me My Life (already published in German, Spanish, Portuguese, Dutch and Russian) Stephan Hausner dedicates the project to the healing potential of family constellations work. We learn by opening the book anywhere and beginning to read that this is an approach for exploring places where people get stuck in their lives, often with physical symptoms, unable to shake loose or get disentangled from what is happening, or what has come before, in their family of origin. For the people he works with, the symptoms often seem to follow an embodied creative adjustment to some relational family dynamic out of awareness. Dynamics have become confused, distorted, and what is needed, what Stephan demonstrates over and over in these cases, is a shift in understanding that allows for love to flow easily and sometimes restoratively.

This work describes what all psychotherapy is about: a way to establish a relationship with clients/patients, a space wherein healing can happen. This involves the patient feeling well enough felt and seen by the therapist to be able to open to some new understanding that allows change we call healing to begin. What so much of complimentary and alternative medicine addresses today is ways we can explore our own increased capacity to find wellness and heal more deeply into ourselves in response to conditions that plague us when we can find the support that makes this possible. And, of course, we no longer think usefully about issues of the mind, without considering the body. Nor do many of us consider our bodies without reflection on the emotional fuel we feed our bodies with. The research being done in neurobiology, integrative medicine, and psychoneuroimmunology, to name only a few relevant disciplines, affirm the many ways we are ingesting emotional messages, perhaps prenatally, certainly from way before we become verbal. We then make whole cloth sense out of these messages. This whole picture we carry in our mind/bodies affects our individual neuronal development, inflecting our disposition and embodied way in the world. How all this informs our intentional behavior and interacts with the life of our bodies, our health, is the subject of wide arenas of research today. One familiar and mainstream example which has been studied only over the last several decades, is the effects of stress on our immune systems.

As a director of this Gestalt publishing house and in the course of readying Stephan Hausner's book for publication by GestaltPress, I experienced it as a framework for self-help. Even as a professional reader I was regularly thrown into deep reflection and reconsideration of long held stories of my own, the ways I've made sense of the saga of my life in order to manage my life. The different possible narratives collected here invited me to reflect more deeply, feel my own sense-making of experiences in a different, more responsible, way. But importantly not as an intellectual exercise. The experience involved feeling into, who I am, how I may have longed for more from my mother than she could ever give, for example. Or how I might have left significant others out of my sense of family connectivity, others such as unborn children. The experience of these reconsiderations was to find and feel some ungrieved losses that help me make better sense of my life story so far, and possibly claim a more active role in how it unfolds from here on.

The aim of this collection of case studies, people's experiences in family constellations groups, Stephan tells us, is to provide a picture of the healing potential of systems constellations with those who are ill. Stephan brings to life profound and sensitive work done with specific patients in constellation groups with his gentle, yet incisive, often moving depictions of the visual and spatial representations of family dynamics at play. The work invites reflection on the strong support this work can be in every clinical or hospital setting where it would supplement medical interventions evoking more successful outcomes in so many instances.

This book can be read several ways: by looking through the Table of Contents and dipping into the conditions or case studies which stir your curiosity. Or you could read it from the beginning – I can warn you that I found it difficult to put down! Finally you could read this book from back to front. The project is a reaching out across the communities of Gestalt practitioners and Family Systems Constellators. For more exploration of the underlying premises of each of these therapeutic traditions, what they share theoretically, you will find a deeply orienting piece from the Gestalt community's (and Gestalt-Press's own) importantly prescient and integrative thinker/ writer, Gordon Wheeler. This, in that Afterword entitled Constellations and Gestalt: a Closer Look for Gestalt Readers.

Also at the end of the book you will find an Appendix that includes a reading list developed by Stephan Hausner for people interested in pursuing further study of Family Systems and Constellation work. Many of these titles are in German for use by the bi-lingual readers among us. There is also a piece here that emerged from a conversation recorded one afternoon in March, 2010, at Esalen Institute, only yards from the beautiful cliff head views of the Pacific ocean. This followed a week long workshop with Judith Hemming on family constellations and an open forum evening session with Stephan. These two experienced and masterful practitioners relaxed for a free-wheeling discussion of the work with Gordon Wheeler, Nancy Lunney Wheeler, and myself. From this, those of you who have not yet experienced the serious value of Stephan's work, or the warmth and easy personability he brings to it, will get a glimpse of the man and how he thinks about the work. Now, I am excited to share this serious, startling and important work with English language readers for the very first time!

Right now, right this minute, there are two forces at work on the human family. There are people being wounded. Think war zones and natural disasters. Think deprivation and desperation that lead to violence. Also think of refugees, or migrating people looking for work, tearing families and communities apart. Then there are deep and angry ways we all sometimes act against each other. We might also think of how, at times, we neglect our loved ones out of our own fears, and misunderstandings, lack of resources or failures to communicate.

At the same time there is the force of love, sometimes revealed in people's healing. Think of the love that grows in a lifelong friendship. The love that takes root between two people and results in a new family, a new baby being born and a child being raised. Love is also taught in the books and stories of spiritual leaders, defenders of peace and justice in the world, and by good teachers and writers of every domain ... and there is certainly love communicated through music, poetry, and the visual arts. There is also the love that constitutes the healing work of great practitioners, therapists, medical and holistic healers. Conscious healers in every tradition know there is some mystery in how healing happens, and the caring of the practitioner for the patient and vice versa does seem to play a part. Read closely and you may find this book to be a meditation on that mystery!

Deborah Ullman, Orleans, MA, USA, March, 2011

INTRODUCTION

'The most worthy basis of medicine is love.'
-Paracelsus

Family constellation work has broadened and developed in many different fields as a method of counselling and therapy. In addition to constellations in organizations and schools, applying this approach to working with illness and disease has expanded the potential for healing effects also in the field of medicine. A view of trans-generational entanglements and family dynamics casts a new light on health and disease and the insights gained from constellations with illness and health problems have led to a more holistic view of those who are ill.

A couple, both internists in a clinic, took part in a constellation group for ill patients and remarked afterwards: 'it is impressive how clearly systemic constellations bring to light the trans-generational connections of disease and traumatic events in the patient's family of origin. This suggests a not insignificant potential for medical intervention and it seems that there has clearly been too little attention paid to the question of these connections in the context of medical care.'

This book is dedicated to the healing potential of family constellation work. It is directed towards everyone in the medical field, including physicians, psychotherapists, alternative medical practitioners, and constellation facilitators, but also speaks to patients and interested readers with no previous knowledge of the topic. For those with no experience or knowledge of constellation work, there is a brief introduction of the basics of this method in chapter one. Anyone who wishes to pursue an interest in the field of family constellations or other forms of systemic constellation work is referred to the reading list for basic literature on the topic.

This book has grown out of my own experiences and thoughts. The case examples included were chosen from my practice as an alternative medical practitioner and over 15 years of leading constellation groups for people suffering from ill health. Rather than using the common forms of 'the therapist' or 'the author', I have opted for the first person singular, 'I'. In choosing to speak directly, I wish to emphasize that my way of proceeding in systemic constellations is only one of many possible approaches, and asserts no claim to being the 'right way' in any broader sense. Patients are referred to in each case as 'the patient' to protect their anonymity.

The aim of this book is to provide a picture of the healing potential of systemic constellations with those who are ill. The application of constellation work is new in the medical field, so there are aspects of the approach yet to be discovered and developed, for example, the specific applications of this work in hospital care.

My intention is to allow the case examples in the main part of the book to speak for themselves. Like observers in a constellation group, readers are meant to participate in the history and process of the constellations with the patients and, entering into the reciprocal effects of family dynamics and illness in this way, experience or have contact with a posture that may support a healing effect in their own lives. From this perspective, the book also offers a possible framework for self-help.

In addition, the patients were asked to speak for themselves. When they provided feedback on their own accord, I have encouraged them to write something of their experience and impressions including when and if they felt their constellation work had been helpful. I have included some of these testimonies and feedback. Any discrepancies between my version of the constellation and the description provided by the patient are products of different perceptions, memories, or interpretations of the process or effects.

In some of the case illustrations, instead of saying 'the father's representative' or the mother's representative', I have simply called them 'the father' or 'the mother'. When a representative is replaced by a different person or by the client, this is specifically mentioned.

At this point, I would like to add a personal word about my professional career path. My original intention was to become a biologist in the area of behavioral research or environmental protection. Eventually, however, my interest was more drawn to people and social environments and I considered a course of study in the medical field. While training in nursing care, I decided to become a physician. Conventional medicine, however, was less attractive to me because I had already been immersed in the context of environmental studies, and was focused on issues of self-regulation in systems. Looking for a more ecological approach, I found my way to traditional Chinese medicine and, while learning about natural healing methods, I was eventually led to homeopathy.

In the field of homeopathy, I became fascinated by the fundamental principle of similarities and, importantly, the phenomenon of spontaneous healing.

This maintains that, given an appropriate healing impulse, the body is capable of re-structuring itself instantly and even severe symptoms and conditions may reverse within a very short period of time. The awareness of the potential for spontaneous remission has greatly influenced my dedication to healing work. Knowing that any healing process is enigmatic and multifaceted, I continue to seek out and optimize effective, holistic treatment methods.

One aspect of homeopathy that I personally found difficult, is the matching of a patient's symptoms to a particular remedy via the homeopathic repertory, and ultimately the dependence on remedies themselves. I am grateful to my father-in-law, K.J. Eick, for introducing me to radiaesthesia. In his practice I learned to test homeopathic remedies for patients, but was also introduced to methods of identifying zones of disturbance in the body. This way of sensing into a situation remains one of my basic tools in constellation work. While learning methods of testing, I began to understand the healing process as a phenomenon of resonance and the field.

I increasingly came to view the doctor or person administering treatment as the substance of the remedy, in the homeopathic sense, stimulating change in the patient through his or her presence. From this perspective, the physician or practitioner becomes the catalyst for change. The doctor does not heal; he or she creates conditions in which self-healing can occur.

At some point, my continuing search for effective methods of treatment led me to a constellation group with Bert Hellinger. Watching Hellinger work with ill people, I saw someone who was able to bring about a healing quality in patients through his presence, insights and interventions, without recourse to medical substances. I had the feeling that I had found what I was looking for.

I was familiar with a connection between health and 'order' from my studies of traditional Chinese medicine and the concept of humeral pathology of ancient Greece, in which illness was seen as a disturbance of order. Bert Hellinger's insights into the orders of love in human systems, as well as their possible significance in a medical context, made sense to me. Observing his use of the constellation approach with ill people, it became unmistakeably clear that one cannot practice holistic medicine without including the family or the patient's relevant social context.

Today, constellation work with illness has become the main focus of my ongoing work. This approach does not stand as an isolated technique but rather, offers one building block in a holistic treatment or therapeutic concept. A constellation facilitator assists the doctor or alternative practitioner and the intention is not to replace their treatment or counselling. Nonetheless, when prescribed treatment methods fail to bring about the desired or expected result, a look at the familial, trans-generational context of illness may open up additional options.

Bert Hellinger provided the foundation of constellation work with illness and, therefore, also the background for this book. Without his faithful support, I would never have dared apply the insights from family constellations directly in my practical work with patients and I feel deep gratitude towards him.

The many patients who have placed their trust in me and my work have contributed a major part of this book. I have felt privileged to share in their lives and in their medical crises. I have learned much from them, and feel deeply connected to all of them.

Amongst my many friends and colleagues, a special thanks is due Dr. Gunthard Weber. Without his support, this book would never have become what it is. Throughout this process, our stimulating exchanges have coordinated, as fully as possible, the thought models of traditional medicine and those of natural healing. This has contributed in a special way to the development of the book.

Other writings on constellation work with illness and symptoms have also been enriching. I ask the reader to make allowances for the fact that I have not always mentioned each of these individually in the text, and I refer you to the reading list at the end of the book.

This book would not have been possible without the faith of countless international colleagues and the often selfless efforts of their translators. Almost all of the case studies included in the book come from their therapy and training seminars, all painstakingly organized and performed. Today, I feel a deep connection through these friendships. Special thanks go to Carlos Bernues, Tiiu Bolzmann, Annelies Boutellier, Michail Burnjaschew, Luisfer Camarra, Carola Castillo, Vicente Cuevas, Mireia Darder, Joan Garriga, Silvia Kabelka, Sonja Kriener, Ed Lynch, Alfonso Malpica and Angelica Olvera, Tanja Meyburgh, Silvia Miclavez, Ingala Robl, Sheila Saunders, Dale Schusterman, Jan Jacob Stam and Bibi Schroeder, John and Susan Ulfelder.

My thanks also to Margit and Dr. Michael Franz, who accompanied this project from the beginning, and to Wolfgang Tatzer who was always available for questions and assisted with the translations of foreign language transcripts.

1

CONTEXT AND GUIDING PRINCIPLES

'Become who you are.'
–F.W.J. v. Schelling

In psychotherapy, it has long been recognized that personal, traumatic experiences can lead to long-term physical and mental disturbances, particularly if they are repressed or closed-off as current demands become more pressing. If those aspects that have been pushed out of awareness can be successfully reintegrated and accepted, many difficulties can be overcome. Family constellation work has delved further into this process and proposes that trauma from previous generations also continues to have effects on the lives of descendents in subsequent generations.

Bert Hellinger opened the way for new developments in family constellations with his insights into the workings and influence of conscience and the question of what entangles one person in the fate of another, within the family and beyond. His continuing observations have also been successful in finding and refining ways of resolving such entanglements.

A BRIEF INTRODUCTION TO THE BASICS OF FAMILY CONSTELLATIONS

Every human being is born into a family and shares a bond with everyone who belongs to that family. Overseeing the conditions and terms operative within the family there is an unconscious authority, which Bert Hellinger calls the 'family conscience'. We are subject to these conditions, whether we choose them or not. The family conscience attends to bonds within the system, the balance of giving and taking, the fate of the family members, and the 'orders' of the family system.

One of these family orders decrees that everyone who belongs to this family system has a right to belong, including those who have died. If one member is excluded, scorned or forgotten – for example, a stillborn child – the collective conscience will ensure that someone else, usually in a later generation, will unconsciously identify with the excluded family member. In such an 'entanglement', the later person may take on similarities to the earlier family member and mirror aspects of that person's fate, without understanding the reason why and with no way to defend against it.

Another order watched over by the collective family conscience involves ranking according to time. Parents have priority over children; a firstborn has priority over the next child, and so on. In the case of sequential families, the newest family takes priority over earlier families. That is, the current family takes precedence over the family of origin, and the formation of a newer family supersedes a previous alliance, even if the new system is established with the birth of a child from an extra-marital relationship. In contrast to our conscious, personal conscience, which informs us directly whether our actions endanger our belonging, this unconscious, collective conscience looks after the internal cohesion and perpetuation of the entire family.

In the core section of this book, actual case examples illustrate the ways in which many illnesses and symptoms may result from our yearning to be close to our parents, or our need to belong to our family. We often see an unconscious need for balance engendering feelings of guilt, or perpetuating some supposed demand. When certain actions or attitudes are disrupting one of these fundamental orders, illness may call a halt to the process.

THE FAMILY AS A COMMUNITY OF FATE

By inquiring into possible family entanglements between individual family members, our work with systemic constellations has revealed a broader context, one that extends to everyone affected by the collective group conscience of the family. Within this framework, all the children in the family belong to the system; that is, ourselves and all our brothers, sisters, and half-siblings – including stillborn children, children given up for adoption or care, and any who were aborted. Our parents and all their siblings also belong, as well as our grandparents, and sometimes even their siblings (particularly if they have had some special, distinguishing fate). Occasionally, even our great-grandparents are included in the systemic group.

Besides blood relatives, the system encompasses all those who have had a significant effect on the family, positive or negative, through their fate or death. For example, one of our parents or grandparents may have had a previous partner who vacated a place, leaving an opening for the new partner, or one who was forced to relinquish his or her place. In this larger sense, victims of violent acts perpetrated by a family member also belong to the family group. A special connection exists between victims and perpetrators so that, in a family in which a member has been the victim of violent crime, the one who did this act also remains a part of the system. All of these people comprise the family's 'community of fate'.

PROCEDURE

Family constellations are the method of choice for revealing trans-generational influences of the unconscious, collective conscience. This is most effective when constellations can be done in a group that extends over several days. In this setting, all participants have the chance to choose representatives for themselves and for the members of their families. These representatives are chosen and placed by the patient according to an inner image of how the actual family members stand in relation to each other. They are set up in a spatial configuration within an area designated as the group working space. One astonishing phenomenon, which has yet to be fully explained, is that when representatives are placed and feel centered, they have a sense of the movements and feelings of the actual persons they are representing. They reflect the feelings of that person and sometimes even develop physical symptoms that mirror those of the actual person. This phenomenon occurs regardless of whether the person being represented is alive or deceased. Based on the representatives' position in relation to one another, their feelings and awareness, what they report, and the impulses they experience, the constellation facilitator and patient can identify which events in the family history seem relevant, and what dynamics in this family could possibly connect to the patient's illness and symptoms.

A group is not the ideal setting for every patient, however. Especially in cases of mental fragility, this issue should be discussed with the patient's doctor or therapist. It is also possible to achieve good results in an individual setting by using small figures or floor markers in the constellation. I will not discuss these techniques in detail in this book. (See Franke (2002), Madelung (2004))

CONSTELLATIONS OF SYMPTOMS AND ILLNESS

In constellation work with those who are ill, it is often helpful to set up someone to represent the patient's illness or symptoms. To maintain a holistic approach and to try to avoid symptom displacement, I, personally, rarely use a representative for an isolated, single symptom.

We have observed that a representative for an abstract structure, such as illness or a symptom cluster, generally stands in resonance with an excluded family member or relevant family issue, often one that is taboo.

At times it appears as though the symptoms reflect the ill person's attempt to preserve the memory of an excluded family member. The patient is still connected in love, whereas other members of the family are holding back or denying the person love and recognition. Setting up the illness or symptoms in relationship to the patient or his or her family often serves to reveal these connections, which usually exist at an unconscious level.

As the patient describes an issue, it becomes apparent what his or her attitude is towards this health problem. It is also a reading on the person's readiness to face the situation and any underlying factors that may be uncovered. If I notice major resistance, or a general attitude of discounting or hostility towards the illness, I usually start the constellation with just two representatives. We set up a representative for the disease or symptoms and a representative for the patient, and allow the representatives to follow their own inner sense of movement. Representatives for family members are usually brought in a later step.

Another option is to begin with representatives for the patient's current family, or family of origin, and add a representative for the illness at a later point.

Clues about what might resolve the problematic dynamics usually come from those representatives who react most strongly to the representative of the illness. Before a patient chooses a representative of the disease, I ask him or her to decide if the person should be a man or a woman. The patient is then obliged to sense into his or her inner feeling about which choice seems right, and may be less influenced by the external appearance of group participants. Often, the choice of man or woman reflects the gender of an excluded person, but the therapist should not rely on this.

THE MISCARRIAGE:
'Dear Mummy, I have what is most important.'
(Patient with breast cancer)

This case involves a woman with cancer in a group organized for systemic constellations around health issues. In presenting her situation, the woman says that her doctor has prognosticated good chances for her recovery, and she also feels convinced that, 'I'm going to make it!'

As this woman says 'I'm going to make it' with such conviction, I am reminded of another constellation concerning a patient with breast cancer. That patient's representative faced the representative of the disease as if she were gearing up for battle. The person representing the cancer said to her, 'have you actually got any idea how dangerous I am?'

In many cancer patients we see an attitude of superiority towards their parents, the fate of some family member, or towards life in general. This attitude is sometimes exhibited in the form of anger or hate but also there is often some illusion that one can protect another person from a difficult fate through one's own suffering.

In this situation, without any further information, I ask the woman to choose a representative for herself and another person for her illness. She chooses two women and places the disease representative closely behind her own representative, with both looking the same direction. To the patient's great astonishment, her representative immediately feels a need to fall backwards and lean against the representative of the cancer. As she does so, she closes her eyes in contentment. The representative of the disease holds her firmly and says: 'As far as I'm concerned, this is fine. If she needs me, I'm here.'

It looks suspiciously like the representative of the illness has something to do with the patient's mother. When I ask the woman about her connection to her mother, she reports that they have always had a difficult relationship. 'In the meantime, we have come to terms with it, but I was my parents' first child and I was supposed to be a boy. My birth was a difficult one, with forceps and ventouse, a vacuum extraction device. Then, I turned out to be a girl! My mother had equipped everything in baby blue, as they used to do in those days. According to my aunt, my mother cried for three days after my birth.'

The patient's answer presents a stark contrast to the caring attitude of the cancer's representative in the constellation. It is clear that, in the constellation, this woman is quite prepared to be there for the patient, but for some reason, in real life, her mother is seemingly not free to really accept her daughter. The discrepancy suggests that something critical is missing.

I ask the patient to add a representative for her mother. She places the new representative at a distance, looking towards the other two. This does not seem to have any significant effect on the two original representatives. The mother's representative, however, experiences a strong physical reaction. It is difficult for her to look at her daughter and her daughter's illness, and she reports: 'I can see my daughter, but as soon as I try to look at this illness, everything gets very blurry and I can't see anything clearly.' The patient's earlier comment about her mother's fixation on a boy, and this reaction from the mother's representative lead me to ask if her mother might have lost a child at some time. She replies, 'yes, before I was born, my mother had a miscarriage and that baby was a boy. I don't think she ever got over the loss.'

When the patient mentions her brother, the patient's representative feels a strong urge to move away from the representative of the disease, and turns to look that woman in the eye. She looks like someone who has just wondrously awakened and is suddenly participating actively in the events of the moment.

The mother's representative cannot bear to watch her daughter looking at the illness representative. She turns away and stares vacantly at the floor in front of her.

Indicating the representative of the cancer, I turn to the patient and ask, 'do you know who's standing there?'

Patient: My mother?

Therapist: I think that could be your brother.

To test out this hypothesis, I ask a man in the group to represent the deceased brother and lie down in front of the mother's representative. The mother looks at her son and begins to weep. At this moment, the patient's representative turns away from the illness and looks at her mother with love and understanding. The representative of the illness, following her own impulse, withdraws from the constellation. She walks out of the circle and returns to her place as an observer.

Finally, I address the patient directly and ask her to speak to her mother. Freely, and with an open heart, she repeats after me: 'Dear Mummy, I consent. I have what is most important and I accept it. I take this, and I will preserve and protect it in me and honor it by taking good care of myself.'

The mother's representative has continued to look at her dead son, but now turns to the patient, her daughter, and takes her in her arms. I suggest some sentences, which she emphatically repeats to her daughter: 'My dear child, live! What is here belongs to me.'

In the final group round, the patient reports how good the constellation was for her. Especially important to her was her mother's statement that she should live, and she feels enormously relieved in response to that sentence. She can see that she has never been absolutely certain whether her mother really wanted her to live. She can also identify what was standing between her and her mother, which actually has nothing to do with her.

There are very few patients who are unable to see a connection between their illness and their family, or their own participation in their illness. This kind of recognition allows the patient to draw clues and guidelines from the constellation.

In the example above, it was unclear at the end exactly whom the illness was representing, but that was not really important in terms of the main issue. Perhaps, in her soul, it has something to do with her brother as well as her mother. The most essential factor was the feeling on the part of the representative of the illness that she was no longer needed. This feeling arose when the deceased brother entered the constellation. He was a key figure, one that allowed the patient's representative to let go of the illness. The patient's mother was clearly unable to overcome the death of her son and thus, was bound and not free to let her love for her daughter flow freely. The relationship between the mother and daughter was strained from the very beginning.

When there is a difficult relationship with parents, children usually look for the causes in themselves. Unable to overcome the obstacles in their path, they are often left to withdraw in despair and anger. Frequently, such children later feel a lack of respect for their parents.

Such disruptions disturb the sense of balance in the soul and, as a consequence, also physical well-being.

Looking at this mother's suffering for her lost child allowed love and respect to flow again. This movement helps the soul to calm, and the resulting peace may have a healing effect on the body.

Each constellation requires decisions about which persons or structural elements should be included and positioned. Those decisions determine the process and the conclusions of every constellation. One difficulty I have confronted in the constellation method is that basically anything can be set up, and a process will emerge that is usually moving. Nonetheless, the core issue, particularly from a medical point of view, is whether or not the constellation actually helps. Where is the juncture where the patient might be able to change something – a perspective, an attitude, a position – so that something in the person's soul and body can make adjustments, flow, or find a sense of peace?

The first contact with the patient and the clarification of the issue are essential factors in constellation work. During this first exchange, I am not attending just to the words that are spoken. While listening as a therapist I am already entering into the situation as a kind of representative of the people and structures mentioned by the patient. I use my inner sense to try to grasp the feelings or qualities present. Often, I sense a discrepancy between what the patient says about a relationship and my empathetic sense of the other person involved. In this way, there may be valuable therapeutic clues about background conflicts that could be contributing to the patient's symptoms (see case example: Early Death of a Parent: 'I am your daughter.' (p. Page reference).

CONSTELLATIONS INCLUDING A DISEASED ORGAN

When someone is suffering from a disease involving an organ of the body, it sometimes feels intuitively as if this organ is not properly embedded in the whole body system. The concept of treatment in alternative medicine, however, demands inclusion to ensure the health and wellbeing of the organs. If I get an especially strong impression of a split between the affected organ and the whole organism, I use the constellation to first look at this interrupted connection. I ask the patient to first choose their own representative and a representative of the diseased organ and set the two up in a constellation. The following is an example of such a constellation.

A MOTHER'S GRIEF
(a patient with recurring respiratory illness)

In a group focussed on physical ailments, a man asks me to work with him because he has suffered from respiratory weakness, ever since he was a child. Frequent bouts of pneumonia have led to chronic respiratory difficulties that have proved resistant to treatment. This information is sufficient to begin with, and I take a few moments to feel into my sense of this man. What I sense in him is a deep, underlying feeling of sadness.

In Traditional Chinese Medicine, the emotion of grief is related to the lung orbit. This means that an overwhelmingly strong or unbearable grief possibly leads to a disturbance in the energetic flow of the lung orbit, which may lead to respiratory difficulties. This can happen even when the grief belongs to another person's experience — someone very close to the patient. In this case, I suspect there is some connection between the patient's complaints and this sense I have of an underlying feeling of sadness. When I allow myself to identify with the patient's breathing and his relationship to his lungs, I cannot sense any connection at all. It feels as if his lungs are shut off from the rest of him.

I ask the patient to choose a representative for himself and one for his lungs. He places his own representative in the middle of the circle. He then chooses a woman to represent his lungs and positions her behind his own representative, at his right shoulder, turned towards him. Without being asked to do so, the representative of the lungs lays her head on the shoulder of the patient's representative. This is clearly an unpleasant experience for him and he takes a cautious step forward. The lung representative keeps her eyes closed and continues to lean against the patient's representative. She shifts her weight forward so that the man cannot continue moving away. As I turn to the patient, I see that he is crying and I say to him: 'It looks as if this picture is familiar to you.' He nods and points to the woman representing his lungs. 'That is my mother. That is how I experience my mother.'

Finally, the oppressive weight proves too much for the patient's representative and he frees himself by taking two steps forward. The lung representative (or the patient's mother) opens her eyes. She remains bent over forwards and looks searchingly at the floor in front of her.

I ask the patient if anyone in his mother's family died prematurely, and he reports that his mother had five miscarriages before he was born. When the mother's representative hears this, she begins to cry and kneels down on the floor.

The patient takes a deep breath and looks knowingly at me in agreement. His breathing has changed during this process, and his chest feels more alive and free. I decide to leave it at this point and I ask him if that is okay with him. With his affirmation, I release the representatives from their roles.

The constellation depicts for the patient a connection between his physical complaints and a familiar theme in his life – his mother's grief and pain. If his symptoms should reappear, he can regard them in a different context and with a different understanding of the connections. This offers him the opportunity to make changes and find a corrective.

In constellations, it is always moving to experience children's selflessness and persistence in carrying the fate or suffering of their parents or significant others.

CONTEXT OF THE WORK AND GUIDING PRINCIPLES

'The appropriate moment determines the quality of the movement.'
–Lao Tzu

In attempting to understand the essential nature of illness, health, and the phenomenon of healing, I have gradually come to the conviction that wherever healing occurs, it is actually self-healing. In this view of healing, we are then faced with the question of how best to accompany and contribute to relief and healing when someone is seeking our help. This may mean creating conditions that optimally support the powers of self-healing. In addition to appropriate medical care for the patient, I have found the work with systemic constellations, especially in groups, to be a helpful and effective complementary tool.

Ever since I began using constellations as part of my healing practice, I have been looking at the questions of efficiency and effectiveness of this method. A healing process can be activated through participation in a constellation group, even in cases of long-standing illness, and even if the patient has not done a constellation of his or her own. When this occurs, what exactly is it that has helped? In addition to the posture of non-intention and a phenomenological perspective, which are integral to the method, are there also other criteria for constellation work that support patients in the process of healing?

In his book Love's Own Truth (2001, p. 2), Bert Hellinger titles one section, The Scientific and Phenomenological Paths of Discovery.

There are two inner movements that lead to insight. One reaches out, wanting to understand and to control what is unknown. This is scientific inquiry. We know how profoundly it has transformed and enriched our lives and enhanced our well-being.

The second movement happens when we pause in our efforts to grasp the unknown, allowing our attention to rest, not on the particulars, which we can define, but on the greater whole. Here, our view is wide, open to receive the infinite complexity around us. When we affirm this inner movement, for example, when presented with a landscape, task, or problem, then we notice how our mind's eye is simultaneously enriched and emptied. We can tolerate such richness only when we restrain our interest in individual things. We pause in the movement of reaching out, pull back a bit, until we arrive at the inner stillness that is competent to deal with the vastness and complexity of the greater whole. This inquiry, with an orientation towards inwardness and restraint, I call phenomenological. It leads to different insights than the inquiry that actively reaches out. Still, the two movements complement one another. Even in an actively reaching out, scientific inquiry, we occasionally need to shift our attention from the narrow to the broad and from what is close at hand to the larger context. And similarly, insights gained by phenomenological inquiry must be tested in their specifics.

CONTEXT AND POSTURE

It is important to create a protective framework for constellation work in a group. This demands personal experience and, especially, a non-judgmental posture on the part of the group leader – one that attends equally to every participant and each individual fate. The less judgement and interpretation there is from other group participants about what emerges in constellations, and the safer the patient feels, the easier it will be for him or her to stay open to dynamics that may be relevant to the illness.

A constellation leader needs to keep in mind that people normally have conflicting feelings about illness. On the one hand, the person is eager to be rid of this constraining, perhaps even life-threatening, illness. On the other hand, we can see that illness may be the person's best efforts to manage the circumstances presented by life.

Rather than looking at illness as a problem, a constellation leader remains closer to the perspective of alternative healing practices; each illness is serving a function and represents an attempt to find resolution. From this orientation, the leader focuses on the underlying dynamics and forces that have led to the illness, and the patient gains the trust that is needed to allow these influences to find resolution in the constellation process.

GUIDING PRINCIPLES

In constellation work with health issues, we have observed that there are certain aspects that seem to interact in shaping and intensifying each other:

- ▸ a person's readiness to say yes to life and to assume the consequent responsibilities
- ▸ children's core love for their parents and their longing for closeness with them
- ▸ the patients' or families' exclusion of persons and/or issues relevant to the system.

'Yes' to Life or 'No'

'Health is not a matter of how you feel but rather of being present.'
–Hans-Georg Gadamer

Traumatic experiences and events in a family generate anxiety in the family members, extending even across generations, separating children from their parents and later generations from previous ones. Nonetheless, those things that are experienced as difficult and burdensome often harbor a very special, deep strength.

The following example of a constellation illustrates the unavoidable ties in a family's history. Our family history belongs to us and is part of us. It influences our personality, strengthening or weakening us.

The Burden

A man in a constellation course describes his issue as, 'I want to get rid of my family's burden'. Without asking any more about what has happened in his family, I ask him to choose two representatives, one to represent him and one to represent this burden. He places the two a distance from each other, but his representative turns his back on the 'burden'. Although the patient's representative seems unusually restless, the representative of the burden remains standing quietly and firmly in place. His expression is friendly as he observes with interest the other representative's attempts to escape. The patient's representative looks increasingly desperate in his inability to get away from the burden and, finally, he tries to hide in the far corner of the room. The 'burden' calmly watches and waits. When asked about what he is feeling, he says, 'I am here and I have all the time in the world'. When the patient's representative hears this statement, his distress flares up anew. He stands up slowly and, without looking around, begins to move backwards. He moves step by step, as if drawn by an invisible force behind him. He is actually moving directly towards the representative of the burden and finally ends up leaning back against the other. The 'burden' lays his hands gently on the man's shoulders, and the patient's representative begins to weep quietly. After a while, he looks back over his shoulder into the eyes of the 'burden', nods in understanding, and the two men embrace. To complete the constellation I suggest that the patient's representative say: 'Yes, I take it (life), even at this price!'

This 'yes' to taking life, just as it comes through one's parents and ancestors, is a difficult movement for many of us. It requires that we agree to our parents, just as they were and are, as well as to the history of whatever family we were born into. Completing this movement does not depend on contact, nor does it have to do with the quality of one's relationship to parents or grandparents. It is a movement that is accessible even to those who do not know their parents or families. It also, per se, signifies agreeing to oneself, to one's personal fate and the circumstances of one's life, including illness, whether acute or chronic, or even life-long.

Experience has shown that the first step towards resolving a problem or healing a disease is often the step of taking over one's own share of responsibility. Based on my observations, I would say that the strength for this movement is connected to a readiness to agree to one's parents and family of origin. This 'yes' to parents and family is equivalent to saying yes to life. As a therapist, I regard this as a prerequisite for constellation work. In my experience with constellation work with the ill, particularly in hospitals, if a patient is not prepared to say 'yes' to his or her actual situation, then that person is often not ready or able to take in whatever may be revealed as a resolving movement in a constellation. In such cases, I first work with the patient's ability and readiness to say 'yes'.

Sometimes, I do an exercise in which I place representatives for the person's parents facing the patient, who is seated next to me: first the father, than on his left, the mother. I put them at a distance based on how much closeness the patient can comfortably tolerate, but near enough that he or she cannot avoid their look. If necessary, I also add the grandparents behind the parents, and sometimes even the great-grandparents.

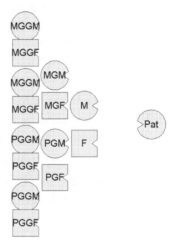

You can feel when the configuration of previous generations is complete or when there is still someone missing. After setting up the representatives, I wait patiently until the patient can really look at his or her lineage. If the person seems resistant to looking, I ask the group of representatives to move in closer, step-by-step, in accordance with what the patient is able to stand. Sooner or later, the patient looks at these ancestors and truly has to look into their eyes, it is then clear that a 'no' to family is impossible to sustain, and there is no choice about this connection to one's origins. Such a confrontation often allows a healing, reaching-out movement towards the parents. In agreeing to this family and their history, the patient finds a 'yes' to his or her own life and fate. The sense of connection to family and ancestors gives us the strength to look at what is difficult and, consequently, also to face illness.

The following constellation involves a woman suffering from an autoimmune disease, and shows how a rejection of parents may indicate unconscious self-rejection.

PREMATURE DEATH OF PARENTS: 'I AM YOUR DAUGHTER.' (Patient with pemphigus vulgaris)

The patient is in her mid-forties and suffers from pemphigus vulgaris, an autoimmune disease that affects the skin and mucous membranes, causing them to thin, bleed, and become extremely sensitive.

When I look at this woman, she seems hard and I feel very little sense of her femininity. As she sits down next to me, she gives me a look of scepticism and reserve.

I wait for a bit and then, following my inner sense, I begin the interview by asking, 'who are you angry with?' She looks at me in surprise, but nonetheless answers immediately, 'my mother!' I have a feeling that this answer is not adequate to fully explain her anger, so I ask, 'who else?' The next answer also comes promptly, 'my father'.

Asking about events in her family of origin reveals that she lost her father when she was nine years old and her mother died three years later. The patient was born in Argentina, but has lived in Spain since she was 20.

When I feel into the roles of her parents, I sense a deep love between them and also love for their daughter. To check out this impression, I ask the patient to choose representatives for her parents. She places the two at a distance from one another, look-ing in different directions. Both representatives turn of their own initiative, smile at each other and embrace warmly. After a while, they drop their embrace and both look at their daughter. The patient is clearly moved and comments in astonishment: 'I have never seen my parents look like that!' I remind her, 'you weren't always there,' which makes her laugh.

The parents' representatives also grin and approach the patient, standing in front of her as she sits next to me. She becomes in-creasingly agitated and avoids looking at them. I turn to her and say: 'Look at them and tell them, "I am your daughter!" I have her repeat this sentence several times until it is evident that she is not just parroting, but resonating with her entire body. 'I am your daughter and you are my parents!' At this, she gives herself a shake, stands up and allows her parents to take her in their arms. They hold her for a long time until she pulls out of the embrace to better look into their faces. I ask her to look at them and say, 'yes'. She looks first at her father and says, 'yes!' and then turns to her mother and says, 'yes! Now I can agree to the way it was!' Noticeably freer, she sits down again, looks at me with a friendly smile and says, 'thank you'.

The next day, during a feedback round, she remarks, 'I cannot even begin to describe how I feel. It seems like my whole life is changing right now. I have never been able to see my parents in a positive light; now, when I think about them, I am filled with gratitude. I have been granted a feeling for life that I have never known before.'

When we resist or refuse to acknowledge those who belong, our symptoms or illness sometimes serve to remind us of who or what we are excluding. Our lives and our happiness are shaped by attitudes influenced by our parents and our family history. Those who live in harmony with their families and heritage can take life in all its fullness and, consequently, perhaps also pass it on.

AN UNFULFILLED DESIRE TO HAVE CHILDREN

This case involves a young married couple who have remained childless over the years, despite a strong desire to have children. The woman has had three miscarriages in the past two years, each occurring between the seventh and tenth weeks of her pregnancy. Clinical tests have not revealed anything of note that would explain the difficulty.

As I talk to the two, I try to imagine how it would be to be their child, and I feel shivers ripple up and down my spine. This sensation leads me to ask the man to first set up representatives for himself and his wife and then, in the next step, to place another representative for a child. The child's representative feels terrible. He is very anxious, and can barely stand the sight of the father or close proximity to him. He immediately withdraws from the parents' representatives and goes to stand behind the circle of the group participants.

I ask the man about events in his family of origin. He reports that he was born in Romania of German parents, is an only child, and has lived in Germany since he was seven. When I ask him if he can explain the fears expressed by the child's representative, he shakes his head. His wife, however, has a very strong reaction. With tears in her eyes, she states that her husband is the only living child in his family. Before his birth, however, his mother had aborted six children.

Hearing this, the child's representative shudders and pulls even further back until he is standing with his back against the wall of the room.

I ask another man in the group to come into the constellation and stand behind the husband's representative as one of these aborted siblings. After a while, he gingerly lays a hand on the husband's shoulder and the man leans back cautiously. This development intrigues the child's representative and, for the first time, he looks at his father. In the meantime, the husband's representative has changed dramatically. The shadow of sadness, previously so present in his face, has now drained away. Having a sibling has clearly done him good. I ask another person from the group to stand behind the two. The husband's representative remains cautious initially, but the first sibling is delighted by the presence of this new representative. The child's representative exhibits his growing interest and takes another step towards his father.

At this point I ask the patient if he would like to take his own place in the constellation. He hesitates, but finally stands up and replaces his representative. As the representative of the aborted child lays his hand cautiously on the patient's shoulder, the man goes pale, closes his eyes, and looks as if he is about to faint. When I encourage him to keep his eyes open, he is able to gather his strength and remain standing in his place. One at a time, I invite four more group members to stand behind the patient to represent the aborted children. It is clear that this demands all the strength the patient can muster, and he can hardly draw a breath. After a while, however, he is able to stand solidly, even with six aborted siblings behind him, and he can look at his own child. The central task facing this patient is to break his loyalty to his dead brothers and sisters. In close contact with them, he must reach out to his own life and, with strength, look at life, at his wife, and at the child.

I recommend to the couple that they not talk about anything in the constellation right away. I send them directly home, with a broad hint: 'Where there's a will there's a way!'

About ten months after this constellation, I received a birth announcement with the comment 'this is the proud result of the constellation'. Fours years later, I saw this couple again because of a health question regarding their child, and I took that opportunity to ask them how they had experienced the constellation described above.

The wife reported feeling very relieved and happy during the constellation and also immediately afterwards. The resolution that emerged strengthened her love for her husband. When she became pregnant, she was very worried and anxious for the first few months, but when the critical time was past, she became more and more confident and had a lovely pregnancy. After the birth, she would often think about her other children and felt sad that she hadn't had a chance to get to know them. That feeling improved over time.

The husband reported having felt completely relaxed at first. As his mother's six aborted children were added to the constellation he became aware of an oppressive sensation coming up. The constellation became overwhelming, something he had not foreseen or reckoned with in any way. He tried to repress his feelings at first, but they finally broke through anyway. After feeling ashamed of his strong reactions and by the end of the constellation he was very relieved. He spoke of a new kind of happiness that came into his life after this constellation work.

BETTER SICK THAN ALONE: CHILDREN'S PRIMARY LOVE

Additional insights have emerged over the years of experience with constellations around health issues, and from patients' feedback regarding changes in the course of their illness and their lives following constellation work.

People representing abstract elements, such as symptoms or disease, often exhibit feelings and reactions that suggest that they are representatives of excluded family members. If those relevant people are given representation in the constellation and the patient gives them a proper place, granting them the respect that is their due, then representatives of the symptoms or illness often begin to feel superfluous. No longer needed, they usually feel as though they want to withdraw from the constellation. From the perspective of the family system, it seems that balance and order have been restored, and this can set the stage for the patient's recovery.

When patients are faced with underlying factors of their illness or symptoms (often trans-generational dynamics), they usually experience insights drawn from the constellation as deeply penetrating, a process that can lead to resolution.

Nonetheless, I have also had repeated experiences when the curative effect of the process is less than expected, or when a symptom diminishes for a while following a constellation, but comes back again after a period of time. The question in these cases is always: to what extent was some factor missing from the perspective of the family system, or was there a movement on the part of the patient that remained incomplete? In my experience, it appears that there is significant potential within the sphere of personal responsibility and the options that are open to the patient.

In this regard, the following constellation provided a key experience for me, one that has encouraged me to focus increasingly on the patient's inner process.

THE DEMAND: 'EVEN IF YOU DIE, YOU WON'T GET ANY MORE'
(Patient with bone cancer and metastasis in the lungs)

This patient is himself a doctor, and has undergone many operations for progressive bone cancer in his right leg. His prosthesis is clearly visible to all. Despite chemotherapy and radiation therapy, it has not been possible to bring the cancer under control. At the time of this group, signs of metastasis have appeared in his lungs, and the patient is suffering from periodic bouts of pneumonia. His wife and teenage children have accompanied him to the group. Although I am initially unaware of the fact, the patient himself plans to only take part in the first day of the group because of his radiation therapy schedule.

During a brief initial interview, he mentions that his parents were just teenagers when he was born. I ask him to choose representatives for him, for his father, and for his mother. He places them in relationship to each other, and we then add an additional person to represent his illness. Judging from the reactions of the representatives, there seems to be some connection between his illness and his mother. When asked, however, the patient cannot think of any information that seems relevant or helpful. He emphasizes that he has, and always has had, a good relationship with his mother. The constellation is vague and reveals very little about the underlying dynamics of the disease. The patient's lukewarm interest in exploring in more depth leads me to break off the constellation at this point.

The patient is irritated by the interruption of the constellation and at the end of the first day he announces that he and his family made a huge effort to come to the seminar, despite great inconvenience, and he is very disappointed. I assure him that I will continue the work on the following day if the experience opens up any new aspects. He rejects my offer and at this point informs me that, because of an important medical appointment, he will have to get a flight home this very evening. I state emphatically that the decision is completely up to him.

The next day he is back in the group again although his family flew home the previous evening as scheduled. The patient appears generally much more relaxed, calm, and collected. I decide to do another constellation of his family of origin. There happen to be a few new participants in the course and I ask the patient to choose representatives from this group, since they know nothing about the constellation from the previous day. The picture that emerges is very similar to that of the day before: confused movements of the representatives, something mysterious about the mother, and little potential for resolution. I ask him to tell me a bit more about his relationship with his mother. As on the previous day, he says that he has a very good relationship with his mother. In this exchange, however, we discover that his mother has no idea that he is ill.

This is clearly the key. I ask him how such a thing is even possible, and he explains that ever since his first operation, he has avoided seeing his mother in person. They talk on the phone daily about everything in the world – everything except his illness.

With this information, I have the mother's representative stand facing the patient and I ask him to tell her, 'Dear Mum, look, I am very ill'. Instead of the reaction that one would expect of a mother turning towards her seriously ill son, her representative staggers dizzily backwards and has trouble standing up. Her movement would indicate that she is overwhelmed and unable to stand by her ill son. I suddenly hear a sentence in my head, and I ask the mother's representative to say to her son: 'My dear son, even if you die, you won't get any more!' The patient is very shaken by this sentence, as if his internal house of cards has collapsed. It is obvious that his body is trying to reorganize after this intervention. The mother's representative feels solid and right in saying this sentence. She has a sense of her own strength again, but keeps her distance from her son. She repeats again that she has given him everything she can and there is simply no more available. When the patient hears these words from his mother, he begins to cry. I put my arm around him, very gently, and hold him for a short while as he feels this pain. When he has calmed again in my arms, he is able to look his mother in the eye and agree — also to her bonds and entanglements — and thank her for everything he has received. This brings a feeling of peace between mother and son. The patient returns to his place in the group a bit taken aback, but with a sense of relief.

About six months after this constellation, the organizer of the group, Susan Ulfelder, received a thank you card. The patient had written: 'Yeah, the computer MRI of my leg and my chest are clear. I want to thank you with all my heart for what you have done for me.

For whatever reason, his medical treatments were finally successful. It is not clear whether the constellation work played any part in this or not.

In August 2006, about two years after the constellation, I saw Susan Ulfelder in an advanced training group. She reported that she had continuing contact with the patient; he was doing well and had completely changed his life around. He had given up the practice of medicine and was running an independent real estate agency.

This constellation illustrates the healing power that can be released through a respectful posture towards one's parents, one that includes all their potential and limitations. In this particular healing process, the nature of the mother's entanglement was not the important issue. The critical factor was the patient's change of attitude towards his mother. Hiding his illness from his mother could be seen as a kind of disrespect for her. There was already a hint of disrespect in the first dialogue, when the patient described his parents as 'teenagers'.

System Orientation – Client Orientation

This and other similar feedback from clients have changed the way I work with systemic constellations. When I began, I was very focussed on trans-generational entanglements as the central underlying factor in illness and key to resolution. Today, my attention is more with the patient during the constellation process, and with those things in the person's basic attitude and stance that might be contributing to illness or affecting the potential for change.

Once, a friend of mine, Dale Schusterman, was in a group as a guest and he commented afterwards that I use the person to change the system, not the system to change the person. I can only confirm this observation. Precisely because we are part of a system, we have influence, albeit limited, on the system as a whole. In one of his books, Bert Hellinger (2002, page 45) included a story entitled 'The Answer':

A student turned towards his master: "Tell me what freedom is?"

"Which freedom?" asked the master. "The first freedom is foolishness. It resembles the horse that, neighing, throws off the rider only to feel his reigns pulled much tighter thereafter.

The second freedom is regret. It resembles the helmsman who chooses to stay on the sinking ship rather than climbing into the lifeboat.

The third freedom is insight. Alas, we only gain this after we have experienced foolishness and regret. Insight resembles a reed that sways with the wind; Because it is pliable it can bend and stand upright again after the wind subsides".

The student asked: "Is that all?"

To this the master responded: "There is the search for the truth. Some people think they can find the truth within their own souls. But there is a Greater Soul, a wider truth that operates beyond the individual soul, permeates it and works through it. Like Mother Nature, this Greater Soul is able to make many slips and errors as each false creation is effortlessly replaced by a new one. If we allow this Greater Soul to support us in the flow of life, we may be granted certain freedoms and swimming with the current, we may be carried to the other side of the river".

Personal Freedom and Choice

When it comes to our parents and our family history, we have no choice and no say in the matter. We are simply connected and subject to the influence of the collective conscience of our particular system. But, we do have some choice about how entangled we are and remain. We can influence how we regard each person in our system, and our attitudes about their lives and fate. Within this realm, depending on our potential and the options open to us, we are free and self-determining to a great extent when we are connected to our families in a good way.

Without a doubt, we have all received from our parents and we each also lack whatever it was that we did not get. It is up to each individual to decide where he or she remains attached. Those who look at what they have received feel the beneficence and usually have something to pass on to others. Those who have unmet demands and are attached to what is missing may feel cheated by their parents and by life. Such a person does not usually do well; he or she has an on-going sense of deficit, and may be unable to give to others. It is an attitude towards life that contributes to depression in many people.

Being in harmony with your parents means taking what you have received and letting go of what you haven't got. This is a very real loss, because there is no one who can ever replace your parents. Your father cannot replace your mother; your mother cannot replace your father; adoptive parents or foster parents cannot replace your biological parents; and your life partner also cannot fulfill these needs. In addition, many children suffer from their parents' unconscious projections and begin to take on a parental role for their own parents (parentification).

The following case illustrates the power of a child's primary love and the potential for resolution that lies in acknowledging one's own fate. In addition, it illustrates something I have observed repeatedly in constellation work with the ill: many patients suffering from illness or pathology are unconsciously caught in the longings of childhood and are holding on because of a deep need to belong. They live and suffer in the hope of getting closer to their parents and receiving more attention — more than their parents are actually capable of giving them. The process of healing means relinquishing this longing for closeness. Being in harmony with one's parents and taking over responsibility for oneself, it is possible to grow into adult autonomy. In a broad sense, an underlying hope of realizing childish desires can sometimes be seen as the unconscious benefit of illness.

NEEDINESS: 'YOU MUST LET YOUR MOTHER GO!'
(Patient with Sudeck's syndrome)

A physically disabled woman is telling the group about her extremely difficult birth. Following her birth, she was immediately taken from her mother and put in a children's clinic for three weeks. As a result of a forceps and ventouse delivery, the new-born's appearance was shocking to her mother. Later, the mother often mentioned how difficult it had been for her to accept this daughter.

As the patient describes the issue, her longing for security and closeness are transparently clear. I also sense a projection of her needs onto the therapist in this situation. Therefore, I ask the patient to first set up two representatives, a woman to represent her and a man to represent me. In the constellation, the patient's representative immediately leans against my representative. Weeping, she lays her head on his shoulder. The projection onto me, as her parent, is also apparent to the patient. I select two group members to represent the woman's mother and father and bring them into the constellation, placing them behind the patient's representative at a distance. My own representative is visibly relieved when I then release him from his difficult position.

The mother's representative shows no interest at all in her daughter and seemingly feels nothing for her. It is clear how difficult this is for the patient, but she is reluctant to expose her pain and tries to hold back her feelings. I decide to interrupt the work at this point to allow the patient a bit of time to more fully experience her own neediness.

The following morning, she reports that since the constellation the day before, she has felt worse and worse physically. She is feeling abandoned and lost in her pain, and is very preoccupied by the image of her mother turning away from her. Her resistance to that picture of her mother is clear, and I tell her, in a quiet but firm voice, 'you have to let her go'.

The patient casts her eyes down in resignation. After a while, she shakes her head and stamps her foot furiously, struggling against my words. I ask the mother's representative from the previous day to come and stand facing the patient, who is seated next to me. The patient continues staring at the floor and again the mother's representative turns away from her daughter. When the patient begins to cry softly, I ask her to look at her mother, to really look her in the eye. Slowly, she raises her eyes, but her mother continues to gaze steadily out the window. Before I can take the next step, the patient drops off her chair onto the floor, wraps her arms around her mother's legs and begins to sob, loudly and dramatically. For the mother's representative, this is unbearable. She tries to free herself from her daughter's grip and shake her off. When the mother's representative finally uses force and manages to get free of her daughter's hold, the patient screams out in rage and pain. The mother takes two steps back, paying no attention to her daughter lying on the floor. The patient does not want to accept her mother's reaction and begins crawling towards her, pulling herself along with her hands, since she is unable to use her legs effectively. She creeps forward, a centimetre at a time, in the direction of her mother. The mother's representative remains quiet, collected, and strong. She continues to look out the window, apparently untroubled. The patient, sobbing loudly, exerts all her strength to get to her mother. When she finally reaches her, she stretches out her hand to touch the woman's feet with her fingertips. As her mother's representative again moves away, the patient cries out in pain and then continues in her attempts to follow her.

When nothing new seems to develop, it is clear to everyone present that the work has to be interrupted. I release the mother's representative from her role and announce a 30-minute break for the group. The patient is still lying on the floor, weeping. When two group members are about to go and help her get up, I indicate to them, without the patient noticing it, that they should leave her alone. I am certain that their help at this point would disrupt the effects of the intervention made by interrupting the work. My sense is that the first step towards resolution must be in accord with the mother, just as she is. Consequently, I act like the mother and also ask the group not to help the patient at this time.

We all take a break and leave the room, very tense and worried, to gather outside on the terrace. To our astonishment, about 20 minutes later the beaming patient walks out to the terrace without the support of her cane. She comes directly over to me to say thank you. We are all impressed that she is managing without her cane. Proudly, she announces: 'this is the first time in years that I have walked out of a house without help!'

About a year later, the woman sent the following report of her own experience.

I had a terrible time throughout the winter and spring of 2004. My physical condition was very poor, and for about six months I was under medication to control inflammation and pain. I was in hospital twice, but nothing helped or brought any relief. Even though the doctors assured me I was on the way to recovery, I had unbearable pain in my heels, feet and hips. Even to take a few steps, I needed the help of a tripod cane, and any movement caused me great pain. I was in such a state of desperation that I decided to try a family constellation.

At the very start of the group, I made my request to work and was chosen as the first patient. As I sat next to the therapist, he looked at me for a long time without saying anything. I felt deeply at peace with his calm, serene look. After a few questions, he said that I should choose a representative for myself, and one for him and place them in relationship to one another. I was puzzled, but I did what he said and put the representatives facing each other. Shortly thereafter, my representative moved nearer the representative of the therapist and, crying, laid her head on his shoulder. This movement came from the representative without any instructions to do so. She then sank slowly to the floor and held tightly onto the therapist's representative, crying all the while.

Stephan Hausner asked me if I thought we had a good basis for therapeutic work. It was clear to me that this was not going to function well at all and I answered, 'no, this looks like the relationship between a child and her mother or father'. Stephan nodded, walked over to his representative and thanked him, and released the man from his role. Then, he chose another man and a woman as representatives of my parents and placed them in the constellation. My father's representative turned lovingly towards my representative, but my mother's representative seemed indifferent and finally turned away. I felt cold when I saw my mother's reaction and my representative had the same reaction. She seemed to be in despair and she tearfully said, 'I feel terrible and I am very cold. I feel like I am dying. My limbs are all going to sleep'. She stood there, crying and shaking, and shaking and crying. Then she added, 'it's too much, it's all too much'. This sentence shocked me because I have lived my whole life with the feeling that it is all 'too much'. At this point, Stephan decided to interrupt the constellation. He said he wanted to leave it like this for the moment and would continue the work the following day.

The next day, as I sat with the other group participants, I told them I had had a difficult time the previous night and I had felt very sad and deeply upset. Stephan did not say anything, but he did something that changed my life. He called up the woman who had represented my mother and brought her over in front of me. He told me to look at her, to look her in the eye, which I finally was able to do. What happened next seemed as though it was instigated by something beyond me. I fell to my knees, forgetting all my pain, and clasped my mother's representative around her knees. I pressed my head into her lap and cried out, 'Mummy, my beloved Mummy! Oh, Mummy, how wonderful it is to be so near you and to hold on to you! Oh, my dear Mummy, I want to stay with you forever, near to your heart, in the warmth of your embrace!'

Then, suddenly, I realized: 'but... you are not embracing me, Mummy! Your hands are not tender and your legs ... my God, they are hard as stone. Now you're turning away from me, just like yesterday. But, it doesn't matter. It's enough to be with you. Just let me stay with you. I need you, Mummy! Just let me stay with you.'

But, she grabbed me with her hard, claw-like hands and violently pushed me away from her.

'Noooooooo!' One single, endless scream, and then death. I had the feeling that my life was seeping out of me as she pushed me away with her hands. Then, nothing – no thoughts, no feelings. I remained lying there on the floor for a long, long time. It seemed like forever.

After this weekend I was no longer the same. I could see that my suffering was also determined by my longing to be near to my mother. My mother had done the greatest part by giving me life, and now it remained for me to thank her and honor her for that and I was finally able to do this.

What astonished everyone, and me most of all, was that I arrived in the group on Friday in great pain, and I was able to walk only with great difficulty. On Sunday, when I left, I had almost no pain and could move almost fluidly. I want to emphasize that this has also lasted. Following that difficult work, I felt better each day, and finally got to the point where I could walk without a cane. I had a wonderful summer.

While doing constellation work in a psychosomatic clinic, I have seen other patients suffering from Sudeck's Syndrome. A doctor in the clinic confirmed that in the family history of these patients, there is often an early separation from the parents, usually immediately following the birth.

Other aspects manifested in the work described above include: finding one's personal strength and resources, taking over responsibility for oneself, and letting go of criticism and complaint as a general attitude towards life.

A child's blind love, with its potential to instigate illness, is not actually directed at the parents. The orientation is actually more concerned with the self. Truly looking into the face of one's parents makes it impossible to hang on this kind of illness in the same way. A child must realize that parents also love and certainly do not want their children to suffer.

The next case is an illustration of a child's readiness to sacrifice her life out of love for her parents.

'FOR YOU! AND FOR YOU!'
(Patient with breast cancer, plus metastasis in lungs, liver and bones)

At an international conference on cancer in Madrid, during a session on constellation work, a 45-year-old woman asks to do a constellation. Her primary illness is breast cancer, and she now has metastasis in her lungs, liver and bones. In view of the clinical findings, I tell the patient frankly that I am not at all certain that constellation work is appropriate for her. She and I can both see that death may be very near, and perhaps I should not interfere with the possible movement of her soul towards death. She understands these reservations, and her agreement makes it possible for me to work with her.

The patient lives alone and has no children. In her family of origin, she is the youngest of four siblings. The first two, a brother and a sister, each died a few days after their birth. She is not in touch with her other brother, who is eight years older. Her parents are separated and both seriously ill, living in nursing care. I ask the patient to choose representatives for her father, her mother and herself, because I have a feeling that there might still be something unfinished between the patient and her parents. This could have the effect of hindering her from living as well as from dying.

She places her father and mother at a great distance from each other, and her own representative about one step behind her father, facing the same direction he is looking.

The mother's representative is crying and shaking from head to toe, staring at the floor in horror. She is most probably looking at the two children that died shortly after birth. The father's representative seems uninvolved, and stares straight ahead into the distance. The patient's representative is breathing heavily. When I ask her what she is feeling, she replies: 'I am very afraid of my father. I don't dare even look at him.'

I ask the patient about any unusual events in her family and she reports that her father sexually abused her. Before her parents married, her father was in Germany as a foreign worker. There, he spent a number of years in prison after killing a German man in a knife fight in a bar.

In the meantime, the mother's representative has dropped to her knees and, exhausted from her extensive crying, lies down on the floor. The patient's representative cautiously moves past her father in order to get to her mother. When she sees her mother lying lifelessly on the floor, she slowly retreats back to her place and turns away. The father's representative remains unaffected.

When I observe the patient closely, I hear a voice inside myself asking the question: 'Who has to die?' When I speak the question aloud, the patient tentatively says, 'me?'

I answer: 'I think it is your father. And who is actually doing it?' She looks puzzled, but I am certain I see understanding in the depth of her eyes. I tell her my opinion: 'you are! - And, you know it!'

She drops her eyes and after a moment of silence says: 'I don't know what to do!'

I respond, 'I don't know if we can do anything for your body, but perhaps for your soul'.

During this exchange the patient's representative has become increasingly restless. We can see that it is becoming too difficult for her to stand, and she sits down on the floor. Slowly, she then lies down on her back, closes her eyes and crosses her hands over her chest. She lies peacefully there, as if in a grave.

After a period of silence, words come to my mind as if from the patient's soul: 'For you!' When these words persist in my head, I go to the mother's representative and ask her to look at her daughter. I ask the patient to look at her mother and say: 'For you!' She does so. Then, I ask her to look at her father and say, 'And for you!' She repeats this to her father as well.

The mother's representative stands up and walks over to the patient sitting next to me. The two look into each other's eyes for a long time and both begin to cry. Finally, they embrace in tears. When the father hears the crying, he looks over at the two. He then joins them, embracing his wife and his daughter. We all sit quietly in silence to allow the process of reconciliation its full measure, and then we end the work.

During the break following this constellation, a doctor from the audience comes up to tell me how touched he was by the work. For many years he has attended the dying in a hospice for street children in Brazil. He says that what many of these children have endured in their lives is unimaginable. Often, they have suffered for years at the hands of their parents or other family members, up until the day they die. Yet, according to this doctor, almost all of these children have only one great longing when they reach their time to let go of life – their parents.

About four months after this constellation, I met a colleague in a continuing education course. It turned out that he was the one who had suggested to that woman that she attend the conference in Madrid and do a constellation. He told me that she was still alive. Along with her medical treatment, she was also in psychotherapy with him and was receiving complementary medical care as well. As her therapist, he found her constellation work to have been a helpful step. Afterwards, the patient was much calmer and more relaxed, which supported the therapeutic work.

Another year after that, I heard that the patient had died. The therapist had accompanied her almost to the end, and he said that, despite her serious illness, she had a good final year.

AS WITHIN, SO WITHOUT: CORRESPONDENCE OF SYMPTOMS.

> *As above, so below –*
> *As within, so without.*
> *–Paracelsus*

I became interested in the doctrine of signatures while studying alternative healing practices. In this approach, diseases and medications are observed carefully, and assumptions made about their inner connections based on external forms and appearance. Also in constellation work with illness, there are often valuable clues to be found through judiciously looking at analogies and correspondence. The issues that are excluded in a family are often expressed with an astonishing correspondence and repetition in the trans-generational appearance of certain themes, diseases, and chronic symptoms.

FATHER'S DECEASED SISTER
(A patient with dental problems)

In a workshop for systemic constellations, a woman describes her severe dental problems, which have pushed both her and her dentist to the limit. An extreme reactivity has resulted in major difficulties. For years, various dentists have attempted to treat this condition and fit her with dentures. Repeated infections, and the woman's intolerance to the materials used in replacements have led to many complications. According to the patient, she has always had problems with her teeth.

In the constellation, the patient appears to be identified with her father's elder sister. This aunt died at the age of three after complications from an abscessed tooth, which led to meningitis. No one in the family ever talked about this child and the patient heard about her aunt only incidentally, through a comment of her mother's. In the constellation, no one even looks at the dead child except the patient's representative. The three-year-old was buried in the family plot, but without a record of her name. In the family, there is never a mention made of her existence.

Besides similarities between the symptoms or organs in question, there is sometimes correspondence reflected in the dynamics. For example, in cases of autoimmune ailments, where the body is aggressing against itself, besides looking at family dynamics, one might also consider forces that belong together, but are not integrated or beneficially joined together.

GREAT GRANDFATHER'S BLESSING WITHHELD
(Patient with Lupus Erythematosus)

The following constellation involves dynamics that have relevance for an autoimmune disease. The case concerns a woman from Jujuy, a province in north-western Argentina, who is suffering from Lupus erythematosus. This is an autoimmune disease of the blood vessels and tissue that produces a characteristic reddening of the facial skin and inflammation of the joints. In the constellation, the representative of the disease feels she can withdraw once the patient is able to bow before her Indian grandmother, who had married a Spaniard. The grandmother's father had refused to bless this relationship and rejected his daughter as a traitor after her marriage. The representative of the patient's great grandfather initially feels bitter, but softens when his daughter shows him his great grandchild. He says that he had felt very anxious about his daughter and was worried that there would be no further generations. The patient spontaneously assures her great grandfather that she will honor him and the heritage of his people.

When there are incompatible differences of ideology, religion or ethnicity between the families of a father and mother, these are usually expressed in physical symptoms in a later generation, for example, through the identification of a grandchild or great-grandchild. In general, we have observed that the deeper the trauma or conflict, the more persistent and long lasting the potential effects in later generations and, conversely, the more serious the disease, the graver the events in the family history.

Sometimes, a patient's symptoms point to the avoidance of a particular movement or attitude. Bert Hellinger found many indications of a connection between back pain and a patient's resistance to bowing down before a parent or other family member who had suffered some special fate.

A case comes to mind that points to this issue, involving a patient who suffered for many years from a neurological disease called cervical dystonia. In this illness, overactive neck muscles lead to a spastic misalignment of the head.

THE ABORTED CHILD
(A patient with cervical dystonia)

This woman of about 35 describes to the group her desire for an abiding, happy relationship – one that would lead to children and a family. According to her, she always ends up with the 'wrong' men.

I ask her to choose a representative for herself and one for a partner. She places the two facing each other at a distance. The woman's representative feels a strong pull on her neck, which she cannot resist and her neck vertebrae tense up in a very painful twist to the right.

When the patient notices her representative's position, she says, horrified: 'For 15 years, I have suffered from a crooked neck with exactly this kind of torsion to the right. I was treated repeatedly with botulinum toxin to relieve the spasms, until one day the problem finally disappeared.'

When the man's representative is asked about his feelings, he says: 'I feel very unsettled. I like this woman, but she also seems sort of sinister'.

The patient's representative is fighting against the painful twist in her neck. The strain forces her to look back over her shoulder to the floor behind her. The difficulties she is experiencing, taken together with the man's comments, lead me to ask the patient whether she has ever lost a child. She says she has not, but I notice a slight distress in her face when I ask her this question. I continue to look her in the eye as a signal that I am not completely convinced by her answer. In response, she adds: 'when I was 17, I got pregnant. My parents were very opposed to the man involved, and also he felt completely overwhelmed by the idea of having a child, so my mother arranged for an abortion for me'.

I ask the patient whether she thinks the baby was a boy or a girl (this question helps the mother make an inner connection with the child). She says it was a boy so I ask her to choose a representative for him. She chooses a representative and places him behind her own representative, who begins to cry. The patient's representative then turns and takes the child in her arms. As she does so, the tension in her neck relaxes.

The man representing her partner reports that he feels very relieved and says that his previous sense of trepidation disappeared the moment the child was mentioned. He had had the feeling all along that something was missing. At the end of the constellation, he says how relieved he feels and as far as he is concerned, there is nothing more standing in the way of a relationship.

EXCLUSION, AGREEMENT, AND HARMONY

'The point is to live everything'
                                    –Rainer Maria Rilke

Systemic constellations demonstrate clearly that many problems, particularly health issues, may have a connection to one or more excluded family members, or to hidden or repressed events in the family history. Conscious or unconscious exclusion usually originates in the emotional overload during a traumatic experience or painful disappointment. When there is an overwhelming flood, damming it up is a first, life-saving step. Often, however, the mechanisms become conditioned patterns of response and are maintained in unconscious projections onto others. Many painful, core experiences later lead to criticism, blame and demands. They reinforce the bonds of relationship, but also serve to separate at the same time. A disease is often the catalyst that brings someone to a halt and facilitates change.

Contrary to the binding, entangling, life-limiting effects of exclusion, we experience agreement, recognition, and harmony as resolving and healing, despite the difficulties they may present us.

Only someone who is in harmonious agreement with the past is also free for the future. One who struggles against the past remains bound to it. This holds true whether it has to do with the person's own life — in the sense of an early loss, an early separation from parents, or a particular decision — or whether it goes beyond the individual to the history of the family.

Systemic constellations involving health issues suggest that simply looking at one's own life is insufficient to provide real relief and healing. Illness must be viewed as embedded in the cross-generational context of a family and not reduced to a personal phenomenon.

❧2❧

Case Studies, Feedback, and Comments

'The more one refuses to hear the message and meaning
in pathology, the more pathological it becomes.'
–Wolfgang Giegerich

In examining the origins and progression of disease, modern medical and psychosomatic research looks at mutual interactions between biological, psychological, and social factors. The idea that there could be any connection between a particular family dynamic and a specific pattern of illness is generally discounted.

Our experience with constellation work and patients' feedback have indicated that in this context, confronting trans-generational family dynamics can contribute to healing and relief, or the capacity to better cope with illness. Each constellation emerges as a unique, personal process, and it is just this that allows the work to have beneficial effects.

The following case examples and commentary document our experience in this area — particularly in respect to dynamics that have been observed repeatedly. They serve to introduce and illustrate the connections and mutually influential relationships in families that may have some bearing on the issues of disease and health. To apply these observations without regard to each individual patient's unique situation and history would not be helpful and might actually do harm.

The case histories are organized according to family issues in order to highlight these interactive relationship patterns. The intent is to place this focus in the foreground of our search for options that support healing as well as the prevention of illness. It is a focus that counters less useful ideas that imply a direct, causal connection between family entanglements and specific diseases.

ILLNESS AND ATTACHMENT BEHAVIOR IN THE CHILD

'It is never too late to have a happy childhood.'
–Milton Erickson

Our parents are our primary link to the strength of our ancestors, a power regarded by all indigenous cultures as the basic foundation for a healthy life. In respectful harmony, we can take life as it comes to us through our parents. Entanglements in the family system or early separation traumas can lead to insecure attachments in the developing child and may stand in the way of deep spiritual fulfillment. I consider inner reconciliation with one's parents one of the most important aspects of constellation work with illness.

Attachment Behavior and Loss

From the perspective of developmental physiology, a child-parent attachment, especially the bond to the mother, serves to protect life. We are indebted to the English psychologist, John Bowlby, for his research into attachment behavior and its influence in the development of the psyche. His observations and conclusions have increasingly attracted notice in psychology and psychotherapy, and constellation work also supports the relevance and importance of his findings. Systemic constellations demonstrate not only the emotional consequences of childhood attachment disorders, but also reveal effects on physical well-being.

The following occurrences have been identified as triggers for attachment disorders:

- a child's lack of early bonding because of a lengthy, serious illness or death of a parent, or because the child has been given up for adoption or foster care, or institutionalized.

- a temporary early separation from the mother or father resulting in an 'interrupted reaching out movement'.

- attachment insecurity resulting from the parents' limited emotional availability due to personal traumatic experiences or family entanglements of their own.

Whatever the underlying reasons for a disruption in the early child-parent relationship, the consequences are that the child is often caught between an unfulfilled need for closeness to his or her parents and a sense of having to hold a line of demarcation and protection. In the context of a constellation group, if the background of this relationship disturbance is brought to light and the patient's emotional splitting resolved, there may be an end to this ambivalence in the soul; there may be a sense of peace, and often healing at the physical level as well.

ILLNESS AND A CHILD'S ATTACHMENT DISORDER BECAUSE OF EARLY SEPARATION FROM THE MOTHER

The mother is a child's primary relationship figure. Therefore, any early loss or separation from the mother has a more serious effect on the formation of secure attachments than does the loss of a father or other significant carers.

PARENTS' SEPARATION: 'DEAR MUM, IT WAS DIFFICULT FOR ME!' (Patient with autoimmune glomerular nephritis)

Two months after having been diagnosed with an immune system disorder affecting his kidney functions, this man is attending a constellation group focussed on health issues. Because of the sudden onset of his symptoms, his doctors are expecting a progressive, advancing disease.

The family history indicates that the patient's mother left him and his father when the child was three years old. She fell in love with an American soldier stationed in their town, and when it came time for the man to return to America, she went with him.

We begin the constellation with two representatives, one for the patient and one for the illness. The patient chooses a woman to represent his disease, and places her facing his representative, but at a distance. My hypothesis is that the origins of this illness could have some connection to a rejection of his mother, so I ask the man to choose an additional representative for his mother. When the mother's representative steps into the constellation, the patient's representative moves away from her immediately, but without noticing that he is also moving nearer to the woman representing his illness. This movement becomes clearer when the mother's representative tries to get closer to her son and he continues to back away, again narrowing the distance between himself and his illness. I ask the representative of the disease how she is feeling and she replies, 'if he needs me, I'm here for him'. Her reaction is enough to support my hypothesis and I stop the movements in the constellation. I ask the mother's representative to come over and stand in front of the patient, who is sitting next to me, and I place her as near as the patient can tolerate. He presses his upper body against the back of his chair and slowly begins to push his chair backwards against the wall.

The man is eventually able to complete a reaching out movement to his mother after he expresses his concerns and difficulties to her. I suggest that he say to his mother, 'dear Mum, it was so difficult for me'. It is interesting to note that he is initially unable to say the words 'dear Mum', but when those words are contained within the entire sentence, he can say it. 'Dear Mum, it was so difficult for me.' I ask the mother's representative to tell him, 'my dear son, I could not act differently. Deep inside, I would have wanted to stay, but somehow I couldn't do anything different than what I did'. When she speaks these words, the patient can finally look his mother in the eye. His resistance melts, and he weeps as he embraces his mother. They hold their embrace for a long time. As he slowly calms, I have the mother say, 'my dear son, even though I had to leave and couldn't choose anything else, please stay!' The patient tells her, 'yes, dear Mum, even though you left, I am staying! I am staying and I now agree to the way it was. I take it (life), even at this price'. The two embrace once more before the mother's representative lets go and moves slowly backwards, step by step. The man watches her retreat a bit wistfully, but with love.

I now choose three more group participants to step in as representatives for the patient's wife and two children. Immediately, the man looks at them with delight. I ask him to say to them, 'even though my mother could not stay, I am staying!'

Just in case the man's rejection towards his mother was based partially on his loyalty to his father, I give him one more sentence to say to his father. I tell him that just to be certain, he might tell his father, in his mind, 'the mother one has is always the best!' The patient laughs and nods in agreement.

A year later, this man sent me the following report:

Two months had gone by since I had been diagnosed with an immune system disease in my kidneys. My doctors prognosticated a drastic deterioration. As a body therapist, I am quite aware of the effects of mental processes on the body and vice versa. Nonetheless, it was not clear to me how my family could be contributing to my illness or could have a healing effect.

I can scarcely remember how we got from the topic of my illness to my relationship with my mother. I remember very clearly the disdain and repulsion I felt towards my mother and how that feeling transformed into a yearning to be near her.

Since the constellation, I have not felt a need to hold my mother at a distance, nor have I felt disdainful of her. I am no longer using any of my strength in that way – quite the opposite, actually, I have initiated more contact with her. Once, during a telephone conversation, my mother had this emotional outburst and said, 'if you push me any more about forgiving your father, I'm not going to be your mother anymore!' For a moment I was paralyzed, as if I had been struck dead; then, as I was moving to the moral high ground, ready to decimate her, words from the constellation suddenly, miraculously clicked in: 'Even if you leave, I am staying.'

I did not hang up, but stayed on the phone in contact with her. I felt an unfamiliar sense of calm and aliveness. I was suddenly 'immune' to her threats of abandonment. Since that moment, I have felt free of the anxiety that was having such a negative effect – also on my marriage. Even my mother noticed her own behavior pattern — perhaps because of my lack of reactivity — and much to my amazement, she apologized. In doing that, something also seemed to be finished for her.

My disease has not gone away, but I feel as though I have become healthier somehow, through that constellation. I have given my kidneys a message to stay. I notice that I more intensely want to stay here, and I experience that intensity in a transformed presence of spirit. Luckily, the disease has not followed the drastic course that the doctors had foreseen. Regular laboratory checks indicate that progression of the illness has almost come to a standstill.

Likewise, in regard to the therapeutic work, I also have more open access to my wife and children now. Just as with the clearing with my mother, the process occurred first in the constellation, then actually at home.

John Bowlby identified various phases in a child's emotional reactions to an early attachment difficulty following a separation (primarily from the mother, father, or other significant attachment figure). At first, the child reacts in fear and panic. Fury and rage follow, to be finally superseded by despair and apathy.

In the resolving movement in this case, I find it interesting that there is a reverse progression of those symptoms in the patient's description of his feelings towards his mother. When she threatens him with her statement, 'if you push me any more about forgiving your father, I am not going to be your mother anymore', he first falls into apathy, followed by anger and rage. With the help of the resolving words from the constellation, 'even if you leave, I am staying', he is able to overcome the rage and at the same time resolve the fear of abandonment that he has been projecting into the relationship with his wife. It would require more specific observation to determine what influence, if any, this has had on the course of the man's illness

In constellations involving immune system diseases, we have often seen similar patterns of rejection towards a parent, so this would seem to merit continued attention.

'NO' TO THE MOTHER
(Patient with dermatomyositis)

Dermatomyositis is a disease of the immune system that results in inflammation of the skin and muscles, causing pain and weakness in the muscles.

The patient, like her mother, carries a genetic defect in x-chromosomes. It is the sort that leads to hemophilia in male children and her brother died of this disease. Her father unconsciously blames his wife for the loss of his beloved son, and the patient has remained loyal to her father. As the woman stands facing her mother's representative, it is impossible for her to look her mother in the eye and say, 'yes'. I have the impression that this 'no' to the mother and her illness is so deeply anchored in her that it is a force turned against herself.

THE MISSING BLESSING: 'THANK YOU!'
(Patient with an unfulfilled desire for children, and two miscarriages)

A very self-confident appearing, 35-year-old woman talks about her desire to have children, which has remained unfulfilled up to now. She has been pregnant twice in the past year, but both times the child stopped growing and died in the eighth week of pregnancy. The repetition of the experience weighs heavily on the patient even though her doctors have reassured her that everything is in order from a medical point of view.

Without gathering any further information, I ask the woman to set up a representative for herself and one for her husband. She places them fairly close, facing one another. They look at each other briefly, smile, each take a step forward and embrace. Finally, they stand, arm in arm, side by side and look together towards a third. I ask the patient to add a representative for a child. She chooses a woman and places her facing the other two.

The representative of the child feels uncomfortable and leans back until she is almost falling over. The patient's representative is immediately at her side, holding on to her. The child's representative allows herself to be held, closes her eyes, but her attention seems to be elsewhere. I ask the patient to choose another representative for whatever it is that stands between her and this child. She chooses a woman and positions her at some distance, looking at the young family. She is hardly in place when she begins moving resolutely, step by step, towards the family. She pushes herself determinedly between the mother and the child, looking sternly at the mother. With this separating factor in place, the child's representative opens her eyes in relief, and regains enough strength to stand on her own feet. The determination of the 'disruptive factor' is striking and leads me to ask the patient if she and her husband received a blessing for their relationship. She reports that her husband's parents died relatively young, but their relationship was always good. Her own father attended the wedding, but not her mother. She has had no contact with her mother for the past 20 years. Her parents separated shortly before her birth. When she was five, her mother met another man, and from that time on she was increasingly left in the care of her grandmother until the age of seven, when she went to live with her permanently. Her mother did not allow her any contact with her father, and she met him for the first time, on her own initiative, when she was 23 years old.

As the conversation proceeds to include the patient's mother, the 'disruptive factor' in the constellation begins to slowly back away from the family, but the child's representative continues to stare fixedly at her with a look of longing. The patient's representative tries in vain to hold the child's attention through stroking and touching.

Because the representative of the disruptive factor reacted so immediately to the mention of the patient's mother, it is clear to everyone present that there is some connection here. Therefore, I ask this representative to change and represent the patient's mother. She has no difficulty doing this and it brings about no change in her feelings or sensations. The patient does not seem pleased with this new identification of the disruptive factor. She says she actually felt that she had finished with her mother. The question in my mind is whether the blessings of her mother might be a key for her and her family. To avoid the patient's resistance to this idea, I work here with her representative rather than working with the patient directly. Based on a sense I have of the mother's representative, I suggest that the patient's representative tell her, 'thank you'.

The representative's expression of thanks leads to a change in the feelings of all the other representatives. The mother's representative is visibly more relaxed, the previous hardness in her face softens, and she looks at her daughter, son-in-law, and the child in a friendly manner. The representative of the child feels enormously relieved and turns, beaming, to look with joy at her mother. They smile at each other and the child moves to be embraced by her parents.

The patient turns to me and says, with some skepticism; 'All very nice. But, what can I do?'

I reply: 'Just what you see here. Say thank you to your mother'.

Her retort: 'Thank you? For what? For life?'

I say to her, in calm voice: 'For example. For life'.

Since the patient is unwilling to take this step that looks so promising in the constellation, I decide to interrupt the work at this point.

Two days later, during the final round of the group, the patient, in tears, asks for a chance to express her thanks to the woman who represented her mother in the constellation. The mother's representative had also felt the absence of a resolving word at the end of the constellation, and she stands immediately and moves to take the patient in her arms.

In this way, the reaching out movement to the mother becomes possible after all. The patient expresses her gratitude as she says goodbye to the group, and reports that she feels good.

Illness Related to an Attachment Difficulty Due to Parental Illness

Children also experience traumatic separations when a parent has a long-term physical or mental illness, or addictive behavior. This becomes visible when the parent's disease, addiction, or psychosis is included in a constellation. We often see a close connection between the parent and the illness. The child, however, is still required to take his or her life from these parents, regardless of what kind of people they are or were, including everything that belongs to them and their fate. There is no way to avoid this step.

Mother's Heart Attack: 'Dear Mum, now I take you, with everything that belongs to you.'
(Patient with chronic headache)

This woman, about 55 years old, has suffered since childhood from headaches that have proven unresponsive to all therapy. In the course of the constellation group, her headache becomes more and more intense, to the point where it is almost unbearable. During the break, the patient asks me to work with her next if possible, as she is afraid that she will have to leave the group because of this extreme pain.

It is striking how many patients suffer from headache when they participate in a constellation group. I consider this a good sign, that in their participation in the group process and being touched by the family dynamics of others in the group they are allowing love to be activated in the depths of the soul. People suffering from headache pain often find it difficult to let their love flow freely towards their parents.

When the patient was two years old, her mother suffered a heart attack. Although she survived, from that point on the mother's heart problems became the central focus of the family. The children were always hearing from their father, 'you know Mother shouldn't get excited'. When she was near, the children were not able to relax and just be children, and a reaching-out movement towards their mother was interrupted.

The constellation confirms that these dynamics are in play. I ask the patient to choose representatives for herself, for her mother and for her mother's illness. She chooses a woman to represent her mother's illness and places her close by the side of her mother's representative. The two smile at each other immediately; they embrace and then turn to look together at the daughter's representative. The daughter very much wants to go to her mother, but doesn't feel confident taking that step. She cautiously takes a few tiny steps in that direction, but as soon as she looks at the representative of her mother's disease, she shrinks back again. She is caught in this movement, taking one step forward and one step back. The mother's representative sees her daughter's need but does not feel able to let go of the illness and go to her daughter.

At this point I have the patient take the place of her representative in the constellation. Just as her representative, the patient cannot look at the woman representing her mother's illness and the path to her mother is out of alignment. I support her by suggesting that she look in her mother's eyes and say: 'dear Mum, now I take you, with everything that belongs to you'.

This sentence indicates respect for the mother's illness and for everything the illness represents. The patient can then look at the representative of the illness and take small steps towards the two. The mother's representative reaches out a hand and they embrace, in tears, in a process that is very moving for all. The representative of the illness is pleased by the loving meeting of mother and daughter, and puts her arms around the two like a protective force. The patient looks at her and says, 'now I can agree to the way it was, and you belong to that'.

As the patient steps out of the embrace, a thought enters my mind and I ask her if she happens to be a doctor. She confirms this in some surprise and then, after a thoughtful pause, her face lights up and she says, laughingly, 'but I think I can now finally do what I have always wanted to do'.

Immediately following this work, the patient's intense headache, which has been present for days, disappears. In conclusion, I suggest to the patient that she write the words 'Dear Mum' on her packet of pain pills.

AN ALCOHOLIC MOTHER: 'A LITTLE GLASS OF SCOTCH EACH DAY' (Patient with basal cell carcinoma)

A woman, about 45, developed a basal cell carcinoma three years ago. The tumor is localized, but destructive and growing. She previously had surgery and radiation therapy but the tumor grew back within six months. Meanwhile, despite four surgeries and very aggressive treatment, the cancer has not been brought under control. Since the onset of the disease, the patient has lost more than 15 kilos (33 pounds), and her pale complexion indicates a generally poor condition.

The following dialogue has been transcribed verbatim from an audio recording:

Therapist: What is your life situation at the moment?

Patient: I am divorced, no children. My husband was an alcoholic.

Therapist: Was there a drinker in your family?

Patient: Yes, my mother. She started drinking when I was still in school. When I was 17, my father left us. I stayed with my mother and took care of her until she died of cirrhosis of the liver. My life actually began after she died.

Therapist: (*after a pause*) I get the impression that you are angry with her.

Patient: No, she drank because...

Therapist: No, no, you are angry with her. One can see it – and this anger is easier than the pain.

Patient: I loved her very much! She died a year before I got ill.

Therapist: So, if there were a cure, what would heal the cancer?

Patient: The doctors?

Therapist: No.

Patient: Me?

Therapist: No.

Patient: You?

Therapist: Oh, good heavens, not me!

Patient: I was afraid of this. My mother?

Therapist: My suspicion is that it isn't going to happen without Mother.

Since this work was taking place in an advanced training group, I address the group to share with them what the patient's body language is saying, thereby also drawing the patient's attention to her own physical sensations.

> *Therapist:* You can see the tension in her body as soon as she mentions her mother. I am not interested in determining what the reason for that is, but it is an indication that the love between her and her mother (that is undoubtedly present) is not flowing freely. I use this tension as a barometer for the intervention and as I place a representative of her mother facing her, I will focus my attention on her physical reactions.

I ask the patient which participant in the group could represent her mother. She chooses a woman, and I ask this woman to come and stand in front of the patient, who is sitting next to me. As the mother's representative approaches and takes her position, the patient immediately moves her chair backwards. This small, instant movement confirms for me the patient's unconscious opposition towards her mother. A voice inside her is saying, 'don't come any closer!' I very slowly and carefully move the mother's representative nearer to the patient, paying close attention to the exact distance needed. Finally, I ask the patient to say to her mother: 'dear Mommy, I am ill.' The woman speaks the sentence but cannot look her mother's representative in the eye as she does so. Instead, the patient reaches out for her mother's hand and wants to hold it against her cheek. I prevent this hasty impulse, because I am not certain that it is a real reaching out movement or if it is a more covert defense. Instead, I ask the mother's representative to again move nearer, and then again even nearer, one centimeter at a time, until she is close enough that the patient leans her head on the woman's belly. She rests here and begins to cry softly. She embraces her mother, who strokes her hair. Slowly the love between the two begins to flow.

In conclusion I tell the group, 'good medicine for this patient might be to drink a small glass of cognac each day'. The patient shakes her head, so I ask her, 'okay, what did your mother drink?'

Patient: Gin or scotch.

Therapist: Good, let's take scotch.

Patient: I hate the smell!

Therapist: Okay, that would be it then. Every day, you take a tiny sip. This is not homeopathy, though! When you begin to like the taste, then you can stop. Then it will be fine.

Patient: I could start with cognac.

Therapist: No, scotch! This is a medical prescription! And, it will only help if you follow the instructions precisely.

Patient: (laughing) Agreed! Now I only have to explain this to my doctor. Thank you.

Two years later I met the patient at a conference for systemic constellations. She asked me if I remembered her, but I had to admit that I did not. She told me that she was the woman to whom I had prescribed scotch two years earlier. She wanted to tell me that it helped and her cancer has never reappeared.

In the following case, a child's fear of her mother's chronic disease prevents their love from flowing freely. When this conflict is resolved, the patient's long-standing allergies also decrease.

'YOU HAVE TO RESPECT YOUR MOTHER'S ILLNESS.'
(Patient with multiple allergies)

In a training course, a woman asked me to work with her as she suffered from various allergies. This course was also recorded on tape, so I will again present a verbatim account of the work.

Therapist: What is the problem?

Patient: I am suffering increasingly from allergies.

Therapist: How long have you had this problem?

Patient: It started about 11 or 12 years ago.

Therapist: Was there any change in your life at this time?

Patient: I was on holiday with my family, with my husband and daughter.

At this point, I am uncertain whether I am getting to the essential information, so I decide to speak more explicitly to her about her physical affliction.

Therapist: Sometimes there are family dynamics underlying allergies. The allergic person is saying, 'go away!' to someone that he or she genuinely loves.

The patient appears touched and nods her head; she drops her gaze and begins to cry. After a while, she confirms the hypothesis. 'It could be. When I was nine years old, my mother became ill with rheumatoid arthritis, a chronic inflammation of the joints, with terrible pain, particularly in her fingers and toes. When I was 18, I moved to Moscow and got married, but I always went back home to visit whenever I had time. This one summer, we took our holiday at the seaside, and that's when I became allergic to the sun.

In the meantime, my mother has died. She was ill for 25 years. Three days before her death, I visited her and I couldn't stand her suffering. I prayed every day that she would die.'

Therapist: Let's choose two representatives – one for you and one for the allergies.

The patient chooses two women and places them at a distance turned away from each other.

After a while, the woman representing the allergies looks round at the patient's representative and then turns towards her. The other woman, however, continues to stare fixedly at the floor.

The representative of the allergies slowly approaches and takes the other woman cautiously in her arms, but the woman remains unchanged – closed and turned away. The representative of the allergies does not give up, but continues to stroke the patient's representative gently until she allows herself to be embraced.

It is clear that the woman representing the allergies is actually representing the patient's mother, and I am quite certain that the patient recognizes this as well. I take her carefully by the hand, and lead her to replace her representative in the constellation. I place the patient in front of her 'mother'. Like her representative, she too is unable to look her mother's representative in the eye. She stares at the floor and seems closed and uncommunicative.

To help the patient get in contact with her own longing and pain, I ask her to say, 'Mummy'. She repeats, 'Mummy'.

Therapist: Dearest Mummy!

Patient: Dearest Mummy!

Therapist: My dearest Mummy!

These words are too much for her and she cannot speak. She begins to weep and pulls back.

I interrupt the work at this point, confident that there will be an opportunity to continue later in the day now that we have identified the first step towards resolution.

I will include here, the patient's own detailed and moving story of her experience (written later):

Dear Stephan,

A training course in Moscow: I see the constellation work for the first time. I find it difficult to understand what is happening. A man is put in the center of the circle as a representative and suddenly begins to cry. I have never seen a man cry. I feel like I have to leave, but my husband won't let me go.

The next constellation has to do with a man and his difficult relationship with his mother. He believes he has been angry with her his whole life. The constellation shows, though, that it has to do with his father, who died very young. The man could not show his pain at that loss. Instead, he reacted with anger and directed it at his mother. At the end of the constellation, when these connections are clear, this man also begins to cry and says, 'dear Mother, I am sorry. Now I can also see your pain'.

Suddenly, sitting in the circle watching, I also start crying and I cannot stop. I have never cried like this. Even when my mother died, I didn't cry like this. The night that her coffin was at home in our house, I sat in the kitchen with her friends and laughed. They were remembering funny stories about my mother's life. Now, when I hear this man's words, I start crying for the first time. After my mother's death, I tried to watch a video of her. The video was filmed nine months before she died, at her 55th birthday party. It was a gay celebration, and she sang songs and danced with my father. You could see how much they loved each other. I couldn't watch this video. Somehow, I couldn't bear it.

I was nine when my mother got polyarthritis. I remember that she wept every morning because it was so painful to touch anything and so hard to get up in the morning. I could not get as close to her as I wanted to, nor could I embrace her, because any touch caused her pain. I learned to live without being near her. My father and mother made it possible for me to go to Moscow and study. Whenever I was free, I went home to visit my mother. After four years of studying, I met my husband, got married and had a daughter. Everything was wonderful.

The only thing we are afraid of in our family is that someone will get polyarthritis – perhaps my daughter or me. My mother's cousin has a daughter who got this illness when her second child was born. She could not get up again from the birthing chair. For me, this is the worst disease that one can have. That's why I married a doctor.

When we had been married for seven years, we had a chance to have a holiday at the seaside with our daughter. That summer, we did not have time to visit my mother, and during this time I became allergic to the sun. My allergy continued to get worse and I began to react to various allergens. Following a theater buffet, I had a skin rash on my thighs and arms that just continued to spread. I tried every kind of medication in Russia, without success. I tried avoiding food that could be a trigger, without any results. I had homeopathic treatments, also with no results. I finally said to myself: just let it be how it is. I can come to terms with what I have. I can live with this allergy – it's only a minor complaint. I am a lawyer, and when I had meetings with clients, I was never sure whether they felt bothered by the red spots on my face or on my arms. Somehow, though, I stopped worrying about it after a while. Two years went by in this way and then I heard about a workshop with Stephan Hausner with an emphasis on constellation work in the healing process. I had a chance to do a constellation there.

Stephan began the work with me by talking about the systemic family influences in allergies. The sentence that touched me was, 'An allergic person says 'go away' to someone that he or she really loves. My throat immediately closed up. When my mother lay dying, I prayed and hoped that she would die. I understood that this allergy was connected in some way to my relationship with my mother.

'Let's set up two representatives, one for you and one for your allergies', said Stephan. I asked myself, why not my mother? Why the allergies? So, I chose a girl for myself, and a very young girl, who did not resemble my mother in any way, to represent the allergies. Stephan asked the representatives to go along with their feelings and follow any impulses to change something, but to do it slowly and in a collected way. To my amazement, the woman representing my allergies embraced my representative like a mother to her daughter. That was the whole constellation.

Stephan released my representative and asked my mother's representative to stand facing me. He asked me to say, 'dearest Mummy!'

I repeated, 'dearest Mummy!' He continued 'my dearest Mummy.' I could not say that. I could not make myself say the word 'my'. It was so painful. My husband and, even more, my daughter were present and I could not show my pain in front of them. Also, this girl who was now representing my mother – she was no longer my allergies, but I also couldn't see her as my mother. Stephan indicated that I should move a bit nearer towards my mother, but I felt like a stone. She put her arms around me, but I stayed a stone. I could not embrace her. Stephan said, 'allergies are easier'. Of course! They are nothing compared to the pain in my soul. They are nothing compared with the death of my mother, I thought, and I agreed with him. I can live with these allergies, but my love for my mother, that is truly painful. Stephan stopped the work at this point.

After two more constellations with other patients, I asked a question about my inner process. 'Mentally I get it, but emotionally I feel cut off and hard as a rock?' Stephan seemed to have been waiting for my question. He looked me in the eye and without answering my question, he simply said, 'you have to respect your mother's illness'.

Dear Stephan, I thank you for this sentence. It was the most important sentence I have ever heard. I understood that in rejecting my mother's illness, I was rejecting my mother as a total being. I understood that the next step for me would be to agree to her illness. It was so painful living for 23 years afraid of coming too close to her. For 23 years, I was afraid that someone else might also get this disease.

The night after this workshop, I wept in my husband's arms.

Two months later, I happened across the video of my mother's party. I was able to watch it and even enjoy it. I heard her sister say, 'oh no, we are already so old…' and I heard my mother answer, 'let's not go to our graves before it's time'. I heard such a thing from my mother for the first time.

Four more months went by. I attended another constellation training group with Dr. Gunthard Weber. Again, I experienced being in this constellation field. The entire three days, my fingers were twisted as if I had an advanced case of polyarthritis, but without any pain. I had no influence over this, my finger just twisted. I understood what it was telling me. It was my mother's illness. But, I wasn't afraid of it any longer. I could agree to having a twisted, alien finger. After two or three weeks, it went away and has never happened again. Then, all of a sudden, I realized that it had been about four months since I had had any allergic reactions. Then it was six months. Now it has been one year.

Sometimes I have the feeling that I want to scratch the places that used to be affected. Instead, now, I stroke my arms and say, 'dearest Mummy, my dearest mummy'.

Last summer I went to the seaside with my husband and daughter. When I noticed that I was starting to want to scratch my arms, I said, 'my dearest Mummy, it is so beautiful here'. I imagined that she was there on holiday with us. I told her she could enjoy with me what she had been unable to enjoy herself.

Dear Stephan, thank you very much. I wanted to wait for a year to write this report, just to be certain that my allergies were truly gone.

My life has changed. In general, I feel more feminine now and I can wear skirts instead of always trousers, as I did previously. My husband and I have begun to dance the tango and we enjoy sharing a coordinated movement of our bodies.

I cannot find the words to express my thanks to you and also to Bert Hellinger. The gratitude is in my heart and I am certain that you and Bert can feel it.

From Russia, with love, S.

ILLNESS AND ATTACHMENT LOSS DUE TO A PARENT'S DEATH
'DEAR MUM, NOW I HONOR YOUR LIFE, AND YOUR DEATH.'
(Patient with fibromyalgia)

Fibromyalgia is a chronic, non-inflammatory disease characterized by widespread pain in the muscles and tendons. It is often accompanied by sleep disturbances and chronic fatigue.

The patient is a woman, about 30, who is married and has a two-year-old daughter. In the constellation group, she chooses a representative for herself and a woman to represent her illness. She first positions the representative of the disease, and then places her own representative in front of the other woman, with her back against her.

The representative of the illness immediately begins to breathe heavily and gasps for air. When the patient's representative tries to lean back against her, the woman representing the illness instinctively takes a few steps back. She then turns away. The patient's representative turns around, looking resentfully at the back of the other woman and stamps her foot in vexation.

When I ask the patient about anything of note in her family of origin, we discover that she lost her mother as a result of a traffic accident when she was one and a half years old. It is probable that her mother fell asleep at the wheel and crashed into a tree. She died on the spot of injuries sustained in the crash. Soon thereafter, the patient's father married his widow's younger sister. Within a year their twin daughters were born.

I suggest that the patient add a representative for her mother to the constellation. When this woman is added, the constellation seems to turn to stone. I ask the mother's representative to lie on the floor, in order to emphasize the fact that she is dead. The patient's representative turns towards her mother and the anger and resentment begin to fade from her face. The underlying pain becomes increasingly visible, until, with tears in her eyes, she kneels down, next to her mother, and takes her hand.

The patient herself also begins to cry and says, 'I was always angry with her for leaving'.

The representative of the illness has also turned round in the meantime and is watching the scene between the mother and daughter. When she sees the movement of reconciliation, she retreats from the constellation, step by step.

I have the patient take her representative's place in the constellation. She kneels next to her mother's representative, takes her hand, and says tearfully, 'I am sorry'. Her mother gathers her daughter to her, and the patient weeps in her mother's arms. Finally, as they finish their embrace, I suggest that the patient say to her mother: 'dearest Mum, even though it was difficult for me, I now agree to how things were. I honor your life – and your death'.

The patient feels very relieved following this work. Two days later, in the final group round, she says that she is beginning to realize how much of her strength had been diverted and sacrificed to her anger. Since the constellation, she has felt an unfamiliar sense of lightness, including when she is around her husband.

In countless constellations with patients suffering from fibromyalgia, I have observed an underlying feeling of anger. It is sometimes, as in this case, the rage of a child who feels abandoned by a parent. Sometimes, the anger is aimed at a partner who has triggered a major disappointment, for example due to a drinking problem. Sometimes, the resentment has been taken over from someone else in the family system, such as a father's previous partner, perhaps anger that the relationship was terminated in a way that was not optimal.

Following

Early loss of a parent can sometimes lead to a different dynamic that might be described as following into death. In this case, the child's desire to be near his or her parents is stronger than the desire to live.

This conscious or unconscious death wish seems operative in many life-threatening diseases and addictions, but also in an inexplicable accident-proneness. There is sometimes a hint of this in an unconscious smile on the patient's face when talking to the therapist about a life-threatening illness.

The dynamics of following can sometimes be resolved in a constellation if the patient can look the other person in the eye and agree to that person's death. In this contact, the patient can see that the deceased person does not really desire this love and closeness at such a high price. The greatest joy for any parent is for their children to live and thrive.

In addition to children following their parents, we see the same dynamics occurring between partners or in parents whose children have died young. In such cases, however, I have generally found that when a patient wishes to follow a partner or child, that partner or child is actually representing the patient's mother or father.

Premature Death: 'My father took a risk...'
(Patient with AIDS, acquired immune deficiency syndrome)

In a training group, I am working with a homosexual man, about 30 years old, who has AIDS. His tanned, fit body implies a healthy life style, and he confirms that he is dealing with his illness in a judicious, sensible manner. When I ask how he got the disease, he says that he was infected many years ago, most probably from a single sexual contact with an older man, an incident that was unpleasant for the patient. He was aware of the risk at the time, but was not strong enough to follow his better judgment and resist.

I ask no further questions, but have the patient set up a constellation of his family of origin. He chooses representatives for his father, his mother, and for himself and places them in relationship to one another. He positions his father's representative unusually far away from the two representing his mother and him.

The father's representative is overcome by powerful physical reactions. His legs are shaking so hard that he finally gives up and sinks to the floor. His legs continue to shake, and also his hands, balled into fists, and his rigid arms. At last, exhausted, he stops shaking. After a while, he closes his eyes and is lying on the floor as if dead. The patient's representative stares at his father in a frozen manner, and initially is incapable of any movement or expression of feeling.

With tears in his eyes, the patient watches the movements of his father's representative. When he is calm, I ask him what happened to his father. 'My father died when I was two years old and I can hardly remember him at all. My Mother and I never had a chance to say goodbye. He was a fireman, and was killed fighting a fire. He ignored the better judgment of his fellow fire-fighters and repeatedly went back into a burning building to try to rescue the inhabitants, who had been taken by surprise by the fire in the middle of the night. He took a risk that he should not have taken.'

At this sentence, the patient stops talking and looks at me thoughtfully. I repeat, 'he took a risk that he should not have taken'. In the meantime, the patient's representative has moved slowly over to the father lying on the floor. He kneels down beside him and lays his head on his father's chest. When he is asked to say how he is feeling, he says, 'here, with my father, I am doing really well'. I thank the representative and release him from this role. I take the patient by the hand and lead him to his father's representative, lying on the floor. He kneels down to this man with love and respect and the two embrace warmly. When they have withdrawn from their embrace, I suggest that the patient tell his father, 'dearest Daddy, although I miss you, I am going to stay as long as I can – then I will come, too'. He speaks these words in a quiet, calm manner. The father's representative smiles, nods in agreement, and says, 'yes, it is good like that'. The son bends down to his father once again and the two hold each other for a long time, until they feel finished.

The patient chooses to withdraw and be alone following this work. He asks the group to excuse him, because he has been taken by surprise by this unexpected connection.

Mimicry

In the constellations, we often see how children unconsciously try to fulfill their longing to be close to their parents by imitating those parents in fatal loyalty. This usually appears in behavior or reactions that the other parent opposes or judges in some way. Children love their fathers and their mothers, regardless of how those parents are or were.

In the constellation of a woman with a brain tumor, the representative of the disease turns into her father, a soldier who came home from the war blind. When the patient's great love for her father is revealed, the constellation leader asks the woman how old her father was when he died. The answer is that her father died at the age of 50, and the woman is now 48. As she relates this, it occurs to her that her brother has always been afraid that he would not live to be any older than their father. When she was diagnosed with the tumor (astrocytoma), she laughingly said to him: 'You can relax now, I was quicker.'

Illness and a Child's Attachment Insecurity due to Trauma

Civil War: 'My dear mum, the father one has is always the best!' (Patient with chronic gastritis)

In an advanced training course, I am working with a man who reports that he suffers from a chronic inflammation of the stomach lining. I can feel a deep sadness in this man and to me he seems like a lost child. I suspect this has some connection to his symptoms, so I ask him if anything special happened in his childhood. He was born in the Belgian Congo, and the war of independence began when he was eleven years old. He was in a small shop when soldiers with machine guns burst through the door and shot at the people in the shop. The boy dropped to the floor immediately and the bullets flew above his head. The two people who had been standing next to him in the queue were fatally shot.

As the patient speaks of this traumatic experience, I sense a deep pain, a feeling of abandonment. This traumatic event perhaps separated him from his parents.

In view of the patient's issue, we begin the constellation with two representatives, one for him and one for his physical symptoms. The patient's representative begins to sway and stares fixedly at a spot on the floor about three meters in front of him. The representative of the symptoms feels lifeless, cut off from everything, and far away. This reaction suggests a possible connection to the patient's traumatic experience. I ask the patient about the gender of the people who died at his side during that incident. He reports that a man stood to his right and a woman on his left. I choose the two representatives and ask them to lie down on the spot where the patient's representative is looking.

The patient's representative is clearly overwhelmed by the sight of these two dead people, and before he drops to his knees, I place two representatives for his parents behind him. This makes it easier for him to remain standing. This seems to be the right moment to put the patient into the constellation. I lead him slowly to the position in front of his parents and have him replace his representative. The sight of the dead makes him weep, and finally he moves slowly towards them, sits down by them on the floor. He touches them and closes their eyes. Then, he just sits there and cries. The representative of the symptoms observes all this very attentively. Slowly, a calmness flows into the constellation.

I trust my intuition that the patient's symptoms are connected to his inner conflict. He has a longing for closeness to his parents but is also unconsciously blaming them for having left him alone in this difficult situation. I tell the patient to look at his parents. As he turns away from the dead, the representative of the symptoms relaxes for a moment and slowly begins to back out of the constellation. I continue the movement by asking the patient to stand and come back to his parents. They try to take him in their arms, but he fends them off, especially his father. He finds it impossible to accept this love and affection. The father's representative says, 'it is so hard for me to see you suffering,' but the patient cannot take that in, either.

I anticipate that this process will require some time, so I interrupt the work at this point.

About three months after the constellation, the patient attends another constellation group.

He reports that he fell into a mild depression after the last constellation. It was difficult for him to work and he needed a lot of sleep. Since it was possible for him to do that, he managed quite well. 'After about a week, as I began to feel better again, the physical changes started. First, the pressure in my stomach diminished. This was a huge relief, since I have lived with that since I was twelve. (*About one year after the traumatic war experience! [Author's comment]*) Gradually, however, I began to experience intestinal problems. I have a lot of gas and have to go to the toilet a lot more often. Sometimes I suspect I might have Crohn's disease. My symptoms have moved down from my stomach to my intestines. So, I decided to come again.'

Without explaining his background to the group participants, I ask the patient to choose representatives for himself, his father and his mother. I ask the representatives to follow their own impulses. The mother's representative is persistent in her efforts to stay between her son and his father.

This leads me to question the patient about his mother's father. To my surprise, the grandfather is not known and there is no information about him.

I decide not to put in a representative for the grandfather to address this problem, but rather, to stay focussed on the patient and look for a resolution for him. I take him to stand next to his father and suggest that he tell his mother's representative: 'my dear mum, the father one has is always the best. I respect whatever is between you and your father, and I leave that with you. For me, my father is the right one'. When these words are spoken, the father's representative puts his arm around his son and hugs him. Cautiously, with one eye on his mother, the patient lays his head on his father's shoulder. The mother's representative takes pleasure in this new closeness between her son and his father, and the patient can close his eyes and relax calmly in the arms of his father.

I ask the patient if this seems good to him and he affirms that it does. At the end I say to him, 'a good place for you is with your father and you have to let your mother go'. He nods in agreement and says 'I know that'.

Four months later, when he is in another constellation group with his partner, I ask him about his prior experience. He reports that in the earlier experience it had not been easy to lay his head on his father's shoulder, but he had finally been able to relax in his arms and could look him in the eyes. That was a very good feeling. After the constellation, he felt very tired at first. He had less gas and slowly lost weight, without going on a diet. He bought some new clothes and noticed that he felt generally lighter and began taking better care of himself. He was more conscious of what he ate and less frivolous about it. The earlier feeling of distress, which had always been with him, had lessened. After a single treatment from a craniosacral therapist his intestinal disturbance diminished and that had remained so. That is one clear change that he had noticed. He rarely had heartburn any more, and a heart problem he had had for years, associated with the intestinal disorder (Roemheld's Syndrome), was no longer an issue.

Trauma and Constellation Work

A detailed look at this important and broad reaching topic is beyond the scope of this book. I would suggest Levine (1997) and St. Just (2006) for a depth analysis of these issues.

In general, I do not consider the methods of systemic constellations appropriate for working with deep personal trauma. However, as constellation leaders, particularly when working with groups, we are likely to be confronted with situations in which earlier traumatic experiences are re-activated. This can affect our patients but also, perhaps even more frequently, other group participants. We try to avoid unnecessary re-traumatization by proceeding in a way that remains focussed primarily on resolution and resources.

The resource that is most constant and among the most easily accessible is time itself. A tempo and rhythm that is in accord with the patient's ability to integrate interventions and constellation events can prevent a possible reactivation of trauma. When symptoms of trauma appear — such as accelerated heart rate, difficulty breathing, cold sweats, tingling, and muscular tension (Levine 1997, page 128) – a possible first measure would be to slow down the therapeutic process and the movement of the constellation.

ILLNESS AND AN INTERRUPTED REACHING-OUT MOVEMENT

We speak of an early interruption of a reaching-out movement when a child loses trust in a parent due to an early separation. The child refuses any closeness to the parent for fear that the experience might be repeated. Even though the parents may have cared lovingly for their child following the separation, the child's anxiety persists. The child resists the attentions of the parent and represses his or her own longing for security and closeness. In an attempt to create distance from the mother without causing her pain, the child may develop physical symptoms to solve the problem. Similar dynamics may also show up later in other significant relationships.

Not only anxiety disorders, but also many other health problems such as asthma, chronic headache, or allergies, may be related to early childhood separation trauma. Such separations would include Caesarean births, a period of time in an incubator, being left in a baby care group or in hospital, or a mother's hospitalization (for example for the birth of another child). Also sometimes parents leave their child in the care of relatives or friends because of work or travel and the child may be unable to feel the same degree of trust for the parents afterwards.

Just as a physical separation can have after-effects, an early emotional separation between mother and child may result in similar effects. These too can originate in the circumstances of the birth. A connection between mother and child might be interrupted if the mother or child is in danger, or if the birth itself is cause for heightened anxiety, for example during a precipitate delivery.

Emotional separation can even occur during the pregnancy. For example, if a mother is concerned about the health or life of the child. She may have previously lost a child or children, or perhaps, her doctor has diagnosed a potential problem or made comments that have led the mother to have doubts about the health of the child. As a result, the mother is no longer free to turn totally to this child-in-utero. From this perspective, labeling a pregnancy as 'high risk' is a step that warrants serious consideration.

The earlier the separation between mother and child, and the longer it lasts, the more difficult it is for the child to resume a movement of reaching out again. Generally this cannot be done without some external help.

The dynamics of an interrupted reaching-out movement can be best resolved in therapy if the child can be held by the mother, even against resistance, until trust is regained. This so-called 'holding therapy' was originally developed by Jirina Prekop.

In a constellation group setting, a therapist can approximate the resolution process by assuming the position of the mother and leading the patient back to the traumatic event, all the while holding the person firmly until resistance dissolves. In this way, the desired reaching-out movement may be achieved and the patient learns to permit intimacy again in the future. The energy of love and life is allowed to flow freely, not only from the parent to the child and vice versa, but also between partners.

SEPARATION AT BIRTH: 'EVERYTHING TURNED OUT FINE!'
(Patient with asthma)

In the next case, when the woman asks me to work with her in
a workshop, I am not aware that she suffers from asthma. She
sits next to me and I slowly enter into the work with her. She
conveys an impression of great neediness, and my sense is that
the most important thing at the moment is to be very present
with her. After a while, she spontaneously lays her head on my
shoulder. I am aware of what this has cost her, and I put my arm
gently around her. Suddenly, as she begins to breathe very deeply
and loudly, I hold her a bit more firmly. She is breathing heavily,
but compared to the vigorous movements of her chest, the rest
of her body is rigid and stiff. Her body is clearly not in accordance with the movement of her breathing. I ask her to express
this deep breathing with a movement in her body and incorpo-
rate her body into the breathing process. She begins to breathe
against the resistance of my arm and integrates her body more
and more into the movement. I give her just enough space so that
she can slowly breathe her way through my arms, just as if she
were moving through a birth canal. When she has come through
the embrace with her upper body, I ask a woman in the group
to act as a representative for the patient's mother, to receive the
patient in her arms. The fearful look on the patient's face suggests a possible birth trauma and I suggest her mother's words:
'everything is fine, my dear child, everything is fine. I am so happy
that everything has turned out well'. The patient becomes calm in
the arms of her mother and is slowly able to breathe quietly and
freely again. What is described here in just a few words actually
lasted almost an hour.

Three years later, I ran into this woman in another constellation
group. She thanked me and told me about the healing effect of that

therapeutic work. Later she wrote a letter explaining that for three years her life had not been disrupted by asthma attacks. For three years she had not had to face the despair, the suffocation, the helplessness, the fear, and the feeling she was about to die. Her last asthma attack occurred during that therapeutic work. Although she could not remember exactly what happened she was still able to feel in her body the feeling of warmth and security of that moment, the feelings of a new born child. Since that work she had felt generally stronger and healthier and, above all, had had no further battles with her bronchial tubes.

Further, she informed me that she had been born by Caesarean section weighing three pounds and 15.5 ounces. She only had to be in an incubator for a few hours since, despite her small size, she was in good health. Her mother had had a difficult pregnancy because of her grandfather's illness and death. He died of pancreatic cancer when her mother was expecting her. The mother had been very close to her father and his illness was very upsetting for her.

TRAUMA DURING PREGNANCY
(Patient with scoliosis)

The woman in this case has already had many years of psychotherapy and has done several constellations with various therapists. According to her account, she has received help resolving many different areas of her life, but has always fallen short of her long-standing goal, which is to be closer to her mother. Throughout her whole life, this relationship has been strained. Even as a small child, she rejected an intimate, close relationship with her mother. She feels an overwhelming need to find peace in this area but, despite her longings, she has not yet found a way to allow the closeness she desires.

I suggest that we try a different therapeutic approach this time and the patient gladly agrees to my recommendation of craniosacral therapy.

Craniosacral osteopathy is a therapeutic manipulation of the cranial-sacral system, in which the spinal fluid flows rhythmically between the skull and the sacrum. This pulsation can be felt throughout the entire body and, unlike the pulse and breathing, these rhythms can be influenced by using techniques of lightly stimulating impulses. Imbalances and blocks of these rhythms can lead to physical, mental, or emotional dysfunction and may interfere with the self-regulation of the organism.

I personally use the patient's cranial-sacral rhythms as a critical factor in the timing of constellation work. If the rhythm slows down or pauses, this is a clue that the patient is involved in a significant process of integration.

In the first consultation, the craniosacral therapist I recommended discovers a twist to the right in the thoracic area of the spine. His efforts to correct this are unsuccessful and he also suspects a link to an earlier trauma. Therefore, in the next treatment, he works with a technique of body-orientated psychotherapy, called somatic-emotional clearing, which comes from the practice of craniosacral osteopathy.

During the course of this treatment, the patient experiences deep sadness. When asked how old she is in her pain, she reports that she is very young. When the therapist asks whether it is before or after her birth, she says it is possibly from before birth. She knows of no complications during her mother's pregnancy.

About two weeks after this session, the patient asks her mother if anything traumatic happened during her pregnancy, and her mother confirms that there was an incident. In her sixth month, her younger brother played a trick on her by coming up behind her and putting a live frog on her right shoulder. The patient's mother was frightened 'to death' and went into labor immediately. She was put to bed until the pains eased off and stopped after two days.

This story touches the patient deeply, because in her mother's anxiety about her, she feels, for the first time, her mother's deep love – a feeling that she has never felt before. A door that had been closed is opened for the first time.

About two weeks go by before she sees her mother again. As so often happens, a small matter escalates into a fight. This time, however, the patient does not turn away in anger. She remains relatively unperturbed and is able to confront the situation calmly. After a short talk, which she experiences as 'a small miracle', she can allow herself to feel the previously repressed pain. The conflict dissolves 'of its own accord', in an embrace with her mother. For her mother, too, this is a surprising turn of events in what had become a routine occurrence. The long desired reaching-out movement can be completed for the first time.

In a final session, the patient mentions that many friends and acquaintances now experience her as having changed in a positive way, without being able to describe exactly what the difference is.

I find it remarkable that the patient's spinal column had taken over, remembering her mother's body movement as she froze in fright, and that the connection between the mother and child was broken.

THE TRANSFUSION: 'THANK YOU!'

Towards the end of a constellation group, a woman of about 30 hesitantly asks to work. Although it is clear that she is feeling a desperate need, her fear of the therapeutic work is also apparent. She sits down beside me very cautiously. This reserved manner in our initial contact suggests an early separation from her mother. To check out this hypothesis, I pull my chair a bit nearer and turn towards her. Her immediate reaction is to lean further back in her chair to maintain distance. This movement of pulling away confirms my suspicion that a reaching-out movement to her mother or father might have been interrupted.

Having gathered this much information from our non-verbal communication, I now ask her about the issue that is concerning her. She says: 'I hardly dare to say what it is out loud. I have always had the feeling that I am possessed. It terrifies me and up till now, I haven't dared to consult a doctor or therapist about it'.

Somehow, I have the feeling that the patient's concern is well founded. There is something 'foreign' in her – something that does not belong or should not be allowed to belong. The fear that this engenders is also palpable. On the one hand, the patient feels relieved when I confirm her feelings, but on the other hand, her tension and fear increase when she abandons the hope that her feelings were not serious. To calm her, I put my arm gently around her and draw her a bit towards me, ignoring her resistance. She begins to cry and lays her head on my shoulder. I hold her this way until she is calm again. When she starts to pull away, I follow my intuition and put my other arm around her, thereby holding her even more firmly. She begins to breathe deeply and tries vehemently to resist my embrace, and I adjust the pressure of my arms to match her resistance. As she begins to breathe faster and deeper, it is clear that the patient is regressing into a birth trauma. I ask her to direct her breathing into a body movement and use that to free herself from my firm hold on her. Slowly, she works her way through my arms. In the meantime, I signal two representatives and indicate to them that, as her parents, they are to receive and hold the now exhausted woman. Visibly relieved, she slides into the arms of her parents' representatives. When she has recovered somewhat, I ask her what happened at her birth. She explains that she had an RH factor incompatibility and required a complete blood transfusion immediately to prevent her dying. She was born in a small hospital in Zermatt, Switzerland. A medical assistant at the hospital happened to have the appropriate blood type and offered to donate the blood she needed. This act saved her life.

I select a representative for the blood donor and ask him to stand behind the parents' representatives, who are seated on the floor. Without any prompting, the patient looks lovingly at him and says 'thank you'. The parents also look at him and say 'thank you'. The blood donor lays his hands on the parents' shoulders and looks with pleasure at the young family.

About a year after this constellation, the patient wrote a thank you note, commenting that she had felt 'like a newborn' since the work. She celebrated the anniversary of this change as a second birthday. She no longer had the feeling that there was something foreign inside her that she had to carry.

ILLNESS AND ATTACHMENT INSECURITY DUE TO PARENTS' LIMITED EMOTIONAL AVAILABILITY

Parents are often not completely free to engage with their children because they have such strong attachments to members of their family of origin or previous partners or because of traumatic experiences in their own lives. Their children sense that something is not quite right in their relationship to their parents. They feel insecure and have the feeling that they cannot fully trust and relax. Children generally react to such feelings by looking for the fault within themselves.

The dynamics that contribute to this mistrust show up in constellations. The representatives of such parents often do not feel close to their children, or find it intolerable to be near them. They sometimes even turn away from the children altogether.

THE RAGE: 'DEAREST DADDY, I WAS NOT FREE'
(Patient with high blood pressure)

This case involves a man of about 35 who has suffered from high blood pressure for the past three years. When I ask if anything special happened three years ago, the man describes the background situation. 'The company I worked for suddenly went bankrupt and I had to find a new job. I am well qualified so I really didn't have to worry much about it, but I still fell into a deep depression. I felt as though the basic foundations of my life had been pulled out from under me.'

In many constellations, we see connections between the way we face professional issues and our relationship with our father. This man's statement about feeling as if the basic foundation of his life had been pulled out from under him, later proves to be significant. It is a clue to an entanglement with someone in his family whose life's foundation was lost.

I first ask this man how he gets on with his father, or if anything of significance has occurred in their relationship. The patient pulls a face and says, in a sulky manner, 'when I was 17, my father left my mother'. I ask him if he is angry with his father because of that.

Patient: Yes, because I had to take over his position!

In order to avoid going further into the patient's anger, I shift to a more factual level and tell him: 'In cases of high blood pressure, we often see family dynamics in constellations that have to do with love that is, or must be, held back.'

The man feels touched by this and he answers, very emotionally, 'I have always loved my father very much, but I've always felt that I wasn't allowed to feel that way because he treated my mother so badly'.

At this point, I ask the man to choose and position three representatives, for his father, his mother and himself. He places his father's representative somewhat apart from the other two. When I ask the representatives to follow their own impulses, the father's representative turns away from his wife and son in resignation. It seems as though he hasn't got a chance with her. The mother's representative says it is all too much for her and – most importantly – she feels that her son is much too close. She deliberately takes a step back and is visibly relieved at the greater distance. The patient's representative, however, follows her at once. The mother's representative begins breathing heavily as her son again ends up standing next to her. She regains her distance from him, by taking several steps backwards. When the patient's representative moves to follow her again, she looks at him very sternly and makes it clear to him that she does not want him any closer.

Asking further about the family history reveals that the patient's mother lost her father when she was five years old. With such a deeply anchored loss, it is difficult for the mother to form an attachment and allow closeness. Perhaps the son also has to stand in for her father, and she shies away from this contact.

In any case, I turn to the patient and ask, who he sees as responsible for the difficulties in his parents' relationship. He responds immediately, 'my father'. I give him a moment to reflect on this, and then ask him what he sees in the constellation.

Patient: My mother!

I ask the man to look at his father and say, 'dearest Daddy, I am so sorry, I was not free'. He weeps as he repeats this sentence. The father's representative instantly turns towards the patient, goes to him and takes him in his arms. The patient cries in the arms of his father, holding one hand on his own heart. He says again and again, 'it hurts so much!' The father's representative holds him firmly and calms him saying, 'it's all right; everything will be all right'. When the mother's representative sees her son in his father's arms, she is also relieved and looks at them benevolently.

In the final group round, the man says, 'no matter how much my heart ached in my father's arms, something was released there. Since that moment, I have felt a lightness that is completely foreign to me'.

When a mother has difficulties with her father and is not living in harmony with him and his fate (and her own), her children often give up their own father. They sense their mother's pain and do not want to hurt her by having a good relationship or closeness to their own father.

From the perspective of constellation work, people who are not able, or not allowed to, take one of their parents into their heart often tend towards depression. This leads to a frequent experience of depressives – the feeling of inner emptiness and abandonment. The cause often lies in an early childhood attachment disturbance (Ruppert 2003), even when the depressive behavior has only appeared later in life, with or without an identifiable trigger.

FATHER'S IMPRISONMENT AND TORTURE:
'A GIFT OF TEN YEARS!' (Patient with piastrinosis)

In a training group in Italy, there is a woman who has suffered for some years from piastrinosis, a chronic, progressive blood disease that involves over-production of platelets in the blood, with a risk of blockage in the blood vessels and thrombosis. There is a concurrent drop in red blood cells, which results in chronic fatigue. The treatment recommended by her medical doctors involves a continuous regime of chemical medication.

> The patient currently lives with her partner. She has been married previously and has a grown son from that marriage. I ask her about significant events in her family of origin.
>
> *Patient:* My father was captured by the SS when my mother was pregnant with me. When she tried to visit him in prison, she was told that she could go home because he had already been executed. Three months later, on March 4th 1944, he was released, having suffered under extreme torture. I was born on April 4th 1944, and my parents named me Grazia [the Italian word for 'thank you'].
>
> *Therapist: (after a pause)* Is your father still alive?
>
> *Patient:* No, because of his terrible treatment in prison, he had lung problems and he died when I was 10 years old. So, I'm only half of a Grazia.
>
> I can feel the effect of her words in my soul and I sense the pain and longing for her father. The response that comes up in me in this situation is 'a gift of ten years'. The patient very quickly says, 'I know...', but I stop her with gesture and repeat slowly, 'a gift of ten years'. She then begins to cry.
>
> I explain the intervention of interrupting to the group. 'One who speaks need not feel.'

There is silence in the room for some minutes. The patient closes her eyes and comes more and more into contact with the depth of her pain. She begins to take deeper breaths. When her breathing becomes faster and louder, I ask her to open her eyes and I position a participant as a representative of her father. When she becomes aware of the man in front of her, she shrieks and embraces him. When she becomes calm again I ask her to look her father's representative in the eye. I suggest that the man tell his daughter: 'In you, I am still here.' After a while, I ask him to say to her, 'I am watching over you'. The patient looks radiant, and her pain has turned to tears of joy. She takes her father's hand, kisses it, and presses it to her cheek. Finally, she lets go of him, clasps her hands over her heart in a gesture of thankfulness, bows her head slightly and says, 'thank you for everything'. I ask her to repeat, 'dearest Papa, thank you. It was a lot, and it was enough'.

Hearing these words from his daughter, the father's representative takes a step backwards. It is clear what it had cost him to survive and stay, and now his need is to pull back. This has to be respected, which the patient also recognizes, and she slowly nods her agreement. The father's representative moves slowly backwards, step by step, and feels relieved as he does so. It is clear that there is a healing link between father and daughter, as well as a concomitant increase in autonomy.

Some time later, I heard that there had been a change following this work so I asked the patient for more information about it. She reported that according to her doctors, this illness was to be treated life-long with a chemotherapeutic preparation. She had to take two pills a day and suffered various side effects such as irritations in her mouth, tongue, and esophagus, gingivitis and loose teeth, hair loss, anxiety, and depression. Directly following the constellation, for the first time in a long time, she was filled with a new feeling of strength and zest for life. She began slowly to regain a sense of trust in life, and decided to risk reducing her dosage from two pills to one and a half per day. Also, around this time she found a homeopath in Pisa. She gradually reduced her medication and at that time had been off the pills for two years. Ongoing medical checks indicated that her blood values were holding within a range that the doctors considered acceptable.

DEATH OF A SISTER
(Patient with Menière's Syndrome)

The following case illustrates how a traumatic event in a family, such as the death of another child, can lead to an emotional separation from the mother. The constellation was video taped in an advanced training group, so the dialogue is presented here verbatim.

Therapist: What can I do for you?

Patient:: I am suffering from Menière's syndrome. This is a disturbance in the inner ear that affects hearing and causes dizzy spells. At first I just ignored the dizzy spells as if they weren't happening. They frighten me but, at the same time, I rather like them. Perhaps 'like' is not the right word.

Therapist: I can feel that ambivalence between fear and yearning. What is the advantage of having these dizzy spells, do you think?

Patient: I don't know. I've given up trying to figure it out.

Therapist: Were you separated from your mother when you were a child?

Patient: Not, physically, no.

Therapist: Was there anything special about your birth?

Patient: Not that I know of. I was born in hospital, and all my siblings were born at home. The next child after me was born 18 months later.

The first contact with a patient often allows the therapist to identify basic patterns. A person frequently reveals here how he or she deals with intimacy and distance in relationships. Is this person trusting and open, or is this someone who is more cautious and reserved, holding others at arm's length? If the latter is the case, it may be an initial indication of an early childhood disturbance.

This woman has a certain air of reserve and I remember that my previous experience of her in the group has been that she is especially helpful and accommodating. She appears to me to have an exaggerated concern about not making a mistake or saying the wrong thing. It appears as if she would go to any extent necessary to ensure that our therapeutic relationship is maintained, so I suspect a transference issue. My suspicion is that the patient was separated from her mother through some traumatic event in her childhood. The pathological neediness of the dizzy spells could be an unconscious expression of her longing for security, for closeness and holding from her mother. To test out this hypothesis, I decide to set up a constellation without asking for any further information.

Therapist: Please choose representatives for you and for your illness, and place them in relationship to each other.

The patient's representative looks accusingly at the representative of the illness.

Therapist: Are you angry with someone?

Patient: The first thing that occurs to me is, with myself, or... perhaps my husband?

Therapist: Why your husband?

Patient: I don't think he understands who I really am.

I have the feeling that this path would not lead very far, so I ask

111

about any traumatic events in her family of origin; if there was anything that happened when she was a child.

Therapist: Did your parents lose a child?

Patient:: Yes.

Therapist: Perhaps that came between you and your parents. Was the death of that child before you?

Patient: No, after me. There were two siblings after me. One sister died of cancer of the kidneys when she was three years old.

Therapist: How old were you when she got ill?

Patient: I was about four. A lot changed in our family with my sister's illness and death.

Therapist: Certainly. Everyone's attention turns to the child who is ill from that point on. The other children cannot understand it and the natural reaction of a four-year-old child would be anger. Choose two representatives for your parents and position them. *(She does this.)*

The mother's representative stares fixedly at one spot on the floor.

Therapist: This mother did not truly 'survive' the loss of her child. You can see it here. In this sense, you not only lost a sister but also your mother, in a certain way. Choose a representative for your sister.

She places her sister's representative next to her mother's. The sister has a difficult time remaining upright. Her knees give out and she sinks to the floor. The mother's representative begins to cry and bends down to her child lying on the floor. The patient's representative looks at her mother, and then goes over to her and lies down next to her little sister, with her head on her mother's feet. The mother's representative now notices her and lovingly

112

strokes her head. At this point, the representative of the illness takes a few steps backward.

Patient: My mother often lay on the floor crying and I couldn't do anything to help her.

When asked for her reactions, the representative of the illness states: 'I want to turn away now. I am no longer needed.'

The constellation confirms the family dynamics underlying the disease, and illuminates the patient's longing, as well as her gain from the illness. The moment the mother touches the patient's representative, the illness is no longer needed. For the patient, this means that if she wants to overcome her illness, she will have to give up her longing to be close to her mother. She will have to let her mother go.

I turn to the patient directly and ask her to say to her mother's representative, 'dear Mummy, now I recognise your pain'. When the patient says this sentence, I also add, 'and now I let you go'. The patient also agrees to this and when she says it aloud, the mother's representative spontaneously says: 'I'm sorry, but I couldn't stay. It was too much for me'. At my suggestion, the patient responds: 'dear Mummy, now I agree to that'.

In this last sentence, I hear a hint of blame in her tone of voice and draw her attention to that quality. She repeats the sentence again in a calm, quiet tone. 'Dear Mummy, now I agree to that.' I can clearly hear the change, so I guide the patient on to additional sentences, which she accepts willingly.

Patient: (speaking to her mother's representative) And now I honor what binds us together as well as what separates us. I got what is truly important and I can take that. For me, it is enough and I take it at the full price that it cost you. I have what I need. The

113

rest I will do myself.

At this point, I put the patient into the constellation. I place her next to her father's representative. He spontaneously puts his arm around her. The patient confirms the truth of the constellation.

Patient: It's true, this is the way it was. After my sister's death, my father paid more attention to us. My mother was, somehow, no longer there.

I encourage the patient to repeat once more, 'dear Mummy, now I agree – with love'.

I cannot resist adding one more sentence at the end: 'and now I will stop picking on my husband'. The patient laughs and responds, 'how did you know that?'

A FATHER'S HANDICAP
(Patient with migraine and sensitivity to weather conditions)

The following case depicts, in a particularly incisive way, the phenomenon of what representatives feel and experience in a constellation process.

When a woman, about 50, asks to work, I follow my inner intuition and do not ask her for any information. Instead, I immediately ask her to set up a constellation with representatives for her and for her headache. The patient chooses a man to represent her headache and places the two representatives facing one another at a considerable distance.

I ask the representatives to follow their own impulses. The representative of the headache cautiously takes a step towards the patient's representative. She quickly backs away in obvious fear. When repeated attempts to move closer to her have the same result, the representative of the headache finally turns away and sits down, cross-legged, on the floor. The patient's representative watches him attentively, walks slowly around him, and finally approaches him from behind. When she reaches his back, she also sits down on the floor and leans her back against his back. After a while the man turns around and gingerly puts his arm around the patient's representative. She snuggles up close to him, laying her head on his right thigh.

As the patient observes this, she bursts into tears and says, 'that is my father!' When she calms somewhat, she explains: 'I am the youngest child in my family – a late addition after the war. My father lost his right leg in the war. He kept having phantom pains, and never got over the loss of his leg. Even at home with our family, he never went without long trousers. One time, when I accidentally saw him in the bath without his prosthesis, he got very upset. He slapped me and threw me out of the room and I was left with the feeling that I had done something that I could never atone for. What I am seeing here is what I always wanted as a child.'

With this information, I remove the patient's representative from the constellation. I ask the patient if she wants to go to her father. She says that she does and cautiously approaches him. She sits down next to him on the floor and gingerly touches his right leg. When the father's representative smiles at her, she lies down in his lap and remains there until she has had her fill.

About six months later, I got a Christmas card from this patient. She wrote that she had experienced the work as reconciliation. Since that time, she has had very few instances of migraine. She said that her migraines were very closely related to weather conditions, and she saw a possible connection here, too, to her father's phantom pain. Her father always complained about how changes in the weather affected him.

ILLNESS AND A CHILD-PARENT ATTACHMENT DISTURBANCE DUE TO FAMILY ENTANGLEMENTS

Sometimes children have to take on the role of being parents to their own parents. In turn, they later project their own needs and feelings of inadequacy onto their children, which can lead to confusion and insecurity in the child-parent attachment.

The following example illustrates a resolution of parentification in a case of a woman suffering from Crohn's disease.

PARENTIFICATION: 'THE GOOD OUTWEIGHS THE OTHER.' (Patient with Crohn's disease)

A woman in a group has been suffering for years from Crohn's disease. This illness is a chronic inflammation, of unknown origin, of the gastro-intestinal system, which creates scar tissue, often requiring surgery to remove sections of the intestine. This patient has felt a strain in her relationship to her mother and her mother's fate in life, but believes she has come to terms with the difficult situation. Her feeling that she has to protect herself from her mother has led her to repress any longing for closeness.

In a very moving process in the constellation, she finds her way to her mother's arms and is able to let in closeness and love.

Because of the advanced, precancerous state of her disease (precancerous means tissue changes with a high risk of becoming malignant), this woman has very regular medical examinations. Immediately following the constellation, there was a surprising and lasting improvement that could be clinically confirmed in the routine examinations.

The work took place in an advanced training course in 2005, with a 35-year-old woman. The session was video taped, so the following record is verbatim.

116

As the patient sits down next to me, she pushes her chair about 10 centimeters off to the side to put distance between us. I observe her very carefully and then say to the group: 'Patients often reveal important information in the first moments of contact and the group leader must not miss these clues, because they are sometimes significant'.

After a while, I turn to the woman, who seems somewhat confused by my comments.

Therapist: What is your issue?

Patient: (The patient collects herself quickly and answers very factually.) I am suffering from Crohn's disease. My doctors tell me it is incurable. I don't want to accept that, but somehow I am not able to find a way to take care of myself, either. Last year they found precancerous nodes on my uterus and I had to have an operation for that. I also suffer from vitiligo (a disease that leads to loss of pigmentation in the skin). All these diseases have to do with the immune system, so somehow my inner defense system is not in order.

Therapist: What is your living situation?

Patient: I live with my boyfriend. He does not want to marry me and he also does not want any children.

Therapist: (asking cautiously) Are you more your father's daughter or your mother's daughter?

Patient: Father's daughter! The relationship with my mother is difficult.

Her quick, resolute answer signals a certain resignation in regard to the problematic relationship with her mother, but also implies an unwillingness to work on this issue. I do not pick up this thread, but continue on.

Therapist: I have worked with many patients with Crohn's disease and up to now, without exception, I have found that resolution lies with the mother. When I say that resolution lies with the mother, I mean a reaching-out movement towards the mother.

Patient: My mother demands too much of me. She is very needy and projects onto me. We look a lot alike and, in addition to that, she even dresses like me. It's all much too close and much too constraining!

Therapist: Were either of your parents in a previous, serious relationship before their marriage?

Patient: No, certainly not, they married very young. They are now separated.

Therapist: Okay. Set up representatives for you and for your illness.

The patient chooses two women and places them facing each other with some space between them. The representative of the disease feels terrible. Following my hypothesis that the patient's mother has a bearing on a resolution, I ask the patient for additional information.

Therapist: Can you say a bit more about your mother?

Patient: My mother is ill. She also suffers from gastro-intestinal problems. She is depressed, and for over 10 years she has been saying that she wants to die.

I ask the patient to choose a representative for her mother and place her in the constellation. The representative of the disease immediately feels better. She turns away from the patient's representative and looks at the mother. Here, we can see the actual connection.

Therapist: (to group) The reaction of the illness's representative shows that the patient is carrying this disease for her mother.

Patient: But she does not even have Crohn's disease!

Therapist: It doesn't need to be that precise.

Patient: I feel confused by my mother's representative. I don't know whether I want to laugh at her or hit her.

Therapist: What happened in your mother's family?

Patient: My mother lost her parents very early on. Her father was an alcoholic. She has a brother who is schizophrenic. *(after a while)* I don't want to see my mother like that. I can't bear that look of suffering.

At this moment, the patient's representative begins to cry quietly and says: 'It hurts so much!'

The patient is also fighting tears now and says: 'She treated me so badly! It was so hard for me.'

I answer her calmly. 'The good outweighs the other.' The patient at first looks at me without comprehension, but slowly she begins to understand. I take another step and have her say: 'dear Mummy, I miss you.'

At this point her resistance melts and she begins to weep. Finally, she is able to say: 'dear Mummy, I miss you so much! It was so hard for me, but now I agree to how it was. Thank you for everything!'

The effect of these sentences is immediately apparent in the constellation. The representative of the illness feels increasingly weaker and says: 'I can pull back now. I have the feeling that I have nothing more to do here'.

Here, I ask the patient to take her own place in the constellation. She goes directly to her mother's representative and the two embrace for a long while. The patient exclaims in amazement: 'it's unbelievable! I can breath now!' She slowly moves out of the embrace and I turn her around so that she can lean back against her mother. I take the mother's hand and place it around the patient on her belly. The patient stands there, very relaxed, holding her mother's hand on her belly. Her breathing is calm and deep.

I end the work saying, 'the resolution comes through the mother.'

The patient sent me a report of her experience about a year after this therapeutic work, to tell me about her healing process. She wrote with deep gratitude for what happened with her after the work we did. When she came into the group it looked as if her condition would move into intestinal cancer if things worsened any more, according to her doctors. She had to take strong medication and was suffering a lot from the side effects. The doctors were offering no solutions and no hope. On the contrary, they led her to understand that she would have to live with this disease. When she heard about family constellations, she registered for a constellation group in Montevideo with some misgivings and nervousness. She had a sense that this work might be an important step for her. There were about 65 participants, and she was the second person in the group to work. She learned it was difficult for her to leave those things with her mother that she had been carrying for her. She reported she would never forget my expression when I told her "the good you have gotten from your mother counted more than the burdens that you carried!" The moment she took her place in the constellation, she wrote of her gut throbbing like a drum, until her mother's representative laid her hand on her belly. From that moment on – exactly that moment – the pain stopped, the pounding stopped, and everything became calm. Five days after the constellation, she had her regular monthly check-up with the team of experts that had definitively diagnosed her with Crohn's disease. They did a colonoscopy and the necessary blood tests. They found nothing. Not even scar tissue in the intestine, although it had been so damaged – nothing! She had never had diarrhea again, let alone with blood. Her blood values were normal, the white blood cells and platelet counts perfect. At that point the doctors wondered whether their original diagnosis was correct. They thought they must have been mistaken and apologized to her.

In doing countless constellations with Crohn's disease patients, again and again I have observed families in which the patient's mother is bound to her own family of origin, a previous partner, or to an aborted or deceased child. This attachment creates a strain in the relationship between the mother and the patient. From the perspective of constellation work, the first step towards resolution for such patients is to acknowledge the mother's entanglements and let her go. This means relinquishing their own child-longing for closeness to their mother. This makes it possible to move away from antagonism towards those factors that are separating mother and child, and to fully take whatever this mother is able to offer.

In one constellation group, a woman asked me to do a constellation for her 11-year-old son, who was suffering from Crohn's disease and was once again in hospital. In a constellation consisting of representatives of the father, the mother, the son, and the disease, we could see a strong connection between the son and his illness on the one hand, and on the other, the child's longing for his mother. In the constellation, this longing remained unfulfilled, since the mother's representative could only stare fixedly at the floor. She was unavailable to all the other representatives, including her son. This scene moved the patient to tears and she told us that a few months after her son's birth, she had gotten pregnant again. In desperation, she followed her doctor's advice and aborted the child.

At my suggestion, the woman placed a representative for her aborted child in the constellation. In a very painful process, the patient's representative turned to this child and took the child in her arms. The son's representative watched this sequence very attentively and finally went to sit next to his aborted sibling on the floor. The representative of the illness followed suit and sat next to him. The father's representative was watching everything at the beginning of the constellation but when the woman reported the abortion, he turned away from the family. The patient confirmed that this reflected her husband's reaction and commented that with the abortion, something in their marriage had been destroyed.

It was only when the woman in the constellation could acknowledge her husband's pain that his representative could respect her decision as well, and the son was able to separate from his mother and the aborted child.

I had the man say to his wife: 'Now I honor your decision, with all the consequences it has for you and also for me.' With these words, the representative of the son's disease moved away from him and spontaneously retreated from the constellation.

In order for a child to feel connected to both parents in love, the parents must have respect for each other. This is a prerequisite for the child to be able to respect his or her parents. With respect, the child can then release the parents in a good way and go his or her own way in life.

ILLNESS AND IDENTIFICATION WITH THE PREVIOUS PARTNER OF A PARENT

Prior relationships of parents and grandparents can have a remarkable influence on family dynamics. Whatever the reason for that earlier separation or relationship termination, resolution requires acknowledgement of that previous partner. If the previous partner is not respected, children from a later relationship may represent that person.

This kind of identification can become especially problematic, resulting in a corresponding tendency towards poor health, when there is an attitude of disrespect for the previous partner. The problems are exacerbated if that person had a particularly difficult fate – perhaps was killed in war, committed suicide, or became seriously mentally ill.

THE ANNULLED ENGAGEMENT: 'I HONOR YOU AS MY MOTHER'S FIRST PARTNER.' (Patient with malignant melanoma)

In a constellation group orientated towards health issues, a woman with malignant melanoma asks to work. The melanoma was diagnosed before it had metastasised and has been surgically removed. From the medical side, aside from regular examinations, there is no need for further treatment, but the patient still feels a need to look into the significance, or possible causes or influence in her personal or family dynamics. We begin the constellation, without further discussion, with representatives for the patient and for her illness. She chooses a man to represent her skin cancer. The two representatives feel a warm connection to each other. They even speak of an inseparable love for one another.

The patient is strongly affected by the movements in the constellation. As a next step, I ask her to add representatives for her parents. This change immediately alters the relationship between the patient's representative and the representative of her illness. The representative of the cancer still has the basic feeling of inseparable love but now his love is aimed toward the mother's representative. The mother's representative finds his attraction embarrassing and she feels very uncomfortable.

The patient reports that her father was not her mother's first choice. Before this marriage, her mother was engaged to a man who was ill treated by the fascists during the Spanish Civil War.

His experiences with prison and torture led to serious illness and a drastic change in him as a man. When he was released from prison at the end of the war, the patient's mother realised that she could not fulfil her promise to marry her fiancé. After the man was diagnosed with a nervous disorder, the engagement was officially annulled.

The reactions and statements of the representative of the melanoma clearly imply that he is representing the mother's previous fiancé, so there is no need to add another representative for this man.

The man representing the patient's father is not recognized at all. In the constellation, the fiancé's representative acts as if the father were not even present, and there is no question of him being the mother's partner. The former fiancé understands full well that the patient's representative is not his daughter, but that does not hold him back in the least. He indicates that he is prepared to take her as his daughter. For him there is no question – this is his family.

This confusion is only resolved when the patient's representative bows deeply before this man. As he comprehends the situation, he begins to cry. He is now able to hear the patient's statement to him. 'I honor you as my mother's first partner. You belong, too. I honor what you have had to carry, and I respect the fact that you made space for my father and therefore also for me. I acknowledge that I am alive because you paid the price.' His pain from this unfulfilled love is heart wrenching, and even the mother's representative cannot maintain her rejection of him. She, too, begins to cry and the two fall into each other's arms, sobbing loudly. They hold their embrace for a long time as the mother's representative repeats, again and again: 'I am so sorry, I am so sorry. I couldn't do anything else'.

When his fate has been properly acknowledged, the fiancé's representative can make space for the new family. He backs away slowly, looking at them benevolently, until he is out of the constellation and he returns to his seat.

In many constellations that have to do with skin cancer, I have noticed that the skin cancer often stands for something that belongs, that is connected in love, but not recognised and loved. I am reminded of another constellation involving a man with skin cancer. The representative of the melanoma represented the patient's elder half-brother who had not been acknowledged by their common father. The mother of this half-brother had deceptively presented the boy as a different man's son.

A MOTHER'S FIANCÉ IN A WORK CAMP: 'I LIVE BECAUSE YOU DIED' (Patient with progressive chronic polyarthritis)

A 45-year-old gardener is suffering from a chronic, advanced case of inflammation of the joints. His hands are the most severely affected, and are swollen and deformed with inflammation. Gardening, especially outdoors in the wet and the cold, is very painful but, as he says, he loves his job, especially the chance to work outdoors. He cannot imagine taking up a different occupation.

To begin with, we set up a constellation of the patient's family of origin, and then, in a later step, we add a representative for his illness.

In the course of the constellation, it becomes clear that the representative of the disease is actually representing the mother's previous fiancé. In the years after the war, her fiancé was taken as a prisoner to a Russian work camp in Siberia where he later died.

The patient's mother had been waiting for many years for him to return, until she finally heard that he was dead.

I recall this meeting between the patient and the fiancé's representative in the constellation as very touching. As the patient replaces his representative and steps into the constellation, he agrees with my suggestion that he bow before his mother's prior fiancé. He bows down with the words, 'I live because you died, and I honor that'. These words move the fiancé's representative to tears and he gazes lovingly at the patient. When the patient stands in front of this man he tries to hide his deformed hands, a habitual response for him. I gently take the man's hands and show them to the fiancé's representative, who takes the damaged hands in his in a loving manner and looks the patient in the eye with understanding and compassion. It seems as though he is very familiar with this pain. This gesture moves the patient to tears and the two look at each other for a long time, occasionally nodding in understanding.

During the break, the patient comes to speak to me, with tears in his eyes, as he is still feeling very moved. He says: 'The moment the fiancé's representative took my hands in his, my hand were without pain for the first time in more than 20 years. I did not even know what that felt like anymore.'

CAUGHT BETWEEN LIFE AND DEATH:
'PLEASE, GIVE ME YOUR BLESSING IF I LIVE.'
(Patient with type 2 diabetes and 'sexual addiction')

Working with diabetics, we have to remember that these patients cannot survive without insulin. In constellations with diabetics, we often see a death wish that is usually outside the patient's conscious awareness. Many diabetics cannot take the life that is offered by medical treatment, and they destroy their health through careless eating, smoking or drinking, or are slipshod about their insulin dosage. Therefore, when working with diabetics, it is helpful to first clarify the person's basic attitude towards life and death.

In an advanced training group in North America, a 50-year-old, very overweight diabetic man asked me to work with him. The dialogue in the following constellation is mostly verbatim.

Therapist: What would be a good outcome of this work?

Patient: A good result for me would be if I could live a bit longer, and if I would develop more self-control and take better care of myself. I eat like a vacuum cleaner. My doctor is putting pressure on me and says he is not willing to continue treating me unless I change my eating habits.

Therapist: It almost sounds as though you would rather work on your dying than on your living.

Patient: In a way, that is true, but in another way it isn't.

Therapist: How long have you been diabetic?

Patient: For five years.

Therapist: Tell me about your living situation.

Patient: I have been married for 35 years. We have one child and one grandchild. My grandchild is the greatest joy in my life. My marriage is in trouble. I have been a sex addict for 24 years and my wife recently said that she was going to leave if I didn't admit that I needed help. Since I have gone into therapy, she has calmed down for the time being. Whether the therapy will help, and if this marriage is salvageable, remains to be seen.

Therapist: What happened in your family of origin?

Patient: Everyone in my family is a musician. We all have a passion for the arts. My mother was a violinist, and my father a composer and pianist. I am the third of six children. My mother was married once before she met my father. That was during the war. There is also a child from that marriage. Her first husband went to Europe in the war and came back as a different man. My mother left him and turned her house in Berkeley into a guesthouse. My father was one of the first guests. He came to Berkeley to study music.

Therapist: I've found out something about artists. You can't marry them.

Patient: (smiles) My wife doesn't know that... *(after thinking it over)* I'm not so sure, perhaps she does know it.

Therapist: She's certainly found it out in the meantime.

Since this dialogue is not leading us further, I decide to begin with the information we already have.

Therapist: Choose representatives for your mother, your father, and for you and place them in relationship to each other.

This is a training group, so I share my hypothesis with the group. 'The question I am asking myself is who is (or are) the dead that this patient is identified with?'

The patient places his representative, very close to his mother on her right side, at an angle. To the mother's left, a bit further off, is the father's representative. The mother is looking towards the father. The son's representative has turned away from the parents.

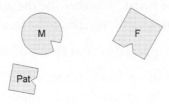

The position of the patient's representative leads me to ask, 'are you Mommy's favorite?'

Without hesitation, he answers: 'Oh, yes! But it's not that I don't love my father...' This convinces me that my suspicion is correct that he has to represent his mother's first husband for her. I ask the representatives about their sensations and awareness.

Mother's Representative: I'm fine. I want to hold my son's hand. I don't have any connection to his father. *(she takes the son's hand)*

Father's Representative: I feel fine here, too.

Patient's Representative: I swing back and forth; I'm sad and then I feel afraid. *(with these words, he frees his hand from his mother's grasp and takes a few steps forward, where he reports feeling better.)*

I turn to the patient and tell him that we need a representative for his mother's first husband. He chooses a representative and positions the man on his mother's left side, between her and his father.

When the mother's first husband is added, the representatives in the constellation experience a change. The patient's representative has the strongest reaction. He can barely remain standing and appears to collapse. He stares at the floor in front of his feet.

I ask three group members to lie down on the floor in front of the patient's representative. They are representing the dead that the mother's first husband must have witnessed as a soldier in Europe. Like so many others, he did not survive the war in his soul.

When the patient sees the dead lying in front of his representative, he begins crying aloud. It touches him to see his representative in this battle between life and death.

Since the patient's representative is on the verge of falling down, I ask him and the representative of the mother's first husband to change places. To make the identification clear, I do not put the patient's representative in position on his father's left. Everyone immediately feels better.

Patient's Representative: It's much better here. I feel like I can stand here. Over there I would have fallen on the floor.

Mother's Representative: This is good. Everything is much more alive now.

I now have the patient replace his representative in the constellation, but rather than putting him between his parents, I place him on his father's left hand side. Finally, I suggest the following sentences for the representatives to repeat.

Patient: (to mother's representative) Dear Mommy, I am your son. Please, look at me as your son. *(the mother's representative nods in agreement)* What was between you and your first husband and whatever is still unfinished between you, I leave with you. What I have carried for you, I have carried with love, but that is over now. A good place for me is by my father.

Patient: (to father's representative) Dear Daddy, I am your son. Please, take me now again as your son. (*The father's representative would like to embrace his son, but the patient is not yet free for this step. He looks again at the representative of his mother's first husband and the dead. It is obvious how difficult it is for him to free himself of that tie. I make another suggestion.*)

Patient: (to first husband's representative) I will now honor you by taking good care of myself.

The first husband's representative can see the patient's doubt and he gives him reassurance.

First Husband's Representative: This is good for me. Live!

With these words, the patient is finally able to receive his father's embrace.

I met the patient again in a constellation group about a year after this work. He reported that he had lost almost 40 pounds in the interim. He thanked me profoundly for the work. He spoke of being in better health than he had been the year before. He felt the constellation work we had done a year before had contributed significantly to this positive change. A year before he had been battling serious depression. This had improved and he had contact with his parents again. He felt better able to deal with his sex addiction. While he had previously found himself in a vicious circle of depression he now saw that his sex addiction had nothing to do with his father's alcohol addiction. Instead of holding the father responsible for his weaknesses, he now saw his problems in the larger context of family, over many generations. When he met other women for the purpose of sex, he did this with a different awareness. He could also see that his wife carried some part of this from her own family background. He now felt like he had a better chance of remaining in this relationship even with these extramarital needs. His blood sugar level was much more stable and he no longer had the feeling that he wanted or needed to die soon. He had been able to lose weight. About two months after the constellation, his daughter remarked that he was less depressed, and his wife was clearly more comfortable in his presence.

When a person is identified with a parent's previous partner, the child loses both parents, at the level of the soul, because in standing in a position of 'lover' for his mother, the son is a rival to his father. A daughter standing in for her father's previous partner is in competition with her mother. When there are only boys or only girls in a family, trans-gender identification can also occur. If the child can resolve the identification, it is usually also possible to complete the reaching-out movement towards the parents.

Mania: 'For your mother, you represent Adolf Hitler!' (Patient with manic-depressive disorder)

Just before the constellation group begins, a man of about 50 approaches me: 'I suffer from periodic manic phases. A few years ago I took part in a group for family constellations. During the group I became manic and the group leader arranged for emergency medical assistance and got me to a clinic.' The man pulls a business card out of his pocked and hands it to me saying, 'this is the address of my psychologist, who has treated me for many years. I would ask you to contact him straightaway if I go into a manic state again. He knows me well and can handle this. Under no circumstances do I wish to end up in hospital!' The psychologist indicated is located locally and I am acquainted with him. I ask the patient if his psychologist is aware of his participation in the group, and he assures me: 'he is the one who recommended that I take part in this seminar'.

During the opening round, the patient reports that he has five children, from three different marriages, and currently lives alone. He has been toying with the idea of emigrating. His issue here in this group is his psychological difficulties, for which he has been in treatment for many years. Both the man and his psychologist are convinced that his problems have some connection to his father, 'a zealous Nazi' and high-ranking officer in the SS. Noticing that the patient seems to be getting wound up, I interrupt him and indicate that this much information will suffice for the moment. Despite his psychologist's diagnosis and hypothesis, I have a strong impression that the patient is more in his mother's sphere of influence than in his father's.

As the group continues, I have a chance to observe the man from time to time during the breaks. I notice that he spends his time exclusively with the women in the group, patently flirting with them.

The following morning, he is the first to request to work. There is a lack of restraint or awareness of personal space that, together with his rather fixed expression, raise my concern that he is on the brink of a manic crisis. I have a feeling that he needs immediate attention, so I ask him to come and sit next to me.

The patient takes the seat next to me, legs planted wide apart, hands braced on his knees, and without taking any notice of me, he looks around the group with bright eyes and announces in a loud voice, 'so, now it's my show!' I look directly at him and ask, 'and how long has it already been going on?' Up to this point, he has not given me a single glance. Now, he sits back in his chair a bit so as to be able to see me, and looks me over. His surprise gives me a chance to continue speaking. 'And where is it going? And what is going to be the outcome?' He softens a bit and then finally announces, 'okay, one-nil for you!' I refrain from any further dialogue and tell him that we will set up a constellation of his family of origin.

Therapist: Have you got brothers or sisters?

Patient: I am the only child of my parents. My father was married before and has a son from that marriage, but I don't know my half-brother. Another important fact – my father was an illegitimate child and doesn't know his own father. His mother was very young when she got pregnant and couldn't, or didn't want to, marry the man.

Therapist: What do you know about your granddad?

Patient: Nothing! Only that he might have been Jewish.

Therapist: Okay. Set up representatives for you, your father, and your mother.

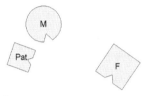

In the constellation of his family of origin, the patient gives his own representative the first position (viewed in a clockwise direction). The mother's representative is exclusively focussed on her son. The father's representative stands off to the side and seems preoccupied with matters of his own. He reports that he feels fine with this. Looking at the constellation, it seems clear that the patient is representing someone for his mother.

When asked about events in the family, or if his mother had any important prior relationships, the patient cannot provide any information that would guide us forward.

I ask the representatives for feedback on their impressions. The patient's representative reports that he is feeling absolutely splendid – powerful enough to rip apart trees with his bare hands. As expected, the mother's representative is interested only in her son, and everything else seems unimportant to her. The father's representative does not feel he has much say in this situation, and is more concerned with matters of his own.

At this point, just to be certain, I want to see what influence the unknown grandfather might have on the constellation, so I ask the patient to add a representative for his father's father. He positions this man behind his father's representative, which both find very pleasant. The dynamics between the mother and son remain unchanged. I turn to the patient again.

Therapist: From what we can see here, it looks like you are representing someone for your mother.

Since the patient appears dubious, I explain this idea in more detail.

Therapist: My suspicion is that this has to do with a previous relationship of your mother.

Patient: (demurs) My mother was 17 when she met my father, and she was 21 when I was born. She loved my father more than anything else! He was the only one in her life!

I remain feeling unconvinced by his objections and still suspect there is something else. I ask the patient to add a representative for a hypothetical previous partner of the mother, just to test this out. When the representative is added, it radically changes the constellation. The mother's representative turns joyfully to the new representative. The patient's representative turns in relief to his father and grandfather.

The representative for the mother's previous partner stands with his feet planted wide apart and his arms folded across his chest. He is looking above everyone's heads, into the distance. When I ask him what he is feeling, he says, in an arrogant tone of voice, 'I am not like these others. I am from a different world!'

This sentence has a striking effect on the patient. In confusion, he focuses on this representative very attentively. It takes some while before he regains a sense of orientation, but in his helpless agitation he seems more natural than before.

Therapist: There must have been a man in your mother's life who was more important to her than your father.

The patient looks nervously from the representative of the 'partner' to his mother's representative and then back again. Suddenly his face lights up and he beams as he states: 'that's true! Basically there was only one man in my mother's life, and that was Adolf Hitler!' His radiance suddenly turns stony and he nods his head in shock.

I give him some time to absorb this insight. Gradually, the tension in his body begins to relax, making clear that he is slowly completing the process of integration. I take him by the hand and lead him over to his father's representative. He looks at him for a long time, and then begins to weep and lays his head on his father's shoulder. I leave him there as long as he appears to need it, and then suggest that he say to his father's representative, 'dearest Daddy, a good place for me is with you – please hold me'. The two embrace again.

Four weeks after this constellation, I received a phone call from the man's psychologist, letting me know that the man had got on very well since the constellation. He also wanted to express his thanks for the work.

About three years later, I saw this patient again. He came into a group to sort out a different issue having to do with his adult son. He reported that since the constellation described above, he had been much improved and had not had any further manic phases.

He reported that, in hindsight, a reaching out movement to his father had been difficult. He had always felt scornful of his father because of his father's involvement in the SS. With the help of his therapist, however, he has been able to take his father as his father, and leave with him the guilt and terrible deeds of the past.

Children often may have difficulty in honoring their parents because what they are looking at are their parents' personal characteristics or actions. What parents have or have not done, however, is a limited, narrow perspective. Parenthood, in and of itself, is much more than this. Respect and honor are possible if we look at our parents in their totality, and also beyond them, at their families and their fate. This is a reverent and humble attitude that leads us to healing. It also counters any impulse to carry our parents' ill-fated needs.

LEAVING AS PROXY: 'I AM STAYING, AND I WOULD BE HAPPY IF YOU ALSO STAY'. (Anorexic daughter)

For about five years, this family has suffered with the 20-year-old daughter's anorexia. The girl needs her father's support in order to walk because, weighing only 61 pounds, she is no longer strong enough to hold herself up and walk alone. The father, mother and daughter are taking part in the constellation group at the recommendation of a homeopath who has been treating the family.

We begin the constellation with representatives for the father, mother and daughter. The patient positions the father's representative off to the side as if he were occupied elsewhere. The patient's representative is placed very near the representative of the mother.

What we are looking at is a young woman caught in the third generation of entanglement. The patient's maternal grandmother died of a sudden heart attack when the patient's mother was two years old. The anorexic daughter has had to stand in for her mother's mother.

When a representative is added for that grandmother who died so prematurely, the longings of the patient's mother surface. I ask the mother to take the place of her representative in the constellation. In a very moving process, she is able to make space for this repressed pain and to agree to the untimely death of her mother. The daughter's representative is then able to free herself from the difficult projection and feels enormously relieved.

In the constellation, with the resolution of the attachment to her mother, the daughter's representative is able to look directly at her father's representative for the first time. This relationship, however, is also under strain. It seems that the father's representative cannot bear to have his daughter look at him. He feels distressed, angry, and afraid.

The anorexic daughter reminds him of the grandfather's victims, who have been excluded from the family memory. This paternal grandfather was an officer in the armed division of the SS during the Second World War, and was active in various concentration camps and prisoner of war camps.

Out of love, with a longing for closeness to his own father, the patient's father has taken over his father's feelings and cannot stand to be seen by this daughter, who is identified with the camp victims.

In the constellation, we add representatives for the grandfather and also for victims of the SS. The patient's representative immediately joins this group and feels comfortable there, with a sense of belonging. The patient's actual father finds it difficult to see his father standing with his victims. I ask him to take his representative's place in the constellation. It requires all the strength he has to follow my suggestion and stand facing his father's representative and bow. He says to him: 'whatever has happened, whatever it is you are carrying and perhaps must carry – I respect it and leave it with you. Whatever has happened, you remain my father'.

Empowered by his son's bow, and empowered by an expression of love that is untainted by what happened during the war or by guilt, the grandfather's representative in the constellation is free to turn to the victims.

With her father's bow to his own father, the patient's representative no longer feels comfortable standing with her grandfather's victims. She can become a child again and reveal her childlike yearning for her father. The father is also now free and can take his daughter's representative in his arms. Deeply moved by the sight of her husband and her daughter's representative in an embrace, the patient's mother turns towards them. Both parents then hold their daughter's representative in their arms. She feels relieved of her burden. I allow the image to work on the patient for a while and then lead her into the constellation. She takes the place of her representative and slips into her parents' arms.

As a final intervention, I suggest that the father and also the mother each say to their daughter, 'I am staying, and I would be happy if you also stay'. In tears, they embrace for a long time. With this image, they leave to go home, and I suggest that they do not talk about what has taken place, but simply allow the constellation to have an effect on them.

A week after the constellation, I get a telephone call from the mother. She reports that the overall situation has relaxed in their home. Her relationship with her daughter has improved markedly. Although the daughter still refuses to eat with the family she has, in fact, put on weight since the constellation, since she has begun to drink fruit and vegetable juice regularly since that time. She assures them that she does have a desire to live and has promised her parents that she will take care of her health, but she continues to refuse solid food. Although there was almost no contact at all between the father and daughter before the constellation, now they battle daily over food and calories. The conflict is exacerbated by the fact that the father is a professional cook, and runs a gourmet restaurant in the same building they live in.

The situation, as described, sounds absurd and I ask the mother and daughter to come in for an individual session. In this session, I ask about any other events, particularly anything that might explain why her daughter is reacting to her father with so much anger. At this point the woman recalls that her husband was engaged when she met him. He broke off that engagement in order to pursue the relationship with her. This is clearly where the daughter's anger belongs. When the entanglement with her father's previous fiancée is revealed, the girl looks radiant and the previous hardness in her face melts away. When I ask her if everything has been taken care of, she responds: 'I think it has'.

Two weeks after this appointment, the mother phoned to say thank you. When she returned home after our session, she told her husband what had happened. After that, he refrained from getting into discussions with his daughter about her eating and they stopped quarrelling. The mother reported that her daughter was taking better care of herself and seemed very confident. About three months later, I heard from the mother that her daughter was eating regularly.

ILLNESS AND THE FATES OF GRANDPARENTS

As already mentioned, constellations often show us the interactive relationship between illness or pathology and the exclusion of relevant members of a system.

Representatives of illness or symptoms often experience urges or feelings that indicate trans-generational connections between the current illnesses of children and grandchildren and the traumatic experiences and conflicts of their grandparents and great grandparents.

Homesick: 'That is mine and I will carry it!'
(Child with neurodermatitis)

A woman tells me about her one-year-old daughter's severe neurodermatitis. When the girl was hospitalized for tests, it was determined that the child's allergy to cows' milk was responsible for the difficulty. A very strict diet, however, has brought about only minimal relief of the symptoms. The girl has to be wrapped in bandages to keep her from scratching herself bloody.

The mother is suffering from Crohn's disease, a gastro-intestinal illness.

We begin the constellation with representatives for the daughter and for the daughter's illness. The client chooses two women in the group as representatives and places them facing one another. Each of the representatives feels an attraction towards each other that borders on love. They draw close together and hold hands.

In the next step, I ask the client to choose a representative for herself and someone to represent the child's father. The father's representative is placed off to the side. He feels helpless and unable to act in this situation. The client places her own representative near her daughter, facing the child's representative. She does not notice that she has placed her representative between her child and the child's father. The position of the representatives indicates that the child has a higher priority for the woman than her husband. The mother's representative feels a strong urge to pull the child to her, which confirms the disturbance in the family order and the exclusion of the father. As a result, the child cannot greet her mother's advances. The daughter's representative pulls away from her mother and retreats some steps backwards, followed closely by the representative of the illness.

This movement suggests that the key to resolution, and the power to take action, does not lie in the parents' generation. The mother's exclusive focus on her daughter and her needy look indicate that this child must be representing someone else for her (the mother). I ask about the client's family of origin.

She is the eldest child in the family. Her father is Serbian and her mother Croatian. When the client's mother was 17, as the seventh child of a poor Croatian farmer, she was sent with relatives to Germany. There she met her husband, the client's father, and soon had this first child.

I ask the client to add a representative for her mother. She chooses a woman and leads her to stand near her own representative. The grandmother does not feel comfortable near her daughter and pulls back away from her. The granddaughter's representative, however, appears very happy with her grandmother's inclusion and tries to get closer to her, again followed closely by the representative of the illness.

The continued inseparability of the child and the illness is an indication that the relevant cause for these symptoms has not yet been found. This leads me to go one generation further back and I ask the client to add a representative for her mother's family. She chooses another woman and places her behind the grandmother's representative, who begins to cry and turns slowly around to the new representative saying, 'I want to come to you. Please hold me'. The other woman also begins to cry and they embrace.

With tears in her eyes, the client says, 'I know. My mother always wanted to go back'.

The daughter's representative mirrors her grandmother's movement, laying her head on her grandma's back. In this position, she appears happy and at peace. This is the first time in the course of the constellation that the daughter's representative and her illness have been apart from one another. The actual conflict – the trauma behind the current effects – belongs to the grandmother.

Now, the question is what the client can do for her daughter. I tell her: 'your daughter's neurodermatitis is connected to your intestinal illness. A resolution for you, and perhaps for your daughter as well, lies in the relationship to your mother. You have to let her go'. With tears in her eyes she answers, 'I know, but how do I do that?'

I ask the client to stand in the constellation in front of her mother and to bow down. She kneels down in front of her mother's representative and bends her entire upper body forward. In spite of her willingness, her inner struggle and tension are obvious. Finally, she stretches her hands forward, palms up and slowly continues to bow lower, until her forehead touches the floor. As soon as the client enters the constellation, her daughter's representative spontaneously moves to stand next to the father's representative. From this distance, she attentively observes her mother's painful process.

The grandmother, in response to her daughter's bow, lets go of her own mother and turns to her daughter. She bends down to her, takes her in her arms and holds her. The granddaughter's representative breathes deeply and turns in relief to her father. As the client completes her embrace with her mother, the grandmother indicates that the woman's place is with her husband and daughter.

Finally, I ask the representative of the illness what she is feeling. She says, 'I am no longer needed. My intention was always to protect the child. When the 'great-grandmother' (the representative of the grandmother's family) was brought into the constellation, my connection to the client's little girl was interrupted. When the client came into the constellation, I was still very alert to what was going on. I was waiting to see what would come next. When she bowed down, I started feeling extraneous, and then it got to the point where I didn't feel anything at all.

The next morning, in the opening round, the client says, 'I don't know how many of you here know what it's like to have Crohn's disease. For me, this usually means spending a painful hour on the toilet every morning. This morning it was a matter of five minutes, without pain, and there was no blood in my stool'.

The positive feedback from this patient confirms my observations about the gastro-intestinal illness, Crohn's disease. The dynamics often involve the relationship between the patient and his or her mother (see p. 96).

In this constellation I experienced the bow as an appropriate ritual for the daughter and also the granddaughter. It honored the grandmother's fate and her pain and, beyond that, the fate of the whole family and the pain of all those who were affected by that fate. (For a discussion of the ritual of bowing down, see Schneider, pp. 148-151)

DEATH IN CHILDBIRTH OF A GREAT-GRANDMOTHER
AND HER BABY (Patient with ovarian cyst)

In an advanced training course for therapists, a woman reports that about three months ago she was diagnosed with an ovarian cyst on her right side. The doctors have recommended surgery to remove the cyst. The woman does not feel ready to agree to surgical intervention immediately, and is taking some time to reach her decision.

When I allow myself to sense into the patient and then into the cyst, I experience the cyst as an independent structure, with no connection or contact to the body of the patient. My thoughts are that this symptom has something to do with some excluded content or person. Therefore, I tell her: 'My image is that the first step that might allow this cyst to retreat, would be to accept it'. The patient looks at me in astonishment, and I tell her a little story.

'Some years ago, I had an amazing experience. My daughter, who was about six at the time, had a wart on the palm of her hand. She kept coming and showing me this growing wart. At first I did not take it too seriously. When it got larger, I began to treat it with homeopathic and herbal medicines, but without any success. I kept thinking about surgical removal, but I couldn't make the decision to do that. One evening, my daughter came to me and said, "look, Papa, now my wart has really got big!" I realised that we had missed the optimal time for an operation, and surgery at this point would leave much too large a scar. As I examined the wart, the thought suddenly came to me that perhaps here, too, there was some excluded topic or person that was having this effect. At that moment, a sentence came to me and I told my daughter that she could tell her wart, "I like you, even if you are gone". She wrinkled her brow and laughed skeptically at her father's idea, but she repeated the sentence. Later that evening, it appeared to all of us that the wart was getting smaller. To our astonishment, two days later it had disappeared.'

The patient does not know quite what to make of this story, and I continue talking to the group:

'If Bert Hellinger is right that what moves people deeply is love, then this also affects and influences illness and other symptoms. We know from what we see in constellations that a movement of the soul can only successfully move towards resolution when love has been expressed to the representative of the excluded or devalued person. In a constellation, for example, a perpetrator's representative can only reconcile with victims when his or her family is no longer standing in condemnation. Negative judgments shut the person out and interfere with the movements that offer resolution.'

Having made these comments, I turn back to the patient and say, 'this cyst can also change only when it is loved and acknowledged as something that belongs'. After a pause, I then add, 'in many constellations we have seen a connection between ovarian cysts and a child who died young'.

The patient feels touched by this and she begins to cry. When she is calm again, she says that in her family there have been many dead children.

The incident in the family that most strongly affects her is the death of her maternal great-grandmother who died in childbirth, along with her baby.

The patient has not even finished speaking before her legs begin to shake. Her attempts to control this physical reaction are fruitless. I encourage her to allow the reaction rather than to fight against it. I suspect that her physical reaction has to do with her great-grandmother's trauma, which she may have taken over. I give her ample time, assuming that her body will calm down when she stops fighting against it. When the shaking does not lessen, it becomes clear that something essential is still missing and further steps are needed. I ask a woman to act as representative of the patient's mother and I position her behind the seated patient. Then, I add a representative for her grandfather, her mother's father, and a representative for his mother, the patient's great-grandmother, as well as a representative for the child who died at birth. None of the representatives know whom they are representing, nor does the patient have this information.

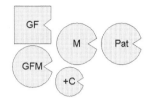

When the patient feels the great-grandmother's right hand on her shoulder, she becomes calm and leans back, relaxed and at ease. After a while, I ask her to turn around and see who is standing behind her and I tell her who each of these persons is representing. When she sees her mother, she embraces her, all the while looking lovingly at her mother's father, and her great-grandmother and her baby.

About two months later I receive a letter telling me that following that constellation, for a few weeks she felt a deep connection and love for that cyst, and even began talking to it.

When she went to the doctor's for an examination two months later, there was no sign of a cyst and her ovaries were clear.

A GRANDMOTHER'S DEATH DURING THE BIRTH OF THE FATHER: 'DEAREST DADDY, IN YOU, I ALSO LOVE YOUR MOTHER'

(Patient with ovarian cancer)

As I begin talking to this patient, she has very little affect, and she seems bitter and negative. Interestingly, she chooses a man to represent her illness. This could indicate some connection with her first husband who committed suicide eight years ago.

The patient states that she married again two years ago and would like to have a child. The issue is weighing heavily on the 35-year-old woman.

In a constellation consisting of representatives for the patient and her disease, the two smile at each other, feel strongly connected and are drawn to one another.

To look at a possible connection with the patient's first husband, I ask her to add a representative for him. There is, however, no change in the constellation when he is present. The representative of the first husband is completely absorbed with his own matters and the patient's representative feels no interest or connection towards him.

I ask about any events in her family of origin. Suddenly, she remembers that her 'granny' is not her father's mother. His actual mother died at his birth. It seems possible that there might be some connection to the illness here. Often, in families in which a woman has died in childbirth, there is an unconscious fear of relationship and pregnancy. Perhaps there is an unconscious loyalty to this grandmother.

I ask the patient to choose a representative for her father and then, as a second step, to add a representative for her father's mother. The reactions of the representatives depict the family dynamics underlying this illness. The man representing the disease is actually the patient's father. The moment a representative for the father is brought into the constellation, it interrupts the warm connection between the patient's representative and the representative of her disease. However, the father's representative is unable to look at his own mother. He looks at the patient's representative with a feeling of love and yearning very similar to the earlier reaction of the illness towards the patient's representative. This would imply that the patient is standing in for his mother.

At this point I ask the patient to take her own place in the constellation and say to her father, 'in you, I also love your mother'. This sentence dissolves the entanglement for the father as well as

148

for the daughter. It moves the father's representative to tears, and father and daughter embrace for a long time. The representative of the grandmother looks at the two with joy.

I have no information as to what happened to this patient, or about the course of her illness.

A GRANDFATHER'S SUICIDE: 'DEAR MUM, NOW I AGREE' (Patient with sleep disorders and digestive complaints)

A patient complains of sleep disturbances and gastro-intestinal problems. She also reports that she was sexually abused at the age of ten by a neighbor. Her parents separated at about this time. She did not tell her parents about the incident with the neighbor.

This much information is enough to form a working hypothesis, so I interrupt the patient here.

In cases of sexual abuse, many constellations of the family of origin indicate that a rape is often basically a displaced incest. In place of the father, a perpetrator steps in, one who does not belong to the nuclear family. The constellations generally reveal dynamics similar to those in incestuous families. Because of bonds to her own family of origin, a previous partner, or deceased children, the mother's soul is not free for a relationship with her husband and her daughter is moved into her place.

With digestive problems, we often see a connection to a difficult relationship with the mother. Sleeping disorders frequently arise out of concerns or fears that a member of the family will leave or die while the patient is asleep. The patient unconsciously wakens himself or herself so that nothing bad will happen.

Here, my suspicion is that the patient's mother is not available in the way the child desires her to be. From the perspective of

149

constellation work, this could be a key to the easing of symptoms or healing. To test this out, I suggest that the patient set up a constellation of her family of origin. She chooses representatives for her father, her mother, and herself.

The mother's representative feels heavily laden, physically, and feels no connection to her husband or daughter. She distances herself from them and eventually moves all the way out of the circle. Here, she is able to breathe again and initially feels better.

In response to my questioning, the patient states that her mother's father committed suicide when her mother was two years old. The mother grew up believing that her stepfather was her father. As an adult, she found out about her biological father's death.

This information might explain the feelings and movements of the mother's representative. Deep in her soul she is drawn to her deceased father. I tell the patient that, 'my image is that all of these symptoms are rooted in the same dynamics. There is one person who needs to be included in the resolution.' I pause here because the patient has turned away from me and is looking stubbornly at the floor. 'Your mother! What would have a healing effect here, is to find harmony with your mother and acknowledge what she is carrying – to agree to the way it was and to take her, including everything that belongs to her.'

In response, the patient retorts, 'but I don't want to!' I try to sense into her statement and after a long pause I tell her what it is that I sense. 'That is not true. There is a level at which you do not want to, and I can also feel that. However, that is only a part of what is true. Deep in your soul, I also feel the love and longing for your mother that makes you strong enough to carry all this for her – the sleeplessness, the digestive problems, and the sexual abuse. All of that out of love for your mother.' The patient listens silently and we sit quietly for a long time afterwards.

To help this patient find a connection to this love, I ask the mother's representative to stand facing her. I wait until the patient looks her in the eye and then offer her the following sentence to speak to her mother's representative: 'Dear Mum, even if you go, you will always remain my mother. Whatever it is that binds us and that separates us, I honor that now.' These sentences move the mother's representative. She looks at her daughter with tears in her eyes and takes her hands. Now the patient can maintain eye contact and she, too, begins to cry. The two embrace. The daughter looks at her mother again and I suggest that she say, 'dear Mum, I agree, and I take it now, even at this price'.

Dealing with Resistance

In therapy or counselling, we generally have to consider that any 'resistance' of a patient has some justification and is serving a function. I respect this, but do not let it deter us in the work. Often we meet with resistance when a patient wants something different from what we want. More precisely, we call it resistance when the patient behaves in a way that would indicate that he or she does not want what we think is right. We could just as easily see this situation as an indication that we as therapists have not correctly judged the patient's capacities. Or, we have not succeeded in inviting the patient into a new way of thinking, feeling, or behaving that, in our opinion, would be preferable.

In this case, I treat the stubborn 'I don't want to' by offering her an unusual interpretation of her behavior. I then confront her with her mother's representative and offer her sentences that I suspect might reach her soul and open the way to a change in their relationship.

MURDERED FOSTER PARENTS: 'IF YOU WANT TO LIVE, YOU HAVE TO LET YOUR MOTHER GO'
(Patient with unspecified stomach ailments)

A man of about 40, from Trieste, has suffered from stomach ailments for as long as he can remember. There is no clear medical diagnosis, but he seems to have intolerance for various foodstuffs, and some doctors suspect Crohn's disease. His symptoms have often been identified as neurogenic, or connected to the autonomic nervous system.

He is the fourth living child of his parents and the 'only' son. Before his birth, his mother lost a male child in the fifth month of pregnancy. While talking to this patient, I suddenly feel an extraordinary heaviness. It takes enormous energy to stay attentive and I have the feeling that something is sapping my own vitality. I share my feelings with the patient and he tells me that it stimulates a memory of two incidents, one being that he almost died when he was a boy. He was playing in the woods with a friend and they found a grenade from the Second World War. When they tried to open it up, it exploded and caused critical injuries to both. He was in a coma for several weeks and his friend lost an arm. That friend later committed suicide at the age of 19, which continues to be of concern to the patient. He cannot shake the feeling that his friend's suicide had something to do with the accident.

The second incident concerns his paternal grandparents, who ran a bar. During the war, partisans often frequented this bar. One day, fascists came into the bar, pulled out one of the villagers and shot him. In the village, it was rumored that the patient's father, who was then 14, had betrayed the man out of fear for his own parents.

As I listen to him talk, I try to feel which of these events seems connected to his symptoms, in order to decide which relationship system should be set up in the constellation. Since I cannot get a clear sense, I suggest that the patient set up representatives for himself and his parents.

The man appears surprised at his own, spontaneous placement of his family. All three representatives are looking in different directions and seem to have no connection with each other.

The patient's representative feels alone, abandoned, and lost. The mother's representative can only stare at the floor, and the father's representative is furious.

As a first step, I ask the patient to add a representative for a partisan. When this representative is guided to his place, he drops immediately to the floor. None of the other representatives, however, feel touched or affected in any way. I ask them about their experience. The father's representative says only, 'it is good that the partisan is dead, but it's not really important. I am so unbelievably furious – at everything!' The mother's representative continues to stare at the floor and exhibits no feelings at all. Since this step does not appear to lead anywhere, I suggest that we add a representative for the brother, the baby that died in the fifth month of pregnancy. I ask him to lie down on the floor in front of the mother. She becomes very distressed when she looks at this child and begins to scream. She seems mentally disturbed. The father's representative cannot stand this hysterical screaming and takes his wife by the hand. Finally, he leads her over to stand in front of the dead partisan. The mother's representative is momentarily silent and looks in horror at the dead. Suddenly, her pain breaks through, and she begins to weep from the depth of her heart.

The patient, sitting next to me, also begins to cry and says: 'I know what this means. My mother's parents came from Danzig. My mother was sent to Italy as part of a children's transport. The Italian family that took in my mother was a supporter of the partisans and she helped to hide them. When my mother was five years old, her Italian foster parents were murdered by German soldiers.'

As the patient is recounting this event, the mother's representative lies down next to the representatives of the dead partisan. Lying there, she feels comfortable and calm. The other representatives are now also at ease. It is only the patient's representative that still feels agitated. He does not know what he should do. On the one hand, he feels drawn to his mother. On the other hand, he seems to comprehend what that would mean.

I leave the representatives in their positions and turn to the patient. I look carefully at him and say: 'My image is that if you want to live, you have to let your mother go.' He affirms this. 'My mother is my whole life. If she were gone, I don't know what I would live for.' In tune with his breathing and body rhythms, I repeat my statement slowly, emphasizing the words. It is obvious that the patient is allowing these words to sink deeper into his soul. With tears in his eyes, he agrees.

The bottom line is that if children want to live, they have to let their parents go. That is, children have to free themselves from their feeling of guilt for relinquishing their loyalty and child's bonds to their parents and perhaps not fulfilling their parents' illusions and desires. This is especially difficult when parents have projected their needs onto their children because their own parents were not available in the way they wished.

A GRANDMOTHER'S DEATH IN CHILDBIRTH
(A son's epilepsy and manic-depressive disorder)

On the recommendation of the attending physician, a woman of about 65 asks to do a constellation for her 43-year-old son. He is not able to take part in the group himself because of a manic-depressive disorder. He has also suffered from epilepsy since he was five months old.

The parents are separated and the son has lived with his father since he was 20. When asked what led to the separation, the woman answers: 'my husband blames me for a lot of things, including my son's epilepsy. I left my husband when my son was seven, and his epilepsy got much better. We were even able to stop his medication. When he turned 16, however he wanted to go and live with his father. I didn't want that and prevented it until he was 20. Then he went anyway. Since he has lived there, he has resumed taking medication'.

I ask the patient to choose representatives for her husband, their son, and herself. She positions the three representatives at the points of an equilateral triangle. All three representatives are looking outwards in different directions. The son's representative feels terrible. He turns around towards his parents, but they remain as they were.

When I ask the patient to choose a representative for her son's illnesses, she selects a woman and places her at some distance from the others, facing the son's representative. He instantly feels worse. His entire body begins shudder and it takes a lot of effort for him to remain standing. One has the impression that the symptoms are sucking all of the son's vitality, as she seems remarkably strong and energetic, and appears happy at the sight of him, even though he is visibly suffering.

Since both parents are looking at the floor, I ask the patient if she has ever lost a child. She says that her first child, a boy, was stillborn in the seventh month of her pregnancy. When we add a representative to the constellation for this son, the patient's representative begins to cry. She goes to him and takes him in her arms. The father's representative, however, stiffens. The presence of this brother and the parents' reactions have no effect on the son or his illness. We might suspect that the father's rigidity has to do with some trauma of his own, so I ask about events in the father's family. When he was 18 months old, his mother died giving birth to his brother.

This information casts some light on the constellation. I suspect that the woman representing the illness is actually the father's mother. It is possible that she is seeking her own child in this grandchild.

To test out this hypothesis, I ask the patient to set up a representative for the father's mother. This triggers changes in the whole constellation. The representative of the illness begins to back away, step by step. The patient's representative looks lovingly at her mother-in-law. The new representative responds in kind, and moves to stand with her son and his wife. The grandson's representative looks perceptibly relieved and looks over at his parents with pleasure. Everything seems to be changing in a positive direction, but the father's representative resolutely rejects the overtures from his mother. Instead, he turns to his son, who flinches and becomes rigid in response.

Here we can see the underlying dynamics of the symbiotic bond between father and son. Apparently the father has not yet been able to overcome the death of his mother.

The question is; what can the boy's mother do in this situation?

The only path open to her is to honor her husband's fate and suffering, and to include his mother. I suggest that the patient say to her husband's representative, 'dear A., I honor your love and also your pain. No matter what happens, the mother one has is always the best.'

According to the patient's initial description, it seems that her husband is transferring his anger towards his mother onto his wife. So, I ask her to add, 'your mother for you, and me for our son'.

The father's representative is now in tears. He turns and looks at his mother. In order to ensure that the grandmother's feelings towards her son do not get mixed up with her feelings for his younger brother, I ask another representative to stand next to her as the father's brother. This addition brings about no perceptible change in the constellation. I suggest that the grandmother say, 'my beloved son, I am sorry I could not stay'. When the father's representative smiles, his mother takes him in her arms. The son's representative turns in relief to his own mother.

The patient is very moved by the reactions of the representatives and comments that a sense of heaviness in her heart that she has felt for years is now gone.

Just as I am ready to end the work, the grandmother releases her son from her embrace and indicates to him that he can pay attention to his wife and son. She retreats slowly from the constellation. At some distance from the others, she turns and lies down on the floor, closing her eyes.

Unfortunately, I have no information about what happened in this family after this constellation. Thus far, in my experience dealing with the problem of epileptic seizures, the constellations have not generally revealed identification to be the underlying issue. More often, epileptic seizures can be seen as a way of solving a dilemma.

R.G. Hamer (1987) also describes epileptic crises as "solutions" that provide escape from a conflict. It is interesting to note, however, that when central relationship dynamics are touched upon and resolved in a constellation, it often happens that the epileptic attacks occur less frequently. I remember an 11-year-old boy who had fewer and fewer and then no attacks at all after his parents sorted out their relationship problems in a constellation group. The situation had similarities to the case reported above in that the boy suffered from epileptic seizures only in the presence of his mother.

ILLNESS AND THE EXCLUSION OF MEMBERS OF THE PRESENT FAMILY

In constellations, we also see exclusion of members of the current family system in connection with illness. The present family, in this context, includes all relevant partners of the patient, including any children issuing from those relationships – also foster children or adopted children with their biological parents, stillborn children, and aborted children, and occasionally even miscarried babies.

UNACCEPTED AND EXCLUDED CHILDREN

The following cases show a connection between illness in the family and children who belong but who cannot be accepted. They also present appropriate approaches to resolution from the perspective of constellation work.

A DISABLED DAUGHTER
(Patient with lupus erythematosus)

This case involves a woman who has been suffering from lupus erythematosus for 13 years. Lupus is a disease of the autoimmune system that affects blood vessels and connective tissue, resulting in a characteristic reddening of the face and inflammation of the joints. This woman experienced her first episode of the disease during her second marriage, shortly after the adoption of a child. She and her husband had made the decision to adopt after experiencing four miscarriages. The patient had a daughter in her first marriage, who was severely disabled due to prolonged oxygen deprivation at birth. Apparently, the difficulty was a result of negligence on the part of the physician. This child died at the age of four.

We begin the constellation with two representatives, one for the patient and one for the disease. The patient chooses a woman to represent the disease, and places her somewhat distant from her own representative. The representative of the illness feels a desire to stand very near the patient's representative. She follows her every movement and tries to snuggle up to her. The patient's representative, however, repeatedly shakes her off, each time more vehemently.

I ask the patient to add a representative of her first child to the constellation. She immediately bursts into tears and puts this young woman at the side of her own representative, very close.

To the patient's dismay, her representative moves away instantly. She cannot stand to have the child's representative near her. The movements of the mother and child are identical, in every detail, to the movements of the patient's representative and the representative of her disease. It appears that the representative of the disease is standing for the patient's first daughter.

At this point, I ask the patient to add another representative, for her first husband. The marital conflict is immediately apparent. They stare resolutely at one another, and neither of them is able to look at the child or at the representative of the disease. The illness had been on the verge of withdrawing when the daughter's representative was added, but now she feels more strongly attached to the patient's representative again.

I speak directly to the patient: 'it looks like the misfortune with your daughter caused you and your husband to separate.' The patient confirms this. 'That's right. My husband couldn't handle it at all. He is a doctor himself. For years, he was involved in lawsuits against the attending physician and, basically, I was left on my own with my pain and our daughter's fate. We were never close again.'

As the next step, I ask the daughter's representative to lie on the floor, to indicate that she died. The patient's representative immediately looks down at her child, begins to cry and sits down next to her. Her husband's representative cannot look at them and turns his back to them.

Something can only be truly over when one has stopped struggling with it. Experience with many constellations has shown how important it is for the living to be in harmony with death and dying. It is essential for the peace of the dead as well as of those left behind. As long as the patient's ex-husband cannot face his grief and pain at the fate of his daughter, it is difficult for the child to find peace and, consequently, for the patient as well. The patient has only limited options, and the first step has to be between her and her first husband.

I ask the man's name, and suggest that the patient look at him and say: 'my dear G., I honor your pain and the way you bear it'.

When the husband's representative hears his wife's words, he turns around and looks, first at her, and then at his daughter. Tears run down his cheeks as he reconnects with the two. At this point I release the patient's representative from the constellation and have the patient take her own place next to her daughter.

The husband's representative takes the patient in his arms and they both weep for their child. I suggest that the man say to her: 'now we are carrying it together'. The patient tearfully adds, 'yes, please, let's carry it together'.

During this process, the representative of the disease feels increasingly superfluous and backs out of the constellation, step by step.

When there is a serious event in a family, such as the disability or death of a child, the parents' relationship is gravely tested. Often, the partners cannot connect in their pain and grieve together. If one of the partners closes against the pain, the misfortune comes between the couple. On the other hand, if the parents can carry the burden together, it will bind the two and the relationship can grow from it.

We must also remember that a man and a woman often experience something like a miscarriage differently, which leads to differences in how they handle it. Women are aware of their motherhood much earlier than men, and the loss of a child in pregnancy shakes the expectant mother at a deep level. The father often has difficulty feeling this, so the woman is frequently quite alone in her pain.

THE MISCARRIAGE: 'NOW WE WILL CARRY IT TOGETHER.' (Patient with mild epileptic seizures)

For the past five years, this woman has suffered from mild seizures at irregular intervals. Neurological examinations have yielded no concrete results. It is assumed that it is some mild form of epilepsy.

Without asking for further information, I ask the patient to set up representatives for herself and for her physical problems. She chooses a woman to represent her illness. In the constellation, this representative feels very attracted to the patient's representative. Unperturbed by the rejection she meets, she attempts to move in close to the other woman, and seeks physical contact even when she is pushed away again and again. When I inquire about her experience, she says: 'What I would really like is to crawl inside her belly'. This statement brings the patient to tears. She explains: 'Six years ago I lost my first baby. That was a terrible time for me. My husband and I were living in Saudi Arabia, after my husband was transferred there. Because he had to be away at work a lot, I was often very lonely, and I did not have many social contacts. In about the fourth month of my pregnancy, my husband had to fly back to Europe for four weeks. I decided not to go with him because I didn't want to take the risk. During that time I had the miscarriage.'

I ask the patient to add representatives for her husband and the baby – a girl, according to her intuitive feeling. The representative of the illness and the baby's representative feel as if they were one, and they snuggle up close to each other. The patient's representative seems cool, and wants to be left alone. The husband's representative tries to get close to his wife, but feels helpless in the face of her rejection.

I suggest that he say to his wife: 'dearest K., now we will carry it together'. At this, the patient's representative is able to raise her head and look him in the eye. Slowly, she is able to feel more, and she finally smiles at him. After a while, she looks at her daughter and very gingerly takes her hand. The husband's representative steps nearer to embrace them both. At this moment, the representative of the illness feels released and begins to move away, step by step.

The situation with an abortion is somewhat different. In this case the parents are not in the same position, because even if they agreed on the decision to abort the child, it is the woman alone who faces the doctor and has the final choice. Because of that, an aborted pregnancy has a quality that separates the partners and if there are already other children, it also can cause ruptures in the family. If this separation is not acknowledged, sometimes illness will come between the couple.

THE ABORTED CHILD
(Patient with Lyme disease)

The man in this case has suffered for some years from chronic headache and cardiovascular irregularities that periodically lead to him unexpectedly passing out. Medical tests and examinations have revealed evidence of Lyme disease antibodies in the blood. Despite two courses of antibiotics, the patient's condition is steadily worsening. His general state of health is seriously affected; he feels extremely weak and sleeps excessively. It is only thanks to his boss's understanding that he still has his job. For the last six months the man has been able to work half time, with flexible hours, but is unable to manage more than this amount of work.

In the introductory round, the patient reports that he has been married for five years and has no children. He knows of nothing special in his family of origin that might relate to his illness. I suggest that we begin with two representatives, one for the patient and one for his illness.

He chooses a man for his own representative and a woman to represent his illness. He positions the two facing each other, with very little space between them. When the representatives are told to follow their own intuitive movements, the patient's representative takes a large step backwards. The representative of the illness instantly follows him. She reports feeling sad when he moves away from her. When the patient's representative takes another step away from her, she is determined to follow him. The expression on her face, but even more, her rather childish obstinacy, lead me to suspect that she could be representing the patient's child.

Although I know from the introductory round that the patient has no children, I ask him again, and the answer is still no. I ask if there have been any children who died, or aborted pregnancies in his family, or perhaps with a previous partner. The patient has a strong physical reaction to my question. He turns pale and drops of perspiration appear on his forehead. He explains that this is typical sign of the recurring attacks of weakness. He barely has time to ask me to break off the constellation before he loses consciousness and falls off his chair.

A slap on his cheeks and some cold water bring him quickly round again. Still lying on the floor, he stammers, 'please don't continue, I can't take any more'.

The following day the patient asks to speak with me privately during a break. He tells me that a woman he previously had a relationship with had aborted a child. I agree there might be a connection, but I plan to work first with the other people in the group who have applied to do constellations and have not yet had the chance. I tell him there will certainly be enough time for him to do something later if he so chooses. On the third day, shortly before the end of the course, he approaches me again and says, 'the abortion did not involve a previous girlfriend; the woman was my wife'. He then immediately adds, 'and under no circumstances do I want to lose her'.

After the break, the work with another participant involves a relationship issue. She, too, has aborted a child and here too, her partner was the father. Since that incident, their life together has been very difficult. The patient with Lyme disease follows this constellation intently, but he does not feel up to continuing his own work on this day.

Two weeks after the group, the patient asks for an appointment for a private session. The last constellation in the group, involving the issues of abortion and relationship struck very close to home for him. He realized that his physical difficulties began a short time after his wife had the abortion.

In the individual session I talk to him about the often far-reaching consequences of an abortion, based on observations in many constellations.

He is especially moved by the case of a woman, about 35, who told a constellation group that she thought she must be the happiest person in the world, because in two months she was going to marry the man of her life. Without any information, I asked her to set up a constellation of herself and her future husband. She positioned them at a distance of about 2 meters from one another. What was remarkable was that whenever the man's representative tried to get close to the woman's representative, she felt pain in her entire body. The pain only let up when the man moved away from her again.

These two people had already had a relationship when they were in school together. When she was 17, she got pregnant and they both agreed that she should have an abortion. They split up about two years after that, and went their separate ways. The woman had a series of relationships and the man got married to a university friend and had two children. After 8 years he left his wife. When the two school sweethearts met again after all those years, the flame was re-ignited and they got together again.

Looking at the constellation, the woman remarked that it was unthinkable for her to marry this man. I told her that perhaps their love could prevail if both partners acknowledged the distance that she needed.

As he listens to this tale, the patient realizes that the intensity and frequency of his attacks is directly proportional to the amount of time he spends with his wife. The episodes of passing out are most frequent when they are on holiday together. He had come to the conclusion that it might be due to his intolerance for excessive heat, so they spent their last summer holiday in the north. It proved to be no easier for him. He can tell by looking at his work records that the majority of the days he has to take off from work because of illness have fallen on Mondays, following a weekend. He usually needs to spend Monday on his own in order to recuperate. In the end, he has to admit that the more space he has in relationship to his wife, the better his health.

It is possible that the patient senses that his wife is no longer free for their relationship in the same way because of a special bond to the aborted child. When he says that under no circumstances does he want to lose her, it may be symptomatic of an unconscious attempt to tie her to him and to hold on to her.

I also strongly suspect that the patient experienced an early attachment loss in his family of origin, either through a personal separation trauma or a family entanglement. None of this, however, relieves him of the responsibility to respect his wife's decision. Therefore, it seems more relevant to focus on the adult component rather than to start with his childhood or family of origin.

In another, similar case, the following constellation illustrates steps that led to successful resolution.

Reciprocal Respect
(Husband's chronic thyroid disease)

A couple register together for a constellation group. They are both experiencing difficulties in their marriage. The man has been suffering from a chronic thyroid inflammation for about three years. His problems began approximately one year after his wife had an abortion. This pregnancy was the third in the space of four years and she felt she could not cope with another child.

Because of an acute medical crisis, it turns out that the husband has to go in hospital the day before the group begins, and so is unable to attend. The woman is absolutely determined to go ahead as planned with her participation in the group because she finds their current situation unbearable.

We begin the constellation with the present family and the woman chooses representatives for her husband, their two children, and herself. She places her representative and her husband's at a distance from each other. The daughters' representatives are standing next to one another, approximately equidistant from each of their parents. All four representatives seem stiff and rigid. Their heads are down and they all seem to be looking towards a place on the floor in the middle. When I ask if there have been any children who have died, the woman tells me about the abortion of the third child. I ask her to add a representative for this child. She chooses a man and leads him to a place between her representative and her husband's. When the representative of the aborted child is given a place in the constellation, all of the other representatives feel better, and the frozen constellation begins to come to life. The representative of the aborted child, however, does not feel well and appears very pale. His legs are shaky, and after a short while they give out and he sinks to the floor, as if exhausted. Before the woman's representative can react, the father's representative is with this child. He pulls the lifeless looking son to him and holds him in his arms, glowering accusingly at his wife.

The patient does not find this movement surprising. She explains that her husband's greatest wish is to have a son.

At this point I ask her to choose a representative for her husband's illness. She chooses a man and places him behind her husband's representative, who is still sitting on the floor. When I ask about his reactions, the representative of the illness says he feels right in this place; he feels strong and good, and connected to the man. The husband's representative is aware of the illness, but shows very little interest in him and moves forwards away from him. As he does so, he pulls his son even closer to him, focussing all his attention on the representative of the aborted child. The woman's representative looks at the two, and feels weak and faint. The two daughters stand close together, holding each other. Their comment is, 'it's a good thing we have each other, because we feel no connection to our parents'.

I turn to the patient sitting next to me in the circle, and ask her husband's name. I have her say to him, 'dear H, I honor your love and your pain. Still, I took the final decision and I will carry that – alone!' when she says this, her husband's representative lifts his head and looks at her. I ask her to repeat it. 'Dear H, I honor your love and your pain, but this is mine. I took the final decision, and I will carry it, alone!' The husband's representative nods in affirmation, and I ask him to say, 'dear J, now I honor your decision, with all the consequences it has for you, for me, and also for our children'. As he speaks, he loosens his grasp on the son a bit. The son's representative opens his eyes at the same time and looks with interest at his mother.

I have the patient take her own place in the constellation and ask the aborted child to sit on the floor in front of his mother, leaning his back against her. She lays her hand gently on his head and strokes his hair.

The husband's representative stands, and the representative of the illness begins to slowly back out of the constellation.

The daughters have been paying close attention to their parents' dialogue, and now feel considerably better. When asked, they report that when their parents expressed their reciprocal respect for each other, the girls regained respect for their parents. They feel good with the contact to their mother and father, and also with their aborted brother. He is in a good place with his mother, whereas the girls feel a bit closer to their father now. They both feel somewhat concerned about his illness in the background.

The information I am given about the father's family of origin is that his parents separated when he was three years old and he had no more contact with his father. As an adult, when he sought out his father, he discovered that the man had died a few years earlier. Presumably, the representative of the illness represents the man's father, but since he is not present in the group, I do not follow this line of inquiry.

It seems appropriate that the woman alone carry the responsibility for aborting the pregnancy. The man has to acknowledge that the woman has the choice in this and he has to honor her decision, whatever it is.

It is a different matter altogether, however, when there is pressure or force that results in an abortion.

THE COMPULSORY ABORTION
(Patient with schizophrenic psychosis)

During a training group, a doctor brings up a case involving a 20-year-old patient. According to the doctor, a few weeks after her mother compelled her to have an abortion at the age of 17, the young woman developed psychotic behavior patterns. She is medicated and stable at the moment. On the recommendation of her doctor, the patient and her mother visit the training group for one morning. Having watched the constellations of two other participants, the patient asks during the break if I will work with her. The following exchange is taken verbatim from a recording of the session.

When I have taken a moment to establish contact with the patient and get my impression of her, I begin the dialogue:

Therapist: You are a good girl.

Patient: Thank you.

Therapist: Good girls go to heaven. *(she smiles)* Good girls often suffer. *(she nods)* Actually, you are not a girl any more.

Patient: I am a grown up.

Therapist: Above all, you are a mother. *(she nods)*

Patient: I am here with my mother.

Therapist: With the conception of a child, one becomes a mother; there is no way to change that. *(she nods)*

Patient: I would like to set up a constellation of me and my unborn child.

After thinking this over briefly, I agree to do that.

Therapist: Is it a boy or a girl?

Patient: I don't know, but for me it is a girl.

Therapist: Okay. Then choose two representatives and set them up.

The patient chooses two women and positions them facing each other, with some space between them. The two look at each other with love and smile at one another. You can see their need to move closer to each other, but they hold back.

I ask the patient to add a representative for her mother. She chooses a representative and positions her directly between the other two, facing the aborted child.

Both the patient's representative and her child's look down at the floor in resignation. The mother, with her hands clenched, moves backwards in the direction of her daughter, forcing her slowly but surely back. The daughter's representative allows this until the child's representative begins to cry softly. At this moment, the patient's representative gathers her courage and tries to go to her child. Her mother's representative, however, holds her back firmly with an outstretched arm, until the patient's representative gives up and sinks to the floor as if dead. The child's representative calls out and then weeps bitterly, turning away in distress. The mother's representative turns around and looks coldly past her daughter lying on the floor. After a while the child's representative turns back and looks beseechingly at her mother. The patient's representative is lying on the floor, but cannot find a comfortable place. She begins to search around, with her eyes closed. In despair, she begins to flail her hands faster and faster, until she is spinning her entire body wildly around her own axis.

When the mother's representative sees her daughter acting so bizarrely, she steps backwards, one step at a time. Without displaying any emotion, she shoves the representative of the baby out of the circle with her back.

The movement in the constellation ends. I turn to the patient, sitting next to me.

Therapist: I think we have seen everything.

Patient: What about my daughter?

Therapist: You are her mother! And you have the choice!

Patient: But my mother won't let me. How can she *(indicating her own representative)* stand up again?

Without answering, I go to the mother's representative, take her by the arm and lead her out of the circle. Then I sit down next to the patient again. The mother's representative immediately turns around and gives me a sour look to show me her displeasure. I firmly admonish the representative to turn away again. She clenches her fist, stamps her foot in rage, and turns around in a huff.

We wait to see what will happen next. The child's representative quietly and cautiously begins to move nearer her mother's representative. As if she can feel the child's longing, the woman becomes more alive. With her eyes still closed, she begins to turn towards her child. The child's representative kneels by her mother, lying on the floor and when they touch, the patient's representative opens her eyes and takes the child in her arms. Crying bitterly, she sits up and begins to rock the child in her arms. The patient, herself, is watching this peaceful scene with pleasure, when suddenly, her mother's representative moves backwards into the circle, nearing her daughter's representative step by step. The patient's representative begins to breathe heavily again and it takes all her strength to turn away from her mother, holding her own child in her arms. When the mother's representative turns and sees that her daughter is turning away from her, with the baby in her arms, her rage turns to despair. She sinks to her knees and lies down on the floor as if prepared for death. The patient's representative breathes freely and turns her attention back to her own child.

I turn to the patient and ask, 'do you want to go to your child?' Her face lights up briefly, but she says, 'I am afraid'. I look over at her mother, who has observed the whole scene, and I ask, 'can she?' The mother says 'yes' very coolly. The patient immediately says, 'I want to!' As if preparing for a sacred ritual, she carefully removes her shoes, walks over to her representative and very gently takes the child from her arms. The child's representative, in the meantime, seems as if she has gone to sleep. Weeping, the patient rocks the child's representative in her arms.

Now I take the patient's mother by the hand and lead her into the constellation. She looks alternately at her own representative lying on the floor and at her daughter stroking the child in her lap, with tearful devotion and without looking up.

Slowly, I lead the mother closer. In tears, she embraces her daughter. The patient, however, senses that her mother is not prepared to accept the baby as well. She shakes off her mother's embrace and presses her daughter to her.

I suggest to the patient that she look her mother in the eye and say, 'dear Mum, look! This is my daughter, your granddaughter'.

For the first time, the mother pays some attention to the representative of the aborted child and the patient is able to look her mother in the eye without fear. I ask the mother to say to her daughter, 'yes, that is my granddaughter, and now I honor your love for her'. It is clear that the mother is not completely free, but she takes a breath and repeats the words. When she very quickly wants to embrace her daughter again, I stop her and ask her to say, 'I honor your love, and now I will withdraw'. With these words, I guide her a few steps backwards. The patient begins to breathe freely in relief.

I end the work and release the representatives from the constellation.

I was surprised and impressed at how present the patient was able to remain during this process and how much she allowed the touching movements to affect her in a good way, even though she was under therapeutic medication. It appeared to me that the patient moved from being a daughter to being a woman and a mother within a very short period of time. Unfortunately, I have no information about what has happened to this patient.

THE SECRET EVERYONE KNOWS: 'YOU ALSO BELONG!'
(Patient with fibromyalgia)

A woman in a group has suffered for about five years from severe pains in her neck vertebrae. Since there is no indication of any organic disorder, a tentative diagnosis is made of fibromyalgia. When I ask if there had been any changes in her life at the time the physical problems began, she says that the pain began after her husband left her. He went to work in the USA and never came back.

Since the work is taking place in a training group, I take this opportunity to point out to the group that, under normal circumstances, a woman does not become ill because of a man – or vice versa.

Since feelings towards a partner are often identical to one's feelings towards one's mother, I ask the patient about her relationship with her mother. She says she thinks they have a good relationship.

I am not completely convinced by her answer, so I ask, very candidly, 'do you happen to be your father's favorite?' The patient affirms this with a smile, followed immediately by tears. She replies, 'my father is no longer alive. But it's true, I was his favorite daughter'.

I inquire about siblings and she tells me she is the second of five children. When I ask if her parents had any previous partners, she says that they were already together when they were 16 and 17, and their first child was born when her mother was 18.

I suggest that we begin with a constellation of the family of origin.

The mother's representative begins crying at the very start of the constellation. The father's representative says he feels calm, but cannot move. The patient's representative feels extremely sad.

When I ask the representatives to allow their own sense of movements to guide them, the patient's representative pulls back and the mother moves to join her husband. He takes her in his arms, but she still feels upset.

I ask if the parents lost a child at some point, and the patient says that a brother was stillborn in the sixth month of pregnancy. I have her add a representative for this child next to her mother, but the change has no effect on the representatives in the constellation. The patient's representative eventually ends up in front of her parents, clenching her fists in anger.

There is clearly something of importance that has not yet been mentioned, so I ask about family secrets. At the mention of the word 'secret', the patient's representative pulls away from her parents as if embarrassed and links arms with her father, on his right side. My image is that she is shielding him in this way.

The patient confirms that there is a family secret, but everybody knows it. Her father has a daughter with her mother's sister. This half-sister is three years younger than the patient.

I ask the patient to add a representative for her half-sister. She places a woman facing the parents.

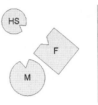

The half-sister's representative pulls back immediately and initially goes to stand next to the patient's representative. When she finds that place uncomfortable, she moves away from the family.

I ask the patient how this sister is doing in her real life. Her response is, 'she has suffered a lot'.

At this point I add another representative for the mother's sister. This touches the half-sister to tears, but when her mother turns away from her, she retreats, weeping, to a far corner of the room.

Since all the representatives in the constellation are frozen, and no one is exhibiting any feelings, I ask the patient to add a representative for her illness. She chooses a man and puts him in front of her parents' representatives. He is now standing in the same position where the patient's representative initially felt so angry, and where the half-sister was first placed.

The most interesting change prompted by the addition of the illness is that the patient's representative can now turn to her half-sister. She lets go of her father's arm and goes to embrace her half-sister.

This indicates a possible systemic connection to the illness. It could be recompense for the patient's guilty feelings, since it is only after the illness is added to the constellation that she can show love for her half-sister.

To resolve the situation, I suggest that the patient say to her parents' representatives, 'she also belongs and I give her a place in my heart as my little sister'.

When she has finished speaking to her parents, I ask her to also say to her half-sister, 'you also belong, and now I give you a place in my heart as my little sister'. As she says these words, the patient cannot restrain herself any longer. She stands and goes to embrace the representative of her half-sister's representative. They remain in this embrace for a long time.

When this feels complete, the patient takes her half-sister by the hand and leads her over in front of their father. She leaves her there and goes to join her own mother, who takes her daughter in her arms and holds her tightly.

When I ask the patient how she is now feeling, she answers, 'peaceful, finally peaceful. Now, I feel like a child'.

About six months after the constellation, the doctor who had recommended the constellation group to this patient reported that her complaints, which had previously been resistant to treatment, had markedly improved in the meantime.

It should be noted that the physical complaints appeared shortly after the patient's husband left her. Here, we see a repetition of a pattern in the patient's family of origin. With the conception of this half-sister, a bond is formed between the father and the mother's sister. A new family system is created, one that has priority over the previous system. In this sense, the patient's father 'left' her mother.

COUPLE RELATIONSHIPS, ILLNESS AND PATHOLOGY

As has already been mentioned, what we have seen in systemic constellations leads to the conclusion that a man does not generally become ill because of his wife, nor does a woman become ill because of her husband.

Most of the time, it is the 'children' who become ill out of love for their parents or other ancestors. In their deep need for closeness, children may unconsciously wish to follow someone, even into death. They may be carrying something for another person, or be drawn to die in lieu of another. It may happen that a child unconsciously identifies with someone else in the family to whom a parent has a stronger connection with more intimacy and closeness.

Still, illness and symptoms play a significant role in a couple's relationship and may fulfil other meaningful functions.

As a protection from too much closeness, or as an acknowledgement of bonds to a previous partner or parents, they can help regulate and calibrate the need for distance in a relationship, although this function is usually unconscious.

REJECTING A WIFE
(Patient with nephrotic syndrome)

This 55-year-old man has suffered since he was 40 from chronic, advanced kidney disease, including an increasing loss of kidney function. He is married with no children. When asked why he has no children, he says that he met his present wife when he was

38. She would have liked to have a child, but it just 'wasn't meant to be'. In his previous relationships he did not consider having children, nor did any of the women.

I am somewhat surprised by the emotional indifference he exhibits when he talks about his wife or the possibility of children, so I suggest that we begin with the current family system. He chooses representatives for himself and his wife and positions them side by side as a couple. When I ask the representatives how they feel, the man says, 'this is much too close. My heart is racing and I'm breaking out in a sweat. I desperately need more space'. It is clear that the representative is suffering, so I ask him to follow his own sense of what movement would help. The man moves decisively three steps sideways. The woman shrugs her shoulders in bewilderment, indicating that she does not understand her husband's reaction.

I ask the patient to add a representative for the illness. He chooses a man and positions him in the constellation. The patient's representative moves so that the representative of the illness is standing exactly between him and his wife. Here, he breathes deeply and is visibly more relaxed. He says that this place feels good. The representative of the illness says, 'I feel like a child here'.

The patient seems affected by what he sees in the constellation and indicates that he feels no sympathy with his representative's reactions. When he assures me that none of his partners was ever pregnant, I ask about his family of origin.

He is the youngest of seven children, and the only one born after the war. His father was in a Russian prisoner of war camp for more than two years following the war. His brother, who is almost 20 years older, was involved with a woman from a refugee camp near their village. The woman got pregnant and had a baby boy. When the patient's mother found out about the pregnancy, she declared, 'if any of you ever do this to me again, I'll kill myself!' When the brother's baby was born, the patient's brother and mother paid the woman a large sum of money on the condition that the brother not be named as the father of the baby, and that the woman leave the area with the child. I asked the patient about how his brother was doing, and he said that his brother had died very young. He had never found the right woman and lived alone, addicted to alcohol.

With this information, I ask the patient to add representatives for his brother, the refugee woman and the child. With the exception of the patient's representative, none of the representatives in the constellation look at the child. The child's representative feels connected to the representative of the disease. I ask the representatives to follow any impulses to move, but none of them change their positions. I ask the patient to add a representative for his mother. When she is put in the constellation, the patient's representative stiffens. When asked how he feels, he answers, 'I wasn't feeling too bad, actually, and I had a good connection with the child's representative, but now I'm not aware of anything but the illness. That is my only point of reference'.

I turn to the patient, sitting next to me, and ask him to look at his mother's representative and say, 'dear Mum, that is your grandson, my brother's son, my nephew. He and his mother also belong, and even though you could not do it, I will give them a place in my heart'. The brother's representative bursts into tears and walks over to the child and the child's mother and embraces the two of them. The representative of the illness pulls back, one step at a time, and the patient's representative looks at his wife for the first time. The entire group is deeply moved by the multiple effects of this 'simple' sentence.

Often, asking about the timing of the onset of an illness or the first sign of symptoms reveals essential clues for the constellation. Many illnesses begin, or worsen in connection to significant changes in family life. Examples of such changes would be puberty, leaving school/home/family and turning towards adult relationships and family. If someone has a function to fulfill in the family of origin, or is standing in for someone for his or her parent, this will limit the young person's freedom to act. It will influence the shaping of life and relationships and create a conflict of loyalties towards the parents and any potential partner.

Other transitional phases that are significant in the development of disease or pathology include engagement, marriage, or the birth of a child. If there is a worsening of symptoms at the time of one of these transitions, it often hints at a connection between the disease and an unresolved attachment in the family of origin.

Illness creates bonds in a couple's relationship, but puts distance between the two at the same time.

ATTACHMENT TO A FIRST WIFE: 'NOW I SEE WHAT YOU ARE CARRYING' (Patient with non-carcinogenic prostate tumor)

A 70-year-old man is suffering from a non-cancerous enlarged prostate. He is determined to avoid surgery, despite a bladder urgency that interrupts his sleep about seven times a night. With a clear medical disclaimer, I agree to do a constellation and ask him about his family situation. This constellation is presented with diagrams and dialogue taken verbatim from a recording of the session.

Patient: I am retired and my wife is considerably younger than me. She is 45. I have six grandchildren from my first marriage.

Therapist: How long have you had this physical problem?

Patient: About seven years. It is getting worse, little by little.

Therapist: Was there any change in your life at the time it began?

Patient: I've been retired for 10 years. I married my wife eight years ago, but we have known each other for 20 years.

Therapist: So, the physical complaints began about a year after this marriage?

Patient: Yes.

Therapist: And you have children from your first marriage?

Patient: Yes, three.

Therapist: How are things going for your first wife?

Patient: Well, I was married another time. My present wife is my third. When I had already met the woman I am now married to, I decided to marry another woman, for reasons that now seem inexplicable to me.

Therapist: Right. Are there any children from your second marriage?

Patient: No.

Therapist: Why did you divorce your first wife?

Patient: It was too difficult to live with her – our life was very unsatisfactory. I have had a lot of therapy and changed a lot. Finally, we just drifted apart. We shared custody of our children, and we were able to manage everything connected to the children well.

Therapist: Right. Let's begin with the current situation. That means, choose representatives for yourself and your present wife.

The patient chooses the representatives and positions the woman on the man's left side. The two look at each other and smile. I ask about their experience.

The patient's representative says, 'I have a pleasant, warm feeling towards my wife. I am happy to see her and I feel good'.

The wife's representative echoes the man's feelings. 'I feel similarly. I also have a warm feeling. I can see him, but I also feel free to look forward.'

Therapist: That all looks perfectly lovely.

Patient: (smiles) And it is, too!

Therapist: I don't quite trust this contentment. Would you add someone to represent your first wife?

The patient chooses a representative and places her to the side of his own representative, but at a distance, looking at the pair.

Therapist: Has anything changed for you?

The patient's representative comments, 'I would like to be a bit closer to my first wife. Now I feel more attracted to her than the current one.' As he says this, he takes a step towards her so that he is roughly equidistant from each of the two women. I turn to the patient and ask, 'what do you have to say about that?'

Patient: That's very interesting.

I ask the current wife's representative how she is feeling, and she replies, 'when I saw the first wife, my feelings of closeness to my husband became more intense and when he moved away from me, it was not pleasant. I still feel free to look around, but if I look at this first wife, I don't feel good.'

The first wife's representative reports, 'I feel unsteady and something is pulling me down.'

At this point, I want to see how the representatives react to the patient's illness, and whether this will produce any changes. I have the patient's representative return to his original position, standing next to his wife and ask the patient to add a representative for his illness. He chooses a man and places him facing his own representative.

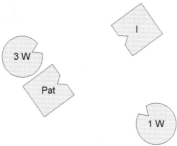

Therapist: What has changed for you?

Patient's Representative: I am thinking about whether or not he disturbs me. Somehow, I felt better when he wasn't there, but I don't experience this illness as threatening. What is different for me is that I no longer feel the urge to move closer to my first wife. I now have that warm, cozy feeling again next to my present wife.

I turn to the patient, 'It seems as though it is easier for you to enjoy happiness with your present wife when the illness is there.'

Patient: The pull from my first wife is enormous. When I separated from my second wife, my first wife was very hopeful that I would go back to her.

Therapist: That was clear in your body reaction earlier when I mentioned that something was still unresolved between you. Relationships live from an exchange of giving and taking. When one partner is less bound, and therefore more available than the other, then sometimes an illness or pathology establishes the required distance. In this way, the illness has had a stabilizing effect in your third marriage rather than a disruptive effect.

Patient: Perhaps there is some other option for stabilizing?

184

Therapist: Right, we'll see what the representatives have to say. How is the first wife feeling?

First Wife's Representative: (laughing) This is good for me. I am relieved of the burden. I wish him well with that *(pointing to the illness)*.

Therapist: It seems as though you don't really have her blessing for the relationship with your present wife. How is the illness feeling?

Representative of the Illness: In the meantime, I have begun to feel a pull to move in closer. As long as he needs me, I am here!

Therapist: How about the patient's representative?

Patient's Representative: Well, the illness actually doesn't bother me at all. Quite to the contrary, I now feel very comfortable with my present wife. That warm feeling I had at the beginning is there again. I can see my first wife out of the corner of my eye, but I can also look forward now, and she doesn't bother me any more.

At this point, I make an intervention in the constellation and ask the first wife's representative to change places with the representative of the illness. In this way, the patient's first wife is directly in his line of vision. When I ask her how she feels in this position, she says she is very hurt. When I turn to the patient, he says, 'I know that, and up 'til now, nothing has made any difference in that feeling'.

I have the patient take his representative's place in the constellation. When he moves into the constellation, the representative of the first wife begins to cry. The patient says, 'I don't have a clue what to do'. Hearing that, the representative of the illness speaks up. 'When he says that, I get all warm again and want to move nearer.' I confirm that impression. 'That makes sense, because basically, you were the solution here.'

When I ask the first wife's representative if there is anything that this man could do, she sighs and says, 'he has already done enough. I can't actually look at him any more. I feel completely alone'. This makes it clear that the heaviness that she is carrying comes from somewhere else, most probably from her family of origin.

I ask the patient what his first wife's name is and ask him to tell her, 'dear M, I can see, now, what you are carrying and I can honor that'. When he says this, she retorts, 'I don't believe him!' The patient confirms, in resignation, 'that's true, she wouldn't believe that from me'.

Therapist: We can see that there is something in her family background that is having a powerful effect. Basically, it has little to do with you, but if it is not honored, she can't let you go. What do you know about her family?

Patient: Her parents got divorced when she was very young. Her grandfather was very reclusive and was forced into retirement at the age of 38. He spent the rest of his life working in his allotment garden. She was very close to him.

Therapist: I am not going to pursue this just now. The most important part is, when you manage to honor what she is carrying, she looks at you. It seems as though that is as much as we can do in this context.

Patient: That's good for me. All those years of dissatisfaction and lack of respect just now evaporated. For her to look at me is truly something new!

The following morning the patient happily reports that he had the most peaceful night he has had in a long time, since he only had to get up three times instead of the usual six or seven.

Whereas the previous case focussed on physical symptoms in a couple-relationship, another case, of a 55 –year-old woman, illustrates a different dynamic. The woman's childhood allergies resurfaced following her divorce. When she separated from her husband, she was once again 'free' to take over the role of mother to her own mother. Her maternal grandmother had died in childbirth when the patient's mother was born. Resolving the parentification allowed the allergic reactions to abate, and the improvement has proved to be a lasting one.

The following case is an example of a child's willingness to become ill in order to win and hold the parents, even at the cost of his or her own life. The quotations in this constellation report are taken from reports from the mother and from various medical reports.

The Divorce: 'Are you finally getting on better with each other?' (Patient with Crohn's disease)

The mother of three children comes into a constellation group seeking help for her son. The son, who is now a young man, has suffered for many years from Crohn's disease and experiences periodic, life-threatening episodes of the disease. According to the mother's report, the son's suffering began with the parents' divorce when he was 14. His father left the family to enter into a new relationship with a young woman. He 'gave up the house and all contact to his children'.

At about this time, the son stopped growing and began to lose weight (eventually, over 65 pounds), and he did not enter puberty. Over the course of many years, various doctors were consulted, but without any real improvement. The boy's constant stomach pains were not considered in the diagnostic process. After three years without any real results, it was recommended that the boy take a 'health cure'. During this time, a doctor in charge of the cure center began to suspect the presence of a stomach abscess, and the boy was referred to a clinic. This diagnosis was confirmed and immediate surgery followed. The operation was successful and the diagnosis read, 'psoas abscess, extending from the liver to thigh, caused by a concurrent perforating Crohn's disease, with intestinal fistulas and a bladder fistula' (first medical report, 1994).

These dramatic developments in the son's condition brought his father back into contact with the family. The previous tensions between the father and mother faded into the background in the face of their son's illness.

With the son's question, 'are you finally getting on better?' his health began to improve consistently. Puberty occurred spontaneously and he gained weight. Although his health stabilized in the following years, whenever there were situations of separation within the family, such as his father's remarriage and move, or his sister's year abroad, the boy again suffered small abscesses in his belly that had to be surgically removed.

In 2002, the young man's separation from his long-term partner led to a dramatic medical crisis.

'Hospital admission was due to clinical evidence of a fist-sized abscess in the lower right quadrant, along with episodes of septic fever. Surgical intervention in response to the abscess in the abdominal wall, revealed a fistula in the abdominal wall that was leaking fecal matter' (Second medical report, 2002).

It proved possible to stabilize the patient and after a few weeks in the hospital, he was able to return home.

'In consultation with the attending internist, the decision is to undertake an immune-suppressive, long-term therapy, initially supported by cortisone.'

In 2003, the mother heard about systemic constellations and because of her son's labile condition, decided to attend a weekend group to do a constellation for her son.

This constellation indicates that the mother is tied to her own father and identified with his previous partner. This leaves her not truly free for the relationship to her own husband. When she recognizes the attachment to her father, it becomes possible for her to accept her share of responsibility for the failure of the marriage. She is able to retract her previously dominant rage towards her husband and, in doing so, she agrees to her son's reaching-out movement and closeness to his father.

I ask her to say to her son's representative, 'my dear son, whatever binds me, I remain your mother and you remain my son'. I ask the son's representative to tell his mother, 'dear Mum, whatever binds you and wherever it takes you, I agree'.

According to the mother's report, following the constellation, her son's medical condition improved and has been stable for four years now. This was also confirmed by the results of his follow-up medical examination in 2004.

'The patient feels well, and is an excellent example of the powerful influence of a sunny disposition on the gastro-intestinal system. The patient is in complete, continuing remission in regards to the chronic intestinal inflammation' (Third medical report).

According to the mother's report, her son became 'a well-adjusted, happy person'. The mother-son relationship was 'untroubled and warm, at an appropriate distance'.

After some years living in a harmonious relationship with a woman, the son married in the spring of 2006. The most recent medical report also confirms that the patient 'happily, continues to be in a sustained remission' (Fourth medical report, 2006).

About a year after his marriage, a new crisis arose. The young man declared he needed more freedom and began to pull away from everyone who was close to him. During this difficult time, his health began to deteriorate. An abscess began to grow once again, and it was highly probable that he would need a further operation.

In concern about her son's health and marriage, the mother decided to come to another constellation group in January 2008.

Without providing the representatives any information about the situation, I set up a constellation of the family including the father, mother and the ill son. The connections and movements of resolution were very similar to those we had seen in the constellation in 2003.

The mother reported after the constellation that it was like a miracle. Her son's abscess had diminished of its own accord. He most probably would not need to go in the hospital, and shortly after our constellation he spontaneously picked his wife up from work and invited her out to dinner. The patient was very thankful.

The interesting thing about this case is that a change in the mother's perspective and attitude following the constellation group, once again brought about an improvement in her son's medical condition, although she had not told him about her work.

ILLNESS AND INCESTUOUS RELATIONSHIPS

In a couple's relationship, when the partners' availability to one another is not balanced because of other bonds and complications, a child may sometimes slide into an incestuous relationship. These dynamics can also lead to illness or symptoms. The following cases illustrate such processes and show how children's symptoms may be indirect indications of relevant issues in the family.

A DEATH WISH: 'MY BELOVED CHILD, I AM STAYING'
(A daughter's cessation of menstruation)

A woman comes to a health-orientated constellation group because her daughter has not menstruated for four years. When her daughter was three years old, the patient left the girl's father. She now lives with a new partner and has a four-year-old son with this man. Two months before her half-brother's birth, the 15-year-old daughter stopped having her periods. She is now 19 years old.

In a constellation of the present family (the woman, both men, the daughter, and the son) the mother's representative is drawn to her own father, who died when she was four. It is only when a representative is added for him that she comes alive and exhibits a desire to be near him. She is oblivious to her first husband, her second husband, and her children.

The mother's longings for her deceased father bring her daughter into a dynamic of sexual abuse with her mother's second husband. The arrival of the second child intensifies her mother's attachment to her second partner and tightens the ties of that relationship. This, in turn, increases pressure on the daughter to compensate for her mother. Perhaps the daughter's body has stopped menstruating as protection – signalling that she is a child.

The daughter's representative is enormously relieved when her mother says to the grandfather, 'dear Papa, now I honor your life and your death. I have everything of importance and I also take that now. I take it and honor it by taking good care of myself. Even though I miss you, I am staying with my husband and my children as long as I can'. She says to her daughter, 'my beloved child, I am staying'.

A Deathbed Promise
(Patient with recurring bladder infection)

Similar family dynamics are observable in the work of a 25-year-old patient who has suffered from recurring bladder infection for the past nine years. The patient's father died of cancer when she was six years old. Prior to his death, his illness was a major issue for some months and the patient's mother painstakingly cared for him at home. She declared him, 'the only man in her life'. At his deathbed, she promised to remain true to him. Eight years after his death, another man came into her life. As the woman and her new partner started making plans to marry and build a new house, the daughter began to have health problems.

In the constellation, it becomes clear that the patient's mother is not truly free, deep in her soul, for this new partner, whom she has married in the meantime. As a consequence, the man's representative begins to look at the daughter's representative. The patient confirms that she was always uncomfortable being alone with him in the house, even though there was no concrete reason to feel this way.

The representative of the patient's health problems pulls out of the constellation when the patient's representative moves away from her position between her mother and her mother's new husband.

Chronic bladder infections in women sometimes indicate an unconscious 'no' to a man. In the above-mentioned case, it is irrelevant whether the patient is taking over the symptoms on behalf of her mother or whether the bladder problems are protecting her from her mother's partner. The patient experiences relief from her symptoms when she recognizes her mother's unconscious inner conflict. Bowing to her mother in the constellation allows her to express her respect and leave what belongs to her mother with her mother.

The next two examples have to do with difficulties that are directly caused or exacerbated by sexual attacks.

THE RAPE: 'DEAR MUM, IT WAS SO DIFFICULT FOR ME'. (Patient with psychogenic voice loss)

In an advanced training group I am presented with a woman who suffers from a condition that ranges from hoarseness to complete voice loss (aphonia). As the woman is a practicing therapist, this condition has been a great strain for the past 20 years.

Without gathering any further information, I ask the patient to set up representatives for herself and her voice problem. These two representatives observe each other for a while, but neither is really interested in the other. When asked about their experience, they have difficulty finding any connection between them.

When the patient adds representatives for her parents, her representative and the representative of her symptoms develop an increasing reciprocal interest. They spontaneously move towards each other and embrace. The mother's representative turns away from the others and states that she would prefer to have no contact with anyone in the constellation. The father's representative looks at his daughter and begins to take small steps towards her. The daughter's representative looks with mistrust at her father. The nearer he gets, the more tightly she holds on to the representative of her symptoms.

An erotic, incestuous relationship becomes increasingly visible. When I ask the patient about this, she reports that she was raped by a neighbor at the age of 17, but never told her parents. I suspect that there is some connection to her voice problems.

This constellation also confirms the observation that rape is often an incestuous impulse that has been transferred to another person. The constellation shows an incestuous relationship between the father and daughter, but in this case, the neighbor was the perpetrator. If the daughter tells what has happened, she brings the family dynamic out into the open and would have to also acknowledge her mother's entanglements. It is easier for her to remain silent than to face this pain and let go of her mother.

I interrupt the constellation at this point and dismiss all the representatives except the mother. I ask this representative to stand facing the patient. At first, the patient is unable to even look at her, and stares fixedly at the floor with her head hanging. Finally, I ask her to say, 'dear Mum, it was difficult for me'. Hesitantly, she raises her head and repeats the words. The mother's representative accedes with a nod and tears flow down her cheeks. She spontaneously says, 'I am so sorry'. I suggest that she also add, 'now I see what you have carried for me and I take it over'. At this, the patient begins to cry. The mother's representative takes her in her arms and holds her daughter for a long time as the movement of reconciliation begins.

I met the patient six months later and she reported happily that there had been a change in her condition. She was suffering only sporadic episodes of speech blockage and her relationship with her mother had improved. I asked her to write something about her experience of this process. An extract from her response is included below.

"It has never been easy for me to talk. It was always difficult for me to say what I wanted. Even as a child, my voice would fail me. The difficulty is still there, but since the constellation it is as though there is a connection between me and this symptom. I have an understanding from the constellation of why I have this difficulty. I did not want to be a burden to my mother under any circumstance. Now, I experience the feeling of 'can't talk about it' as a part of me, as if it belongs to me. I got a new perspective from the constellation and I can look at my symptoms with a bit of distance from the emotional aspects. This has given me increasing strength to say what I feel. What is new for me is that I am speaking up more often and even feeling comfortable doing so. My voice can come out and also be heard. I am very thankful for this."

SEXUAL ABUSE: 'I LEAVE THIS NOW WITH YOU, WITH LOVE.' (Patient with nightmares)

A man of about 75 has come to a constellation group at the urging of his daughter. In the opening round, he says that he has had the same nightmare every night since he was a child. When he was nine years old, his 19-year-old brother shot their father. His mother was hospitalized as a result and the patient was put into the care of a Catholic seminary where he was sexually abused by a priest every night. When he was 16, he was able to leave the order. The patient feels as though he has worked through this past, but every night he continues to dream of his traumatic experiences in the seminary.

We take a break after the opening round and as we reconvene, this man is the first to raise his hand to work. I agree to begin the work with him, and ask him what a good result would look like. He says, 'if the nightmares would stop and I could just sleep in peace'.

I ask him to choose three representatives, for his father, his mother and himself. The mother's representative does not feel connected to either her son or her husband. I ask her to follow any urge she might feel to move and she walks slowly out of the circle of participants and finally lies down on the floor.

The patient looks at me with a nod and sighs, saying, 'yes, that's how it is'.

I give him time to make space for this pain and finally say, 'I am going to make a suggestion that you probably won't understand right now, but it is not important that you understand it'. He says that he trusts me.

I dismiss his representative and the father's representative from the constellation. I ask the mother's representative to stand up and I position her facing the patient at a distance of about one meter. I ask him to look into the eyes of his mother and tell her, 'dear Mummy, what I have carried for you, I have carried in love, but now it is over. Now, I leave this with you, with love'.

As he speaks these words, the patient seems to fall into a trance, crying bitterly. He drops from his chair down onto his knees and bows down to the floor in front of his mother. The mother's representative moves as if to pick him up, but I signal her to let him complete his process without interruption. When he slowly comes round again, I gesture to her and she goes to him. She lifts his hands from the floor and he straightens up. Now, kneeling before his mother, he is embraced by her.

It is obvious that the man was moved by something that he could not control. He looks at me questioningly and says, 'I don't know what has just happened'. I reassure him that he does not need to understand it, nor does he need to remember it.

The next morning he comes into the group beaming. In the opening round he says, 'I still don't know what happened here yesterday, but last night I slept very well. It was the first night in years without a nightmare'.

Because of this man's open, easy going nature, he is often chosen as a representative in others' constellations and he is usually very willing to participate in this way. In the afternoon, however, he refuses a request from a course participant, saying, 'I don't always want to represent these 'nasty' men'. I pick up on his answer and suggest that perhaps he is being asked to represent these men so that he can find peace with the 'nasty' men in his family. These words move him to tears. To allow him to remain in his personal process, I ask the participant to choose a different representative.

Then again, on the third day of the workshop, a woman chooses him to represent her father. The woman's father has always rejected his own father because of the father's involvement in the genocide of Jews as an SS officer. As the man stands as a representative of the woman's father, facing her grandfather, he feels like he is going to faint. Every time he closes his eyes, he slips into his own history and sees his brother, who murdered his father, standing in front of him. When he follows my suggestion that he bow to the perpetrator, he feels a sense of peace in his soul.

At the end of the course, in the closing round, he says, 'it's a mystery to me what has happened here, but I feel like a newborn baby. I don't think this is just due to the good sleep I'm now enjoying, but rather, to a deep feeling of inner peace'.

In January 2008, the man's daughter took part in a constellation group and relayed greetings from her father. I requested that she ask him to let me know if there had been any changes for him since his constellation. He wrote that in that constellation on the first of June 2006, he had raised the issue of his childhood experiences with a pedophile theologian. Unfortunately, he could not actually remember the constellation himself, but could say with certainty that since that time, those experiences had disappeared from his mind. The man sent his heartfelt greetings and gratitude.

To deal therapeutically with incest and sexual abuse, we must first determine how much distance the patient has that will allow him or her to face the events. As long as the person is still caught in outrage and blaming, it is difficult to find a movement of resolution. In both of the situations described here, the people involved had already achieved enough distance to work with an orientation of resolution. This means giving the traumatic events themselves as little room as possible, and not involving the father or other perpetrator in the process of resolution. I would suggest that to develop a satisfying and healing attitude and posture in relation to these extremely stressful experiences, what has priority is usually acknowledging the bonds of the mother. These bonds usually appear in a constellation of the family of origin.

When, as here, the perpetrator is consciously left out of the movement towards resolution, it does not mean that the guilt and act of perpetration is unseen or excluded. This intentional shift of focus intensifies and optimizes the process of resolution, allowing the child's love to stand in the foreground.

ILLNESS AND A NEED FOR RECOMPENSE AND ATONEMENT

'Suffering shared is suffering doubled'
–Bert Hellinger

Along with our longings for closeness to our parents and our need to belong, deep in the soul there is also a trans-generational striving towards justice and reparation. In many cases of chronic illness, the patient is unconsciously responding to these needs, either as atonement or relief from guilt feelings generated by real or imagined guilt.

Often, what is experienced as guilt is actually a matter of fate, with no personal influence involved, such as a mother's death in childbirth or, as in the following case, the death of the patient's younger siblings due to an RH factor blood incompatibility.

RH FACTOR INCOMPATIBILITY: 'I WILL STAY AS LONG AS I CAN, AND THEN I WILL COME, TOO'.
(Patient with immune system deficiency AIDS)

The patient is a man, about 45 years old, who became infected with HIV virus more than 20 years ago through drug use. According to his own account, ever since he was diagnosed he has made a great effort to live in a healthy and mindful manner. Most of the time he is free from complaints, but from time to time he experiences lengthy crises. During these periods, he has an increased awareness of the limitations of his body's defenses and vitality. Currently, he has been battling a chronic respiratory infection for about three months. This affliction is extremely enfeebling and he suffers from excessive weakness and fatigue. Because of this he can only attend the constellation group for a few hours each day.

When I have a picture of his condition, I ask him to choose a representative for himself and position this person inside the working area. The representative feels weak in the legs and searches the floor uneasily. Periodically, he looks with horror at a single spot on the floor, but then immediately reverts to his roving glance. I comment that this representative looks to me like a living person looking at a number of dead people. The patient confirms that he is the only living child of his parents. Following his birth, there were four siblings who, due to RH factor incompatibility, were stillborn or died immediately after birth. Based on this information, I ask four course participants to lie down on the floor to represent those children. The patient's representative's face relaxes from it's earlier strained expression. He kneels down by his siblings on the floor and finally finds a place for himself amongst them. He makes a special effort to lie so that he has body contact with all of them. When he has found this position, he closes his eyes contentedly.

The patient is very moved by the sight and says, 'I have always felt guilty about being the one who lived, and somehow I've also felt responsible for the deaths of the others. I always thought that if it weren't for me, my brother would be alive.'

I ask the patient to look at his brothers and sisters and say, 'I will keep you in my memory and I hold you in my heart'. After a pause, I then have him say, 'I will stay as long as I can, and then I will come, too'.

When the patient repeats these words, his representative opens his eyes, sits up and looks around. He remarks that he is suddenly aware of these dead siblings in a different way. Before this, he could not really look at them. Now, he feels very connected to them but yet, also more distant from them. Finally, he stands up and takes a few steps backwards out of the circle of the dead. He looks around the group of participants. I suggest that he look at his brothers and sisters again and repeat the sentence, 'I will stay as long as I can, and then, I will come, too'.

Although the patient is able to say the sentence strongly and confidently, his representative does not seem altogether relieved of strain, and the image of the constellation does not seem to be complete. I ask the patient to add representatives for his parents. The pain is too acute for the mother's representative and she cannot look at the dead children. It is only when the father's representative puts his arm around his wife that she has the strength to look at her children. With tears in her eyes, she sinks slowly to her knees and sits with them, stroking their heads. The patient is touched, watching his mother's painful process of reconciliation. At the end, I ask him to tell her, 'dear Mum, I honor what you have to carry and I leave it now with you'. With these words, his representative suddenly gets some color back in his face and with a feeling of relief, he moves a few steps further away from his parents and deceased siblings. The patient also feels relieved and we end the constellation.

Under these or similar circumstances, it is not easy to take life and happiness in the face of the death or difficult fate of other family members. We sometimes find that such patients secretly take pleasure in their unhappiness or failure, or in their pain and suffering from disease. Now and again, a fleeting smile or an unusually relaxed tone when the patient is speaking of complaints hints at this unconscious satisfaction.

In the foreground, such atonement may be experienced as relieving but where does it actually lead in reality? Who benefits from this kind of recompense? Penance on the part of the guilty party or beneficiary brings no relief to the one who has paid or suffered. Rather, what seems to be helpful and resolving is to honor what has happened. That means acknowledging guilt or blame where there is actually guilt or blame, and grieving or looking compassionately at those who have died or suffered harm.

ILLNESS AND SURVIVORS' GUILT

Survivors of war, natural catastrophes, or accidents also experience guilt feelings that instigate a need to compensate for fate. They may feel guilty for having survived when others died, or perhaps feel they did not do enough to try to rescue others. The emotional and psychosomatic reactions of 'survivors' syndrome' are well known in psychosomatic medicine and include depression, anxiety, disruptions in memory or concentration, chronic headache, and sleep disorders.

There is less known about the connections of fate that extend over multiple generations. Children or grandchildren may also suffer chronic illness and afflictions when the traumatic events, or the individuals who suffered injury or death have been excluded from awareness in the family.

THE FALLEN COMRADES: 'DEAR DADDY, NOW I CAN SEE WHAT YOU HAVE TO CARRY'. (Children with neurodermatitis)

A woman in a constellation group presents an issue concerning her daughters, aged 16, 14, and 11. All three girls have suffered from serious neurodermatitis, a form of eczema, since they were small children. This, of course, would also suggest a constitutional vulnerability. The resistance of their condition to treatment has brought the patient to a constellation group focussed on issues of illness.

In the patient's family, there is no indication of anything remarkable, so we begin the constellation with five representatives for the current family.

The patient positions the daughters' representatives far off to the side, as if they do not belong to the family. She is astonished by her own configuration, but when she again checks out her inner feeling, it still seems to be right. It is also interesting that all three representatives of the daughters instantly feel itchy, and one of the daughters experiences actual skin pain. The children's parents are placed next to each other and feel connected to one another, but sense little connection to their daughters' representatives. None of the representatives feels a need to change anything. The mother is sorry not to have contact with her children, but feels fine standing next to her husband.

This constellation reveals none of the family dynamics often seen in cases of neurodermatitis, such as a parental conflict that draws in the children, or a daughter's identification with an earlier partner of one parent.

At this point, I remember a constellation Bert Hellinger once did in a group in Glarus, Switzerland, in which a patient with neuro-dermatitis mentioned that his grandmother had died in a fire. I ask this patient if perhaps someone in her family was killed in a fire, but she is unaware of anything of that nature.

Coincidentally, an acquaintance of the patient, who comes from the same village, is also taking part in this course. Much to my astonishment, he is very affected by my question about fire, and asks to share a story. The patient agrees. He reports that he plays in a brass band with the patient's father and whenever they play a particular march, her father starts to cry and has to stop play-ing. The lyrics of the march have to do with comrades burned in a firestorm. The woman confirms that her father was in Russia during the war, but has never spoken about it.

In response to this clue, I ask the client to choose a representative for her father. The representatives of the three daughters imme-diately feel drawn to their grandfather and move to stand next to him. In this position, they feel much better and the grand-father's representative finds the nearness of his granddaughters very pleasant. I ask three more participants to lie down on the floor to represent the grandfather's fallen war comrades. The grandfather's representative cannot bear the sight of these dead fellow soldiers, and he turns away. The three daughters, howev-er, are fascinated by the dead men and feel very drawn to them. When the daughters start to follow their impulse to move closer to the dead, I intervene. I lead the grandfather's representative to stand between his granddaughters and his dead comrades. He looks at the dead men for a long time and kneels down to them, in tears. He gently strokes each of their faces, closes their eyes, and finally lies down with them. The girls' representatives feel a sense of relief and freedom when he does this. For the first time, they are able to turn to their parents. When the client sees this, she gets tears in her eyes and says, 'I have always felt that there was something standing between me and my children, but it never occurred to me that it could have anything to do with my father'. I suggest that she face her father's representative and tell him, 'dear Daddy, now I can see what you are carrying, and I honor that. Please look benevolently at me, and at my husband and our children. When the father's representative hears his daughter's voice, he opens his eyes and gets up. I ask him to say, 'my dear child, this is mine and I carry it'.

After we end the constellation, the representative of the eldest daughter reports, 'when the grandfather touched the soldiers, it was as if he were touching me. I felt like he was stroking me, and my skin started to relax'.

About two months after the constellation, the client called me to report that since the constellation, her father had been feeling worse and worse. One afternoon, when the family and friends were all together, he could no longer hold back. He began to weep and started talking about the war. In Russia, as they were retreating, they had been trapped in a village. He and three others separated themselves from the troops and were able to escape. The rest were all killed, and from a safe distance he watched as the entire village went up in flames.

THE CAMP DOCTOR: 'I WILL HONOR YOUR SUFFERING BY TAKING GOOD CARE OF MYSELF'.
(Patient with migraine headache)

In the course of an advanced training group, a homeopathic doctor asks to work. Even in her childhood she was plagued by headaches, initially triggered by a case of meningitis when she was very young. Everything she has tried in hopes of relief has proved fruitless. The patient is the only child of her parents, who separated when she was six years old.

We begin the work with a constellation of her family of origin. The patient chooses and positions representatives for herself, her mother, and her father. The mother's representative has the strongest reaction. Shudders run through her body and she feels leaden, anxious, and has a distinct sense of horror. I ask the patient to add a representative for her ailment. She chooses a woman and places her behind her own representative. The migraine representative feels good and in the right place. She lays her hands on the shoulders of the patient's representative.

With the addition of the new representative, it is again the mother's representative who has the strongest reaction. Her breathing becomes very labored as her condition worsens, and it takes more and more effort for her to remain standing. I ask about the history of her family.

The patient's mother was born in 1929 as the second child of a Jewish family in Prague. When the ghettos were evacuated, the family (father, mother, and two daughters) were deported to a camp. The patient's facts are a bit uncertain, but she believes they were able to flee to Ukraine through the help of a Czech organization. There, the family survived in the woods, helped by Russian partisans, among others. With this information from the patient, I ask her to set up representatives for her parents. The next step is to add a representative for all those who were instrumental in the survival of her mother's family. The addition of this representative is very touching for the mother's parents, and the mother's representative feels much better. All of the family members look thankfully at those who provided the help that allowed them to survive. Only the representative of the symptoms remains untouched.

The patient is also very moved by what she observes in the constellation and needs some time to internalize this. Since the headache's representative has not changed, I say, with some concern, 'I think something essential is still missing here. Frankly, I cannot imagine how they would have been able to escape from a camp without help from Germans as well.' The patient reflects on this for a moment, and then her face lights up as she says, 'that's right! There was a woman doctor in the camp who must have helped them'. She heard about this once from her aunt, her mother's elder sister. Years after the war, this aunt tried to find that woman to thank her, but she found out that the family's escape had been noticed and the doctor had been severely punished for her participation. Miraculously, she had survived the torture, but suffered the after effects for the rest of her life.

I ask the patient to add a representative for this doctor. As she chooses a woman, she looks into her eyes and begins to cry. She leads the representative to her place in the constellation, where the woman experiences severe pain in her head and neck, aching limbs, and legs like lead. This corresponds closely to the experience of the representative of the illness. The patient is very touched and I decide to work with her directly at this point. I ask her to take her own place in the constellation and suggest that she look this doctor in the eye and say, 'I thank you for my life and I honor the fact that you had to suffer for that. You belong, and I give you a place in my heart'. The patient painfully repeats these words and the doctor's representative answers in relief, 'that feels good. Now I can breathe, and I am also able to stand here more easily'.

The patient comments, 'for me, it is almost too much. I can't bear to see her suffering'. The doctor's representative spontaneously answers, 'seeing you alive gives me great joy and deep satisfaction'. With these words, the two embrace and hold each other for a long time.

The moment the patient finds a way to meet the camp doctor with love and without regret, the representative of the migraine begins to pull back out of the constellation.

STARVATION: 'WHO NOURISHES THE BLOOD?'
(Patient with anaemia)

This case concerns a middle-aged woman who has suffered for years from severe anaemia. She regularly takes iron supplements and from time to time she gets a blood transfusion to compensate for the continuing deficiency of red blood cells.

When I hear the diagnosis of this gaunt, pale woman, a question spontaneously arises in my mind and I ask, 'who nourishes? Who, here is the nourishing figure?'

The patient does not understand my question. I repeat the question slowly and clearly. 'Who nourishes your blood?' The patient cannot make sense of the question, so I answer, 'your mother'.

As soon as the word 'mother' is spoken, the patient has to fight back tears. She says, 'that makes me very sad, and I see images of the war and starving people. I was born shortly after the end of the war in London. It was a terrible time of indescribable poverty. Starvation was so rife in the city that my parents sent me to relatives in the country because they were afraid that I would not survive. When I was 17, I came to the US as an exchange student for one year. When I was 24, I came back to the States again and have remained here ever since.'

I interrupt her story and choose a representative for her mother and place this woman facing the patient. She takes some time to face her mother, and as she slowly allows a connection to develop between them, I repeat the question, 'who nourishes?'

At this point the patient can no longer hold back her tears and she moves to embrace her mother with her pain. They hold each other warmly. After a while I offer her the sentence, 'dearest Mummy, thank you! Thank you for everything you have given me. From you, I received my life. Thank you!'

The patient is able to make the reaching-out movement to her mother, but the mother's representative still cannot stand securely and keeps looking at a place behind her on the floor, to the right. Following her line of vision, I ask three participants to stand at this spot to represent those who did not survive the time of hunger in London.

Seeing these dead, the patient can hardly breathe, and leans more heavily against her mother. I suggest that she tell them, 'I will remember you. In honor of you, I will take what has been given me'.

With these words, the patient's face surprisingly takes on color. I repeat the original question once again, 'who nourishes your blood?' This time the patient nods knowingly and says, gratefully, 'my mother – and I can actually feel that working in my bones!'

I met this woman, a year later, when she was attending an advanced training group to deepen her experience with constellation work. During a break, she told me about the positive results of our short work the year before. I asked her to write down something about her experience, which she was happy to do.

The reason I applied to do a family constellation was an on-going concern about my low red blood cell count. My doctors were talking about indications of incipient leukemia. I also used to have eating disorders; first I was anorexic, then I became bulimic. My mother was pregnant with me when the bombs were falling on London near the end of the war, and I was born shortly before the end of the war. My brother was born 18 months later and almost died of malnutrition. I was sent to live with relatives in the country because there was more food available there. Around that time, I had a terrible experience in the hospital after I had lost consciousness for no apparent reason.

What has stuck in my memory about the constellation is that a representative for my mother was put in front of me. Later, representatives for the war's starving people were added.

The impressions that have had a continuing effect from the therapeutic work in the constellation group are:

1. The first sentence, which simply established the connections between blood, nourishment, and mother. This sentence brought the fundamental issue with my mother into the foreground.

2. As I sat in front of my mother, I had a very precise feeling of resistance in my body but at the same time, the need to be there for her.

3. When I spoke the sentence, 'from you I have life. Thank you!' I could feel the resistance lessen and I got generally softer.

4. The embrace and being held.

5. The sentence to the people who starved during and after the war: 'I will remember your suffering.' With this sentence, I understood my past eating disorders as belonging to me and I had the feeling of moving into a feeling of harmony with the hardships of war that have caused my family suffering over three generations. I recognized a connection between my ongoing eating problems and the fate of my ancestors.

Since the constellation, there have been dramatic changes in my life. First the physical ones: My red blood cell count is now in normal range. My bone density has improved and the diagnosis of osteoporosis has been reduced to the lesser condition of osteopenia. I have also begun to eat without any sense of constraint. I've put on weight and many people have commented on how good I look. I feel strong and full of energy. My relationship with my mother is deeper and warmer, and both of us are more open. I know that I have a place in her heart and she in mine. I feel love and respect for her. The relationship with my daughter (now in her late 20s) is more affectionate. I feel more of a connection to her and at the same time I can handle distance better. My relationship with my husband has also deepened and my private practice as a psychotherapist has begun to grow, which I attribute to my increasing aliveness.

My mother has just gone through a series of colds in the last three months, and was greatly weakened. In our talks, she confided in me that she could feel her energy diminishing, and I am aware that she is preparing for her death. She will be 91 in August. During these three months, I did not feel well, either. First I had a gastro-intestinal flu, then a very bad cold that I had trouble getting over. One night I woke up with very painful cramps in my leg, exactly the way my mother is awakened with cramps because of constricted arteries and veins. In this phase, I have started eating unhealthily – too much sugar – even though the doctors say I have a higher risk of becoming diabetic as I get older because I already had high blood sugar problems when I was pregnant. Once again I have felt a longing to be close to my mother before she dies and I have again started feeling resentful about things that happened when I was a teenager.

In the constellation group, as an observer participant, I became aware of the connection between the onset of my symptoms and my concern that my mother was about to die. I have realized that my desire to have a closer connection to my mother and the appearance of these old resentments from puberty were a return to a child-like longing. Once more I was longing for more from my mother than she can give me. One sentence in someone else's constellation that gave me some comfort was, 'dear Mummy, you are the right one for me. What you have given me is enough and I will do the rest myself'. I can see now how much the war drained my mother, and what strength and courage it took to stay alive amidst all the dying.

The constellation a year ago helped me to say 'yes' to my mother and to feel thankful that she gave me life. This weekend, although I have just been a quiet observer, has helped me to really agree to how she is and to take in that what she has given me is enough.

During my last visit, I told my mother that she is the best one for me. She was very touched and I felt free afterwards.

I am deeply grateful. The constellation a year ago and the participation in this group have changed my life in many different areas in a healing way.

Warmly,

K.

A JEWISH HISTORY: 'I BELONG WITH YOU.'
(Patient with type II diabetes)

'A doctor in a training group introduced a 55-year-old man. This patient developed diabetes at the age of 25, one year after his father died of war related injuries.

The patient looks very healthy and gives the impression of someone who takes good care of himself. He reports that, in light of his illness, he tries to live his life very consciously.

I ask him to choose representatives for his father, his mother and himself, and set them up in a constellation.

The father and mother are facing in different directions. They do not feel connected to one another and exhibit no interest in each other. The patient's representative is standing between them and feels lost. Since there is no movement to be seen in the constellation the patient has set up, I suggest that he add a representative for his illness.

The father reacts most clearly to the new representative. This indicates a possible connection between the disease and events in the father's family. The family was Jewish, and the patient's father was the only one of his family to survive Auschwitz.

I ask some participants to act as representatives of the father's family members who died in Auschwitz. This includes his parents and his grandmother. When they are added to the constellation, the father's representative cannot bear the sight of his murdered parents and turns away from them in pain.

At this point I ask the patient to take his own place in the constellation. He looks cautiously at his murdered relatives. Spontaneously, he bows deeply to them, all the way down to the floor, as he has perhaps seen in other constellations. Eventually, he is lying on his belly before them, with his face turned to the floor and his hands stretched upwards, palms up. He remains in this posture for a while, weeping. When he looks up again, I ask him to say, 'I am your son. I belong with you. And now, I will take this (life) even at such a price'. (What is intended here is recognition of his Jewish ancestry and an agreement to the fate of his people. When he earlier mentioned his Jewish roots, it was clear to me that such an agreement would demand a great deal of him).

He remains lying on the floor for a while, then stands up and embraces his grandmother, then his grandfather, and finally, also his great-grandmother.

Descendents of survivors often find it difficult to completely embrace their lives. They hold themselves back because of their unconscious loyalty to those victims and they feel guilty if they are doing too well in their lives.

I met this man a year after this constellation. He told me that his blood sugar levels had gradually improved. After about six months, his doctor put him on insulin pills instead of shots, and has slowly reduced the amount of insulin so that the man has now reached a minimal dosage.

In constellations, we repeatedly see cases of diabetics who are not able to take from their parents or ancestors for various reasons. Also, in the case cited above, the process of taking from parents had been interrupted in several generations. I remember quite a number of patients with type 2 diabetes, who have experienced a lessening of symptoms and better coping mechanisms following a constellation.

For those of Jewish heritage, constellation work often brings up the issue of acknowledging a connection to the communal fate of Judaism, even if the Jewish background seems unimportant to the patient. In view of the many dead, a deep identification and agreement to a Jewish identity can trigger anxiety and may lead to blocking out or rejecting persons or events.

I remember running into these dynamics in a constellation with a family whose 8-year-old son suffered complications following a case of the measles and developed meningitis. It is unclear, and also unimportant, to what extent the work was significant in the easing of the symptoms. Regardless of what it was that actually helped, the father's report, four years after the constellation, was very moving.

Dear Stephan,

As you remember, my wife and I were in a constellation group in the spring of 2004 with our son, who was eight at the time. We were in despair because none of the doctors we had seen were able to offer us any hope. The diagnosis made around Easter in the St Anna Children's Hospital in Vienna was of subacute sclerosing panencephalitis, [a rare chronic, progressive encephalitis]. This had also been confirmed in other clinics. The first symptom was that Sami began twitching, and then his personality started to change in peculiar ways.

When we came to the group, Sami could hardly stand up and a few weeks later he was wheelchair-bound. Happily, the nasty course of the illness took a good turn.

Sami is now almost 12 years old. He can once again ski and ride a bike. He is in the fifth class and takes the underground to school each day. If you did not know the background, you would never believe what had happened.

Sami still has to take antiviral medication every six hours (isoprinosin), but there are no appreciable side effects.

We do not know what influenced this turnabout. If you consider the prognosis of SSPE in medical literature, we can only speak of a miracle. We pray every day that it will remain as it is.

Warm greetings,

G.

GUILT AND ATONEMENT FOR ONE'S OWN ACTIONS

Every therapeutic intervention is aimed at reconciliation and re-integration of something or someone that has been excluded. In fear of losing our right to belong, we tend to reject or repress parts of ourselves, even though we know, deep in our souls, that they belong to us. This would include, for example, personal responsibility or blame for something, such as an auto accident or perhaps careless or inconsiderate behavior.

In the following example, we are not concerning ourselves with the extent to which the illness and guilt are connected.

THE DEAD CHILD
(Patient with scleroderma)

The patient in the constellation group is about 55 years old, attractive, and youthfully dressed.

During the opening round, she says she is here at the urging of her friend, who is also in the group. Her friend is undergoing homeopathic treatment with me and has already taken part in a constellation group. This patient is new to alternative healing methods and has had no experience with psychotherapy. Because she so clearly has reservations, I suggest that she watch a few constellations of others, and if she feels like she would like to look at her own issue, she can just let me know. The patient reiterates that she is only here because her friend talked her into it and was willing to accompany her.

On the third morning of the course, she asks to work. She states that she has suffered from scleroderma for about 15 years. This is an immune system disease that involves hardening of the tissues, resulting in inflexibility, particularly of the hands. When inner organs are affected, it may severely restrict functioning and can lead to death.

I consider the first critical requirement for a clear-cut therapeutic process to be a clarification of the issue and the decision whether or not it should be addressed in a constellation. If so, the next question is who or what should be set up. One of the problems with systemic constellations, in my opinion, is that basically anything can be set up in a constellation and will generally reveal new and moving connections. The core question, however, is whether the constellation is revealing something that will support the patient in relation to his or her presenting issue.

Already in our nonverbal communication, I am searching for an answer to these questions. I try to feel into the patient's situation the way a representative does. I sense my way into the illness or symptoms, and into the patient's parents. I also form an image of a potential outcome of the work.

What stands out for me with this patient is that I suddenly feel a noticeable pressure in the area near my stomach. At first, I have difficulty connecting this sensation with the patient. Then, however, the pressure increases and turns into nausea, of a kind I have never experienced before. I decide to take a closer look at the patient's relationship to me. I ask her to choose a representative for herself and one for me. At first she is very reluctant, and emphasizes that she wanted to set up a constellation of her family of origin. I reassure her that we can certainly do that later, but it is more important for me to first have the two of us in a constellation, so that I am certain that I am in a position that will be in her best interests.

She chooses the representatives and leads them to the center of the circle. When I ask her to proceed in a collected and precise way, she places her representative first and then mine, at some distance, to the right of her representative.

My representative is staring numbly at the floor in front of the woman's feet. He turns pale and grabs his stomach, complaining of headache and severe nausea. The patient's representative is untouched by the stark symptoms of the therapist. She looks out the window, indifferent and almost amused.

It appears that the therapist could be in contact with a dead person who has been excluded by the patient or by her family. To follow up on this assumption, I ask another participant to lie down on the floor in front of the patient's representative. My representative breathes out in obvious relief and asks if he can move a few steps back and I agree. The further he gets away from the patient, the better he feels. The patient's representative is unaffected and turns away completely.

I ask the patient if she could say something about the reactions of her representative. She says that she doesn't understand the sense of the constellation and has no explanation. I suggest that there is perhaps a dead person in her family who is not being recognized, and judging from the strong reaction on the part of my representative, it could even have to do with a murder.

The patient shakes her head and we interrupt the work at this point.

About four weeks after this constellation group, the patient's friend visits me for a homeopathic treatment. She says that her friend was in some turmoil after the constellation weekend, and finally confided in her that it is possible that a child she had lost did not actually die a natural death. The baby was a so-called screaming infant and never slept without body contact with her mother. One morning, as the woman laid her baby down to sleep, the baby screamed as soon as she moved away. On this occasion, the mother could not bear to hear the screaming. She arranged pillows around the baby and left. When the child calmed, she thought she had gone to sleep. When she came back to check, a while later, one of the pillows had slipped over the baby's face and her daughter was unconscious. She called for emergency medical assistance, but it was too late. The doctors diagnosed sudden infant death syndrome and the woman did not have the courage to admit what had happened.

Constellation of Patient and Therapist

The longer I work with systemic constellations, the more attention I pay to my own sensations and the therapeutic relationship. Earlier, I used to concentrate primarily on the patients and their issues; today I focus far more on the pattern of the therapeutic relationship. Particularly at the beginning of the work, I consider the question of how the patient might feel after our work, but also how I will feel after this work. How much strength will it take from me, and how much engagement and attention is the patient willing to contribute? Sometimes, this process leads to the conclusion that therapeutic work is not appropriate or useful at this time. Rather than sending the patient away puzzled and frustrated, I often ask the person to set up a constellation of just two representatives, one for the patient and one for me. This depicts how the patient stands in relation to me, and brings out any potential transference and counter-transference issues. It provides information about the patient's attitude and readiness to find resolution, and also about what options are open to me as a therapist.

In just such a constellation, a patient with prostate cancer put me in the position of his father, who had died of prostate cancer at about the same age the patient had now reached. My representative felt terrible in the constellation and only felt better after I had asked the patient to add a representative for his father.

The patient's attention was immediately diverted to his father's representative and my representative was able to pull back in relief. In this way it was possible to resolve the transference and re-direct the patient's focus towards a resolution. (This case is available on DVD in German with English translation, published by Steinhardt Verlag, Hausner 2005)

ILLNESS AND GUILT OR ATONEMENT THAT BELONGS TO ANOTHER

Guilt that is denied or not acknowledged can often have effects that extend across generations. Many illnesses and symptoms in later generations have some connection to a previous denial of a victim's fate, or to the guilt of the perpetrator. When a family excludes or denies in this way, members of the system in later generations may show a corresponding identification with the excluded victim or perpetrator. Children and grandchildren remember the victims' suffering through their own illnesses or take on the guilt of the perpetrators and atone with suffering.

ILLNESS AND IDENTIFICATION WITH VICTIMS

DEPORTED JEWS: 'WHOEVER GETS ON HERE WILL NOT GET OFF ALIVE'. (Patient with aerophobia)

A woman in a constellation group talks about her fear of flying, a fear that has plagued her for years. Twice she has tried to visit her daughter in America, but was unable to actually board the plane. Both times, just as she was about to board, she experienced severe tachycardia and near collapse. She felt certain that if she were to get on the plane, she would not get off alive. A friend had mentioned her own experience in a constellation group, and this woman began to wonder about a connection that is later confirmed in her constellation.

Her father was a secondary school educator in Vienna and at the beginning of the Second World War he was transferred from a suburb to a school in the city center. As part of his transfer package, he was granted a subsidized flat in the city, which is still occupied by the family.

In a constellation of her family of origin, the representative of the patient's complaint is seen to have a connection to the Jewish family who owned and lived in this flat before their deportation. Suddenly, the patient's feeling 'whoever gets on here will not get off alive' communicates its true meaning in this larger context.

The representative of the fear feels superfluous once the patient has bowed down, all the way to the floor, to this Jewish family and has acknowledged their fate.

I stood in this constellation as a representative for a member of the Jewish family. I remember vividly how appropriate the patient's symptoms seemed to me. I felt my righteous anger transformed into sympathy when she bowed down before my family and me.

In many cases, a perpetrator is unable to face up to what has happened. We see this in constellations when the person's representative obstinately refuses to look at the victim. It is only the love of their own family that allows them to eventually weaken, admit to their guilt, and see humanness in themselves and others. This makes way for a process of reconciliation.

Family members have to resist judgement, take the victims and the perpetrator into their hearts and acknowledge all as having equivalent value. Such a resolution is the theme of the following case example.

A FATHER IN A PARTISAN WAR: 'WHATEVER HAPPENED, YOU ARE STILL MY FATHER'. (Patient with panic attacks)

A woman in a group has suffered from panic attacks since she was a teenager. She is the eldest of four siblings. After a short description of her family situation, I ask her to choose representatives for herself and for her symptoms. She chooses a man to represent her panic attacks.

The representative of the disorder feels strong and powerful, and is totally focussed on the patient's representative. She feels fearful of him and searches about helplessly for a place to hide. When she cannot find any retreat, she squats down and buries her face in her hands. The representative of the panic attacks moves towards her in small steps. She turns her back on him and edges away to maintain her distance. These movements are repeated several times. The patient's representative attempts to evade the man's eye, but he follows her unwaveringly.

At this point I ask the patient to add representatives for her parents. When her father's representative enters the constellation, the situation changes. The representative of the disorder loses his importance and influence and feels an urge to pull back. He looks for a good place from which to observe whatever happens. There is no change in the patient's representative's fear, but it is now focussed on her father.

In response to my questions about her family or her father's family, the patient states that, as a young soldier, her father was in Italy towards the end of the Second World War. She has no information about this, since her father has never spoken about this time. Once, in a conversation with family friends who had been on holiday in Tuscany, her father said that he could never go there because he had experienced too much horror in that place. So, the time her father spent in Italy was a taboo subject in her family.

Knowing that in the partisan war in Italy the Nazis enacted many reprisals against civilians, I ask five group participants to come into the constellation and I arrange them as a group of men, women, and children, without revealing whom these people are representing. The father's representative turns away immediately, which visibly relieves the patient's representative and she is able to breathe again. She straightens up, takes a few steps backwards and pulls back from the scene. The representatives of the Italian civilians draw close together, and the fear is now located in this group. Two of the representatives, standing in the front of the group, feel increasingly unwell. Their faces are pale and it looks as though life is seeping out of them. Slowly, they drop to their knees and crouch in a pose similar to the daughter's previous position. The father's representative turns cautiously towards them and stares frozenly at the five-person sculpture forming before his eyes.

The patient watches the constellation with intense concentration and finally asks for an explanation. I briefly describe the situation of the Italian partisan war and clarify whom it is that the five representatives are standing for in the constellation. I also share with her my suspicion that her panic attacks are caused by identification with victims of her father or his troops during the war. She looks doubtingly at me for a long time. What consequences might this statement have on her relationship with her father? The inner conflict is palpably present.

After a while I break the silence and ask her to look at her father and say, 'dear Daddy, whatever happened, I honor it. And, whatever happened, you are still my father'. This statement allows the father to soften and he begins to cry at the sight of the Italian victims. He looks back and forth in anguish between them and his daughter.

The representative of the panic attacks has been observing everything very attentively. Now, he returns to his seat. I focus my attention on the patient and her relationship to her father. We end the work with her saying, 'dear Daddy, what I have carried for you I have borne with love, but now it is at an end. Now, I honor what you are carrying and I leave it with you.'

For a few days after the constellation, the patient feels well, up until the following weekend when she gets together with her father. She notices immediately that their relationship has a different quality, which unsettles her. She does not know how to behave towards him. To her amazement, her father starts talking about the war. The woman, however, feels completely overwhelmed and finds an excuse to leave. That night she has a panic attack again. She continues to avoid any contact with her father over the next week, but after a few days she comes to the realization that this is not a good solution. In addition, her panic attacks are occurring more frequently than ever. She also has the feeling that her father is especially eager to have contact with her, and as soon as she is alone with him, he begins to talk about the war.

The patient feels extremely strained in this situation and after about four weeks, she calls for an individual appointment.

In the individual session, we go through the constellation again, step by step. Her father had traumatic experiences that he could not work through. The daughter has to agree to her father's ties to this trauma, leave his guilt and his difficulties with him, with love and respect, and still acknowledge him as her father.

The healing posture for children is to respect their parents' unresolved entanglements. This respect creates a bond between the parents and their children at a higher level and can overcome the separation caused by the traumatic experience.

The patient comes three more times, once a month, to gain support for her process of resolution. She is increasingly able to find a healthy distance to her father, her panic attacks occur less frequently, and now that she understands the background and knows where these symptoms belong, she is less frightened of the attacks, experiencing milder fear when they do happen. The vicious circle has been interrupted and she is getting better and more and more adept at dealing with her difficulties.

It requires great strength and solidity to acknowledge one's parents as perpetrators and, at the same time, to take them as parents with love and respect. Not every child is able to achieve this complex movement. The effects of unacknowledged guilt often appear first in the generation of the grandchildren.

GRANDFATHER WAS A CONCENTRATION CAMP WARDEN (Patient addicted to heroin)

A 20-year-old heroin addict comes to an appointment in my office. He is in a heroin detox program using replacement drugs, and is seeking an accompanying homeopathic treatment as support. At this time, I have only been familiar with family constellations for a few months and I am not yet working with this method. Nonetheless, due to my participation in several constellation groups, I have changed the way I look at patients and their symptoms, including having more awareness of possible family connections. When I look at this young man, with his shorn head, undernourished appearance, dark rings under his eyes, and wearing the same ragged, blue and white striped t-shirt at the second appointment, I am reminded of pictures of concentration camp prisoners. At the end of the session, I ask the patient if I can tell him my impressions. He agrees and I say: 'when I look at you, you remind me of the pictures of Holocaust victims.' This statement has a powerful effect on him. He turns pale and asks if he can sit down again. After a while he says: 'There is something that is never spoken of in my family. My grandfather was a warden in the Dachau concentration camp.' I tell the patient: 'it looks as though you are identified with the Dachau victims and are bringing your family's hidden secret out in the open in this way'. He responds instantly. 'My elder brother also did that. He was an enthusiastic member of a Klezmer music group. It annoyed my father enormously, because he could not stand to hear the Jewish music. My brother was also a heroin addict and died two years ago from a "golden shot".' As the patient speaks about his brother, there is an unmistakeable gleam in his eye.

His girlfriend cancels his next appointment. He has voluntarily admitted himself to a clinic and has unexpectedly been accepted into a withdrawal treatment program. He sends me the message that he is still thinking about the connection to his grandfather's victims, and even though he finds it shocking and frightening, he can feel it bringing him strength for getting his life in order. He says he will be in touch with me after his treatment, but I have never heard from him again. I still remember the light in his eyes as he spoke of his dead brother.

ILLNESS AND IDENTIFICATION WITH PERPETRATORS

GRANDFATHER IN THE ARMED SS: 'HE IS CARRYING IT FOR YOU' (Son with a brain tumor)

In a group organized and focused on constellation work with illness, there is one woman who stands out. Although she follows each constellation with intense interest, she denies every request to stand as a representative for someone else. On the last day of the course, shortly before the end, she asks to work.

When asked about her issue she answers: 'I have come because of my 19-year-old son. He has an inoperable brain tumor about the size of a plum, located on the corpus collosum, the bridge between the two halves of the brain. The doctors have said that if the tumor continues to grow as it has so far, my son has only a few weeks or months to live.'

When I feel into the image of the son, I sense a very deep connection to the client as 'my mother'. There is an almost eerie closeness and I feel like there is no space to breathe or to live. It feels very clearly like the son is carrying something for his mother.

My rational thinking clicks in again immediately and I ask myself who would be helped if I were to say this aloud to this woman? How would her life be with this comment if her son dies? I trip over my own thoughts and feel shocked when I suddenly realize that in thinking this, I have already given up hope for the son.

I can see the woman's determination and readiness to do anything possible for her son and it gives me the strength to say, 'my image is – and I would be happy to be proven wrong – he is carrying this for you'. To my surprise, the woman nods in agreement. She stares silently at the floor for a while and then looks me in the eye again as she speaks. She is clearly affected, but also self-contained. 'I know this. I have known it for two days now.'

After a few minutes of heavy silence, I can feel that she has got the most important piece and that she can handle it. I ask her if we can leave it like that and she says, 'yes'. I wish her all the best and she nods and returns to her seat.

About three months after this seminar, I receive a phone call. The same woman wants to register for another group. I remember her name and ask what she wants from an experience in the group. She says: 'I would like to do a constellation of my family of origin'. She does not expect me to remember her situation and is taken aback when I ask about her son. She says, much to my surprise, 'at the moment he is doing amazingly well. He is still getting cortisone, the tumor has only grown a minimal amount, and everyone, including the doctors, is as satisfied as is possible, given the circumstances'.

In the group, we begin the work with a constellation of her present family. This constellation shows her cancer-afflicted son standing in the position of his mother's father. His attention is focused on his grandfather's victims. The grandfather was an SS officer who was active in the murdering of Polish Jews.

Constellations with descendents of victims and perpetrators imply that there is a bond of fate between a perpetrator and his or her victims that is stronger and more intense than all other family ties. Dignity for the perpetrator requires that this bond be recognized, along with an acknowledgement of the guilt.

For this woman, that means letting her father go. She must also include an image of her father's victims whenever she now looks at her father. In this way, a process is initiated in the soul – one that allows her son to move out of his identification with her father.

Unfortunately, I do not have any information about what happened to the son after this time.

BOWING DOWN BEFORE THE VICTIM
(Patient with depression and violent fantasies)

The following is a report from a 43-year-old man describing a process that resolved his identification with a perpetrator. This is based on his experience in a three-day constellation group.

As long as I could remember, my life was defined by depression fed by feelings of guilt, low self-esteem and self-doubt. I also had recurring fantasies of violence that ran through my mind like scenes from a film. Since these were mostly concerned with violence against women and children, I did not feel free to have an intimate relationship or family.

I heard about family constellations from a friend of mine and it awakened my interest. I wanted to consult by telephone, first, to inquire whether this kind of therapy might be appropriate for me. Even though I did not say why I was calling, the conversation came round to my issue. The therapist thought it would be a good preparation from my side if, before the beginning of the group, I could clearly formulate what I hoped to accomplish and also what had changed in my life that made this effort worthwhile.

I immediately began to think about my situation. Confident of my ability to express my needs clearly, I asked to do a constellation. I went into the group without any prior knowledge of what would happen. Everything was new for me and yet, I experienced the constellations I saw as clear and 'right'. I decided to wait until the evening of the second day to do my own constellation.

When my turn came, I felt extremely nervous. The therapist asked what my issue was and I said, 'I don't want to be a bad person'. It had taken me months to feel and formulate this sentence. I was shocked when I heard his response: 'That is a general need and not a personal issue.' He said he would only work with concrete, personal questions. I was outraged and became very angry, but before I could put words to my indignation, he continued in a calm tone, 'however, I can feel that you mean this seriously. Most of all I can feel your need! So, I suggest we set up a constellation of your family of origin. Please choose a representative for your father, your mother and for yourself.' I did so.

I quickly found representatives for my mother and my father, and then a representative was in position in my place. He was a tall, imposing man, but as soon as he was placed in the constellation,

228

he fell to his knees and began to gasp heavily and hoarsely for air. It was only when the mother had almost left the circle that the poor man in the middle could breathe again. The 'father' stood impartially nearby. I watched the whole sequence in astonishment. The feelings I experienced were very familiar to me, yet I did not recognize their connections. I only began to understand the situation when I took my representative's place and felt the familiar tension I always feel in the presence of my parents. The therapist continued to work with me, but the only part I can still remember is the situation when I was to bow down in front of my father. My back was so stiff it would have broken rather than bend.

Me – a child without a mother, and an indifferent father. Yes, I knew this and it felt good to see it. Finally, I could sort out all my feelings and I felt free of self-blame, because it simply was so.

I drove home and slept peacefully with this confirmation of circumstances that I had never allowed myself to speak about. The next morning, I dressed in a peculiar fashion – black leather trousers, black motorcycle boots, a blood-red t-shirt, and a grey woolen pullover with a very high neck. I steered my car towards the last day of the constellation group, with diminished interest. I had already worked and now all that was left was to sit through a few more hours.

When I arrived and took my place and listened to the opening round, I felt astonished at the sympathy expressed for my work on the previous day. My constellation had touched many other participants. Many were surprised that I had had a good night. Certainly it was not an easy situation, but it also was not new to me. My feeling was more along the lines of – it was as it was and here I am today. I've survived.

The constellations began and a man in his mid-seventies had his turn to work. He was grieving for his deceased sister who had died at the hands of the Russians when his family fled. I suddenly felt very sad and felt a growing impulse to cry. Once again, bloody war images flashed through my mind. I got warmer and warmer. I took off my boots. The old man was crying and his pain made me cry as well. I noticed that I was crying louder and louder and I had no control any more. There were images I recognized from church visits and meditations – women raped and tortured, children slit open, men impaled, and so on. But, why was I seeing these things here? I couldn't leave, either. My feet would not support me any longer. The whole room was swamped in my sobbing. Something pulled me to the floor and the voice of the therapist penetrated into my ear. I only felt him place my hands on someone's feet. I had barely grasped these feet when all those familiar images of the raped and tortured women and the dead children and men again ran through my awareness. I was a barbaric pharaoh, a Greek prince, and a vicious, cruel man... I knew these pictures and I had seen them often enough. Sometimes they were in historical places, like once when I was in Greece in a small chapel where torture was depicted. I knew these events. I was there – back then.

After a while, the rush of images receded and I felt as though I had been emptied. The man whose legs I had been holding staggered and fell to the floor. The therapist helped me up and held me. I could hear his heart beating. For the first time in my life, I could consciously hear a heart beating.

As I drove home, I felt ineffably lightened. So much was suddenly clear to me. My fundamental belief that I was a murderer or rapist – a belief I never really dared to feel but that, nonetheless, had determined my life for years – was gone or understood.

With the exception of one incident, I have not had any of these images since my participation in the constellation group four years ago. Prior to that time, those pictures were a constant feature in my life.

Since that experience, my basic mistrust in life has eased away and I feel much more confident in my profession as a business consultant. It is also easier for my clients to trust me.

Heartfelt thanks and best wishes,
M.

The most important piece of constellation work is not the constellation itself. Many times, people ask to do their constellation with the idea of getting it behind them. In reality, they have it in front of them afterwards. As with many other psychotherapeutic methods, constellation work serves the goal of integrating and working through aspects of the soul that have been split and excluded.

In the example above, it may remain unclear just who is the perpetrator and who is the victim in the patient's family. What is significant is the correlation between the patient's violent images and the very probable fate of the other man's sister.

As the therapist in the group, I focussed on and followed the pain of the patient and his impulses to move. He spontaneously fell to his knees with a loud cry. His body position corresponded to a bowing down to the floor, so I placed another participant in front of him and laid the patient's hands on this man's feet. In this way, his inner movement led to the completion of a resolving bow. He remained in this position until he felt calm again.

There is hardly a German family that has not been affected by the consequences of the Second World War and the Nazi regime. It may have involved family members directly or indirectly in the Nazi regime, or victims of persecution and terror, refugees fleeing the war zones, prisoner of war camps, hunger and want; these things are dealt with in a wide variety of ways. The consequences of this period are still seen in the generations of grandchildren and great-grandchildren. It is not only in mental disorders such as depression or psychosis that we find connections, but most probably also in a large number of physical ailments. Since a medical model is currently predominant in our culture, and medical treatment seldom considers contextual factors that may have contributed to the origin and propagation of diseases, such connections are rarely taken into consideration and brought into the open.

RESOLVING LOVE
(Patient with multiple sclerosis)

Sometimes, guilt and atonement that has been taken over from another can be put to an end. This becomes possible when descendents are able to regard both victims and perpetrators with love and respect and give them all a place in their hearts. The following is one patient's report of her experience.

In January 2004, on the recommendation of an alternative medical practitioner, I attended a family constellation group, because I am ill with multiple sclerosis.

At that point, I had been living with this diagnosis for seven years. The disease had progressed periodically with intermissions; at the time of the group I was doing relatively well physically, but my soul was crying out for help.

On the second day of the seminar, I asked to work. I talked about myself and about my family of origin. We began the work and I chose representatives for my mother, my father, and myself. My representative turned away from my mother and kept staring at the floor. In my conversation with you, I said that my grandmother, my mother's mother, had hanged herself. At that point I did not know why, since it was never spoken of, even though I had asked.

You told me to choose a representative for my grandmother and have her lie on the floor. When my grandma came into the constellation, my representative suddenly felt terrible. She began to cry and could only look at her grandmother. Slowly, as she moved nearer to her grandma her posture became more and more stooped. Just before she reached the grandmother, she stopped and said, 'I want to lie down with her'.

You agreed that she should do so, and then turned to look at me, sitting next to you. As my representative lay down next to her grandmother, my mother came closer and also kneeled down next to her. At the same time, I began trembling so violently in my chair that you took me in your arms and held me tightly until I calmed down again. Then, you explained to the other participants what this image might mean.

There must have been some terrible event in my mother's family of origin, perhaps even some kind of crime. Since I did not have any further information and in addition, I could not continue the work at this point, you interrupted the constellation. You advised me to ask my family about this and then perhaps come again.

The next few days at home were terrible. I couldn't sleep, couldn't eat and couldn't work. I could not get closure with this constellation. A week later I had another appointment with my alternative health professional. I told him about the work and how awful I felt. He began a kind of client-centred therapy with me and finally got me to the point that I could continue. He supported me in doing some research into my family of origin.

In April 2004 I came back to you again – with mixed feelings, I must admit. On the one hand I felt rather happy about it, but on the other, I was terribly afraid. Again, I asked to work on the second day, but this time we began much differently. You remembered what had happened in the constellation in January, but much to my surprise, you did not ask me what had happened in my family. No, I should choose a representative for you and one for myself. Then you asked your representative if he could do anything for me. The man said, 'no, she has to do that alone'. I must admit, I felt rather snubbed and I looked at you very perplexed. We sat there for a while until you said, 'perhaps we can still do something'.

You stood up and chose two people. You positioned one on the left side of the room and the other facing her on the right side. Without any further explanation, you sat down next to me again. The two representatives looked at each other for a long time. When they finally began to move slowly towards each other, I had a strong feeling that if I didn't get between them, my heart would be torn apart.

You kept me from standing up and then, all of a sudden, my heart calmed as the two representatives reached out their hands to each other and looked deeply into each other's eyes. Suddenly, I could breathe again. You explained that you set up these two as representatives of a perpetrator and a victim from my family. The two found peace when they were able to meet in love.

Without saying anything, you looked at me for a while and then said that you could do something for me, but only if I really wanted it. When I agreed, you asked the two representatives, the victim and the perpetrator to stand next to each other in front of me. They each put an arm around the other.

Although this frightened me somewhat, I had to keep my eyes on them the whole time. I had a very peculiar feeling. On the one hand, I felt sorry for them and wanted to touch them, but on the other hand, I was afraid of them and I also felt absolutely furious with both of them.

When you suggested that I could move nearer to them and touch them, it was impossible for me to do that at first. At your suggestion, I said 'thank you' to them and 'I honor and respect whatever happened and I now leave it with you'. Having said that, I was able to stand up. As I stood in front of them, you gently took my right hand and laid it on the heart of one of the representatives, and then my left hand on the heart of the other one. The moment that I was able to open my heart to both of them, all my fear and anger disappeared. All I could do was to weep and hold the two of them tightly to me.

I will never forget the beautiful feeling of relief I experienced. I had felt the true meaning of reconciliation and harmony. Actually, it was just a few words that led to this path. I only said 'thank you' and 'I honor and respect whatever happened and I leave it with you'. I am certain that I am on the right path, because this work has not only helped me, but also my elder daughter. She also knows now where her place is and our relationship has changed, very much for the better.

I can also report, to my great delight, that since the work in April 2004, I have had no further crises with multiple sclerosis.

Once again, my heartfelt thanks.
W
March 2008

ILLNESS AS PROTECTION?; 'THEN I WOULD KILL MY WIFE!'
(Patient with multiple sclerosis)

Years before I knew anything about the work with family constellations, I had an experience in my homeopathic practice with a 45-year-old patient with multiple sclerosis. He was almost fully lamed from the neck down. Although his disease was in a very advanced stage and his breathing was restricted by the muscle deterioration in his chest, the patient was quite convinced that he could recover. Because of his exceptionally strong will to get well, the question came to mind what he would like do if he actually did become healthy again.

Much to my shock, he replied, with the same degree of conviction and devoid of any emotion, 'then I would kill my wife'. I still remember the relief I felt when he left my office. There had been no mention of a further appointment.

Often, in constellations of patients with multiple sclerosis we can see the patient's identification with a perpetrator; the patient's representative sometimes expresses more or less concrete, murderous impulses. The lameness incurred by the disease could be serving as a protection against violent impulses.

We have seen similar dynamics in constellations with patients suffering from serious, progressive rheumatic diseases, and also in cases involving compulsions and tics. These could also be understood as actions designed to hide the actual urges as well as the guilt in the family background. A resolving movement in constellations is to make the dynamics visible and acknowledge the guilt or crime, even when it is not known exactly what happened.

ILLNESS AND HIDDEN EVENTS THAT ARE SYSTEMICALLY RELEVANT

There are taboo topics and secrets in every family. Some of them serve to protect and preserve individual family members or the entire family.

But when there are events that are relevant to the system (the conception of a child, paternity, or a violent death, for example) and these are not spoken of, or have been denied or forgotten, the systemic order is disturbed by the exclusion of relevant people and events. These sorts of secrets come to light, regardless how fiercely they are shielded. They find expression through the behavior or symptoms of a child in the family, either in the same generation or a following generation. Experience has indicated that many people, including the experts, do not notice these clues, or fail to understand their significance. Sorting out connections of this kind and resolving relevant entanglements is often impossible without external help. This is an area where systemic constellations have an important contribution to make.

GRANDMOTHER'S DEAD CHILD: 'WHO TOLD YOU THAT?' (Patient with cervical dysplasia)

The next patient is dealing with a probability of cancerous alteration of cells in her cervix. A clinical examination (colposcopy) has substantiated the initial diagnosis. I suggest that she set up a constellation with representatives for herself and her medical problem. The woman who is chosen to represent the illness is placed directly behind the patient's representative. The two seem like mother and daughter. When the patient's representative feels the representative of the illness put her arms around her shoulders, she relaxes and leans back, and lets herself be rocked. The patient agrees that this image fits her mother and herself. She feels comfortable changing the representative of the illness into a representative of her mother rather than adding another representative.

Even though the two feel relatively good, they appear rather lost and powerless. Since the pathology has to do with a female disorder, I suggest she add a representative for her grandmother, her mother's mother. The patient places this woman very near to the others. The mother's attention is immediately drawn to her, but the grandmother takes no notice of her daughter. Instead, she stares sadly at the floor. It is impossible for the mother's representative to approach the grandmother, who anticipates her every attempt and turns away.

I ask another participant to lie down on the floor in front of the grandmother. The grandmother begins to cry and turns to the representative lying on the floor as if to a small child. In response to this movement, the mother's representative says, 'now it's fine', and turns happily to her daughter again.

In a different constellation group six months later, the patient approached me during a break and asked if I remembered her. I had to admit that I did not. She reminded me that 'due to pre-cancerous tissue in the cervix, my doctors had recommended surgery soon because of the danger of cancer, and I did a constellation. When I got home from the constellation group, I asked my mother if her mother had perhaps lost a child. "Who told you that?" was my mother's astonished reaction.'

A further clinical examination, two months after the constellation, revealed no observable cellular change in the cervical tissue. Aside from the constellation work, the patient had had no therapy or treatment, nor had she changed anything else in her life.

Sperm Donation: 'That is your father'
(Son with anxiety attacks and depression)

This family comes in for an appointment with their 12-year-old son. The parents emphasize the boy's above-average achievements in school, but report that for the past two months he has suffered from depressive moods. The onset of the depression followed a nervous collapse at school. Since then, he has been unable to leave his parents' house alone. Away from home he suffers from anxiety states, ranging from rapid heartbeat and sweating, to complete collapse. The depression is worsening and he has lost interest in everything that used to bring him joy. His life is increasingly centered on computer games and the Internet. More and more frequently, he has expressed a fear that he is going insane.

Since psychotropic drugs have failed to bring about the desired results, the parents are inquiring into homeopathic treatment, and I also recommend that they participate in a constellation group. The boy feels relieved when he hears that he does not necessarily have to be involved in this. Up to this point, he has been the center of the various therapeutic interventions and he feels as if everything is resting on his shoulders. The parents are prepared to attend a group.

We begin the constellation with three representatives, the father, mother and son. I first ask the mother to set up the constellation and ask the representatives to note their positions. Then, I let the father set up the constellation. The two pictures show very few differences. In both constellations, the son is placed between the parents' representatives, separating the two. The three representatives form a half-circle, with the mother in the first position, her son to her left, and then the father.

The mother's representative does not feel well in this position, but cannot describe her feelings explicitly. The son's representative has no sense of orientation and the father's representative does not feel as though he belongs and, strangely enough, does not feel as though he wants to.

Hoping to bring some clarity into the constellation, I ask the mother to choose a representative for her son's difficulties. She chooses a man and places him at some distance behind her son.

The son's representative is extremely upset. He feels afraid, his hands become sweaty and his eyes begin shifting back and forth, faster and faster, between his father's representative and the representative of his illness. He looks as though he is going insane. Suddenly his glance settles on the patient (the mother), who has been strongly affected by the reactions of her son's representative in the constellation. In anguish, he bursts out, 'you lied to me about my father!' Then he looks at me and, nearly in tears, he repeats, 'she lied to me about my father!'

The patient, next to me, does not react to the son's words, but stares expressionless at the floor. Before I can ask her about the meaning of this odd sentence, her husband speaks up and says, 'perhaps it is important here to mention that I am not the boy's father. We had been married for some years and wanted a child, but my wife did not get pregnant. The results of examinations showed that I could not produce a child. We did not want to give up our desire for a child, so we decided to use sperm from a sperm bank. Our son does not know anything about this.'

I answer quietly, 'well it looks like he knows. If I take seriously the representatives' reactions and what the constellation is showing us, I have to assume that he knows'.

The son's representative adds his conviction to this statement. 'When the representative of the illness was put into the constellation, I did not know anything anymore. All of a sudden I did not know which of the two was my father, and I felt a peculiar sense of betrayal from my mother.'

The boy's father (actually his step-father) asks what can be done at this point. I have the father's representative say to his son, 'that is your father (the representative of the illness) and that is your mother (indicating the mother's representative). She and I take care of you, but that man there is your father'.

The son's representative smiles and says, 'that's fine. I can live with that.'

Out of curiosity, I ask the representative of the illness how he is feeling. He says he wants nothing to do with any of the others.

I say to the child's representative, 'that's how it is' and he nods. Finally, I tell the two clients, 'I think that is all that I can do for you'.

About two months after the constellation, I received a call from the step-father. He wanted to thank me and tell me how astonished they were when they got home from the group to find their son in distinctly better condition. Within a few weeks he was back to 'normal'. This gave the man and his wife the strength to find an opportune moment to tell the boy that his presumed father was not his biological father. The son's reaction was similar to his representative's. When I last heard of them, the boy was doing well.

Children are their parents and they recognize their parents in themselves. So, you cannot fool children when it comes to their parents. If they are kept in the dark about their actual parents or given false information, it leads to a split and uncertainty in the child. The child sees his or her 'parents', but does not feel like their son or daughter. Children generally seek the source of such discrepancies first in themselves. What does a child think when an adoption is first made known when he or she turns 18, or is told that a different, biological father exists, or when a child somehow discovers such facts?

Constellations often reveal family secrets, but I must issue a clear warning against misusing this method. If there is a sound reason to believe that a father is not the biological father, then only a paternity test will bring about certainty. As long as a father or a child is in doubt, love cannot flow freely.

AN AFFAIR WITH CONSEQUENCES
(Patient with chronic sinus infection)

This case involves a German woman who has lived in Barcelona for 18 years. She is married to a Spaniard and they have a four-year-old son. For a long time now the woman has been thinking about separating from her husband and returning to Germany. In this stressful situation, she has developed a chronic sinus infection that has proved resistant to all antibiotics. In January 2005, the patient had to have surgery because the infection had spread into her ears and there was a danger of infection of the membranes in the brain (meningitis). The operation and subsequent intravenous penicillin prevented the disease from spreading but did not lead to a cure of the problem. In March 2005, the symptoms again worsened and at the time the patient came to a constellation group in Barcelona, she was suffering again from severe headache and increasing sensitivity to light.

I decided to do a constellation of the illness in the context of her current conflicts. The woman's symptoms disappeared within two hours after the constellation and she later wrote to me to express her thanks. Since I could not fully remember the details of the constellation, I asked her to write me a report of her experience.

'The original problem I was hoping to sort out with a constellation was whether I should accede to my increasing desire to go back to Germany and, if yes, how that might be accomplished. When my health deteriorated again, my original question receded into the background. I heard about a constellation group for people with illnesses, and spontaneously registered for this group. During the group, my physical condition got much worse and my only interest was a burning desire to get well again, including staying in Spain if that was necessary.

Before we did the constellation, I described my current living situation, and you asked me if there was anything of note in my family of origin. I have a younger sister and a half-sister who is only a year older than me. My father and mother met when they were very young and it was their first real love. When they had been in a relationship for some years, my father went to Sweden over the Christmas holidays with some American friends – soldiers that were stationed post war near his village. Two of the Americans had girlfriends there. The soldiers left the day before my father, and my father had a one-night affair with one of the women. On that night, my half-sister was conceived.

When my father found out about the pregnancy, he refused to believe that he could be the father of the child. He assumed that it had to be the American who was in a relationship with the woman. For him, it was always clear that he would stay with my mother. The whole escapade remained a secret until my half-sister, at the age of 36, came looking for her real father and found him.

Since then, I have stayed in contact with her. Although we don't see each other often, since she lives in America and we are in Europe, we are on good terms.

The Constellation

First, I was asked to choose a representative for myself, and one for my illness. The two representatives circled around each other, whereby my representative turned demonstratively away from the illness and did not want to have anything to do with her.

After a while, you asked me to add representatives for Spain and

Germany. My representative immediately went to 'Spain' and leaned against the representative. The woman representing my illness took three steps backwards. You were mistrustful of this movement and I had to add representatives for my mother and my father. Then, later, we added a representative for my half-sister's mother and finally, also one for my half-sister.

My mother's representative had no connection to the other representatives. My mother had lost her father when she was two. As her representative showed, my mother seemed caught in that early trauma. My father's representative wouldn't let himself feel anything for anyone and watched the whole thing with a defiant look on his face. My half-sister and her mother felt very angry with him.

At this point I was to move into the constellation myself, and I was placed in front of my half-sister, at a distance. I immediately burst into tears and felt a mixture of relief and joy at seeing her, but also tremendous sadness for the long years of loss. A representative for my younger sister was added and you turned us away from our father. I felt a huge relief. I had given my half-sister a place, on behalf of my father, so to speak. I had taken over responsibility that was his to carry. I felt that I had to give this up and entrust it to my father. He had to carry it alone. I turned to him several times, and each time I could feel that old familiar loyalty. Even though I knew that it was right, it was difficult for me to leave him 'alone' with it. Of the final image, I only remember the three of us sisters, with a good connection, standing with our backs to our father, who stood behind us at a distance. In the background, as far as I can remember, there was a group watching with interest, including my mother, our father, and the representative of my illness. I cannot remember any longer where the representatives for Spain and German were standing. What I will never forget, though, is that you said that perhaps I had gone to Spain to save my life, and if I were to leave Spain, it should be in deep gratitude.

My headache stopped on the same day and my nose started running. I had a runny nose for about two weeks, and after that I was really healthy again. During this time, I decided to return to Germany with my son. My husband and I agreed to a time-out. We stayed in regular contact and things were good between us. We also started going for couple's therapy. Now, we are living together in Germany and have a second child. During my pregnancy, I had a slight relapse of my sinus infections, but was able to manage it with homeopathic treatment.

What continues to be significant for me is having recognized, in the constellation group that my difficult relationship with my mother is partially due to my loyalty to my father. This was shattered when I stepped into the constellation and looked my half-sister in the eye. I experienced it as an important and healing movement to find a good connection to my siblings without a guilty conscience, and to leave the difficulties with my parents.

It was two years later that I suddenly became aware that the story with my half-sister actually started in Spain. About six months before that trip to Sweden, my father and his friends had first met the Swedish women during a holiday in Tossa, a town about 80 kilometres from Barcelona. The two Americans began their relationships with the women at that time. Later that same year, at Christmas, they and my father went to Sweden. Could this be the origin of my attraction to Spain (which I felt, even as a child)?

'MY FATHER INFECTED MY MOTHER WITH AIDS'
(Son with behavioral disorder)

In a constellation group, a mother talks about her 12-year-old son, who is exhibiting rather disturbed behavior. In school, he steals from his classmates and is often involved in fights. When confronted with his behavior, he reacts either aggressively or with total denial. Because the violent outbursts are becoming more frequent and more intense, the school staff see no alternative at the moment other than to expel him from the school and send him to a special facility.

In a constellation of the present family, the patient positions her son near her on her right. The child's father is to her left, at an appreciable distance. If one looks at the representatives in a clockwise manner, the son is standing in the first place, and has priority. This is a disruption of the natural order of things, but in this case the son does not feel uncomfortable in this position. He is standing up straight, appears strong, and feels superior to his mother. He is not even aware of his father. The patient's representative expresses her fear of her son. The father's representative cannot see any options for action and feels as though he has been left alone to hold the fort.

Judging from the son's position in the constellation, he must be representing someone for his mother, so I ask the patient to add representatives for her parents. She positions them facing each other, behind the representatives of her son and herself. The mother's mother does not give her husband so much as a glance. There is obviously a major conflict represented here.

When I ask the patient if something had happened between her parents, she answers, 'yes, but I can't say what it was'.

The effect of this statement is immediately apparent in the constellation. The son's representative takes a step back so that he is standing between his mother's parents, and repeatedly stamps his foot furiously. I say to the astonished patient, 'here you can see how that secret continues to work in your son when you guard it and keep it hidden'. The patient begins to cry and then she explains: 'My mother is ill. My father infected her with AIDS.' When asked how he got infected, she scornfully says that it came from prostitutes.

So, the gravity of the issue is out in the open. The question that arises is what posture the patient can hold in relation to her parents, particularly her father, to ensure that what is between her parents does not continue to have a negative effect on her and her children? A resolution first calls for a step in the relationship between the patient and her father.

I ask the representatives to stop moving at this point and ask the patient to look at her father's representative. It takes some time before she can look at him, and when she finally manages that, I suggest that she say, 'whatever happened, you remain my father'. After a short pause I have her add, 'and what was and is between you and Mum, I leave with you now'.

When the patient speaks these sentences, the son's representative steps out of the field of tension between his grandparents and turns to his father's representative, who claps him happily on the shoulder. The son's representative seems like a different person. Now he radiates the lightness of a child, and his joyful expression allows the patient to relax. Finally, I suggest that she might tell her son, 'the father that one has is always the best!' With some hesitation, but then smiling, she repeats the sentence.

PATRICIDE: 'NOW I TAKE IT, EVEN THROUGH YOU'
(Patient with Hashimoto's thyroiditis)

Hashimoto's thyroiditis is an immune system disease of the thyroid, with possible degeneration of thyroid tissue. Without thyroid hormone supplements, the disease can lead to death.

A woman of about 20 years old has been suffering for some months from a seriously progressive form of degenerative thyroid disease. In cases of aggressive, autoimmune thyroid disease, I have frequently encountered indications of crime in the family history. When I mention this observation directly to the patient, she reports that in her family there is a strong suspicion that her mother's eldest sister poisoned their father. This aunt was a pharmacist, was single and childless, and lived in the house next to her parents. The grandfather died from eating a mushroom dish that another person had also eaten the day before. The patient's aunt was the last person to see him alive. A few years after the grandfather's death, the aunt committed suicide.

We begin the constellation with a representative for the patient and one for her illness. She chooses two women, and positions them so that the representative of her disease is standing behind her own representative. The representative of the disease feels exceptionally powerful. She puts her arms around the patient's representative and says, 'she's mine'.

There is no escape for the patient's representative. All her attempts to free herself from the grasp of the illness are in vain and it appears that she is at the mercy of this disease. I ask the patient to choose representatives for her parents and to add them to the constellation one at a time so that we can observe the effects of each on the constellation. Adding the father leads to no marked changes and the father's representative has no sense of being influential. The mother's representative is very affected by her daughter's difficult situation, but also feels helpless and without recourse.

As the next step, I ask the patient to choose a representative for her mother's eldest sister. No sooner is she positioned than she feels a sense of being driven by restless unease. She feels no connection to any of the others in the constellation. She is only able to calm down when the patient adds a representative for her grandfather, her mother's father. He is instantly a focal point for the aunt. Between these two there seems to be some kind of love-hate relationship. They do not feel like father and daughter, but rather man and wife. In answer to my question, the patient confirms that this aunt was the grandfather's favorite.

I ask the patient to add a representative for a possible earlier partner of her grandfather. This woman's entry into the constellation changes everything. With her head held high, she slowly moves to a place from which she can observe everyone else. They all watch her tensely and dare not move. She radiates an awesome power. In response to the anxious looks of the other representatives, she says in a ringing, haughty voice, 'I have you all in my grasp. You all are mine!'

For a moment, all the representatives stand as if frozen. The first one to cautiously begin to move is the representative of the disease. She lets go of the patient's representative for the fist time and moves slowly, step by step, out of the constellation. The patient's representative sinks to the floor in exhaustion. Her mother takes her daughter in her arms, and cradles the lifeless body. Then, the aunt's representative breaks away from her father and comes to kneel by the two, lovingly stroking her niece's head. All these movements are performed with utmost care and attention and all the while, the representatives keep an eye on the grandfather's previous partner.

The conflict that was previously seen between the grandfather and the aunt is now apparent between the grandfather and his previous partner. She feels a murderous rage towards him.

The patient suspects that the relationship in question occurred during the grandfather's years as a soldier during World War Two.

In the meantime, the representative of the disease has moved out of the constellation completely. The patient's representative is still lying lifeless in her mother's arms. The power is still in the hands of the grandfather's 'partner'. The scene transmits a sense of the portrayal of a curse.

To make space for whatever might be missing, I ask a participant from the group to act as a representative for whatever it is that remains unfinished between the two. I ask him to enter the constellation and follow his own feelings or impulses. He cautiously approaches the grandfather's partner and sits down at her feet. The woman's rage turns to an immeasurable pain. Her whole attention is focussed on the representative at her feet. She drops to her knees, takes him in her arms, and rocks him like a baby. The grandfather's representative remains hard and after a while he turns away.

Slowly, the patient's representative begins to feel better, but still lacks the strength to stand up.

At this point, I am wondering who of the representatives might serve as a resource for the patient, and from whom she could draw the strength to step back into life. Is such a person even present, or is someone perhaps missing who must be added? As I cast an eye over the constellation, my attention is drawn to the mother's sister. She had taken on the murderous rage of the father's previous partner, which has burdened the family like a curse, and she it is likely that she took revenge on him, acting in place of his previous partner. This identification actually cost her her own life, and that fact has to be seen and acknowledged as well.

I ask the patient's representative to say to her aunt, 'I now take it (life), also through you'.

When the aunt hears her niece's words, she is moved to tears. She smiles at her and responds on her own. 'Live, my child, live!' The patient's representative beams in response. To strengthen her movement towards life, I suggest that she say, 'yes, in honor of you, I will now live'. The two women embrace and then the patient's representative straightens up and slowly moves away from the constellation. When she reaches the edge of the circle, she turns and looks forward, into the future. The representatives of her mother and father close in behind her in support. The aunt's representative gazes at them benevolently. She appears pleased and peaceful and goes to stand next to her father. These two look at each other for a long time and then melt into an embrace.

The patient looks exhausted, but relaxed, at the final image of the constellation. She remarks, 'I have always longed for this peace, and now I will take it with me. Thank you.'

THE ABORTED SIBLING
(Patient with suicidal tendencies in pregnancy)

This 30-year-old woman initially comes in for homeopathic treatment. She is happily married, has two children aged three and five, and is now in the fourth month of pregnancy with a third child. For about a month now, she has suffered from depression, anxiety, and general unrest. She cannot sleep and more and more frequently she finds herself having thoughts of taking her own life.

I begin a homeopathic treatment and recommend that the patient attend a constellation group at the same time. She is pleased to follow my suggestion, since her suicidal thoughts are becoming increasingly concrete.

We begin the constellation with representatives for the patient and her symptoms. As this configuration offers no useful indications, I ask the patient to add representatives for her parents. When a representative for the patient's mother comes into the constellation, the woman representing the disorder feels immediately drawn to her and dissolves her connection to the patient. The mother's representative, however, turns away from the symptoms' representative, who nonetheless continues to follow her, and finally lies down at her feet like a small, sleeping child. The patient dismisses my suspicions that this representative might be a reminder of a child who has died, either the mother's or somewhere else in her family. She explains that she has a very open, trusting relationship with her mother and if there were such a child, she would have known about it.

What the patient is able to conclude from the constellation is that these symptoms actually belong to her mother. Bowing to her mother, she feels relieved and the mother's representative is prepared to take over caring for the symptoms.

The patient leaves the group feeling more confident and visibly less tense. A week later, however, she reports that after two days of relief, her condition has deteriorated again. At my suggestion she asks her mother to attend a separate constellation group.

In the constellation of the mother's current family system, the representatives display movements similar to those of her daughter's constellation, although these representatives have no information about that previous constellation. In tears, the mother confesses that she aborted her third child. In the constellation, when she is able to take this child, her daughter's representative is freed of the need to support her mother and can let go and turn towards her husband and children.

After her mother's constellation, the patient feels somewhat better. About a month later, as she is going into her seventh month of pregnancy, her husband phones me in despair. His wife has required constant supervision for some days and, they would like an immediate appointment before they move to a psychiatric consultation.

I agree, and I am shocked by the woman's condition and appearance. After a brief clarification of the current state of affairs, it is clear that she is in need of psychiatric help. Nonetheless, I decide to first contact her mother to ask if she would release me from the bond of confidentiality, in view of her daughter's extremely critical situation. She agrees, and with her consent I tell the patient what I know about her family.

The patient is shocked, but as she hears of her mother's abortion, her expression clears. The feeling of the destructive, all encompassing turbulence calms into a stunned silence. When her husband gently takes her in his arms, she bursts into tears. He holds her for a long time, and when she is calm again, they leave for home. From this moment on, all her suicidal, murderous thoughts vanish.

When this third child is about three months old, the patient and her mother attend a constellation group together. Again, we set up a constellation without sharing any of the previous information about the patient's family of origin. Again, what appears is her tendency to carry her mother's burden. In this constellation she is able to leave this problem with her mother in a beneficial way. She can agree to the consequences of her mother's decision and once more take life through her mother, with full recognition of what has occurred. At the end of the group, both mother and daughter agree that the topic can now be put to rest, and they leave for home with a positive connection to one another.

This constellation and others have shown how important it can be for even aborted children to have a place in the family. It calls into question an earlier belief in constellation work, that an abortion only concerns the parents. Above all, constellation work with chronically ill children often points to a connection between the children's illnesses and aborted siblings or half-siblings. A terminated pregnancy can shake the whole family structure and influence the relationship of the living children to their parents.

OTHER ASPECTS

In addition to the interconnections already described above, I would like to mention a few other influences and aspects that may play a role in illness and poor health. These are all issues that I have encountered in my constellation work with ill people.

BLESSINGS AND CURSES

A curse is the weapon of the underdog
  −Masai saying

The Masai differentiate between three different kinds of curses in terms of intent and effects. There is a 'harmless curse' that ceases to have an effect after it is spoken. This would roughly correspond to our sense of an immediate expression of anger, without any real intent to cause damage. Therefore, it is described as 'weak and without actual value'. Influential curses include the 'justified curse' and the so-called 'all-destroying curse'. Both of these are adjudged to have powers that can extend across generations and cause illness.

When I think about curses and their effects, I am reminded of the constellation of a patient who was feeling grave concern for himself and his sons. All the men in his family, over three generations, had died at a relatively young age, either of heart failure or in accidents. The patient's great-grandfather was a German soldier who had fought in Russia during World War Two.

We set up representatives for the patient, his deceased father, two of his father's brothers who had been killed in accidents, his grandfather, who died of a heart attack, and his great grandfather. When the representatives were left to find their own places, it was clear that they were all focussed on a point on the floor some distance away.

Only the great-grandfather remained motionless in his place. There was general agreement amongst the representatives that there must be a woman lying in the centre of the half-circle they had formed. The patient chose a participant and I asked her to lie on the floor in that spot in the constellation. She had barely lain down when she remarked, 'I am most certainly not dead!' She stood up briskly and glared at the men with a furious, nasty expression. The men all felt under a spell cast by this woman and her unrelenting hardness caused them to shudder.

The woman herself was only able to relax her frozen severity when it was acknowledged that something terrible must have occurred. Not only the great-grandfather, but also all the other men bowed down before her. She felt unbelievable pain rising up in her and she dropped to the floor, sobbing. Slowly, she was able to calm down and finally close her eyes.

The patient followed this painful process with bated breath. As the woman lay lifelessly on the floor, he asked permission to approach her. In tears, he knelt down in front of her and bowed down, all the way to the floor. When the woman became aware of him near her, she laid her hand on his head as if in blessing, stroking his hair. The patient felt as if he had been relieved of a heavy weight.

In his book, *Der Austausch,* Bert Hellinger (2002, p.136. and p.223) describes a curse with the potential to cause illness in connection with a case involving neurodermatitis. In constellations with patients who suffer from neurodermatitis, there is often an indication of a parent's previous partner feeling rage. The lingering rancour acts like a curse on the new relationship, but instead of affecting the partner, it shows up in his or her children.

A reconciling move towards this previous partner can have a healing effect. It may be important, for instance, to assure that there is honor and respect for that person's love and pain. The previous partner may be asked to remain friendly and to really look at the child who is ill. This can lift the curse and perhaps even turn it into a blessing.

THE WITCH TRIAL
(Patient with paranoid schizophrenia and her son with ADHD)

A woman of about 45 and her mother have come to a constellation group in Mexico on the recommendation of the woman's doctor. During another participant's constellation, this woman becomes increasingly upset and begins to quarrel loudly with her mother. The mother vehemently admonishes her daughter to be quiet, but during the break, the daughter can no longer contain herself and she screams at her mother to leave.

Then, the daughter's tone of voice changes and she cries in panic, 'go away, grandfather! Leave me alone!' Her mother attempts to subdue her, but the daughter flails against her mother's embrace, biting and scratching. The mother does not know what to do about her daughter's mounting aggression, so I decide to step between the two. I hold the patient firmly in my arms until she calms down.

After the break, the daughter returns to her seat, but seems inattentive. I begin the group work and offer time for questions from participants. At this point the woman drops to the floor and crawls on her hands and knees to the middle of the circle. She makes threatening gestures and hisses like a wild cat. Her mother freezes at the sight of her daughter behaving in this peculiar way.

I turn to the patient's doctor, who shrugs his shoulders and explains that he has only known the patient for a few days and these seemingly psychotic symptoms are also new to him. The patient had originally consulted him for help with anxiety states, sleeplessness and nightmares.

Action is called for, so I ask the mother to come and sit next to me. Her face is white with shock. Before I can start questioning the mother, the daughter notices her mother sitting next to me. Slowly, she crawls over to us on hands and knees until she is kneeling in front of her mother. She hisses and begins to scream aggressively again. 'Go away! Go away, Grandfather! Leave us in peace!' I ask the mother about the grandfather, but she is not able to respond. I then ask another participant to stand behind the mother as a representative of the grandfather. Looking at the man, the shrieks in a wild frenzy, 'There is the Devil! Be gone, Satan! Go!' Luckily, my friend and colleague, Marianne Franke-Gricksch is present, and I ask her to stand behind the grandfather as a representative of 'the Devil'. I feel, intuitively, that I could not ask a Mexican participant to take on this role. The mother, sitting next to me, shudders and goes completely rigid. The daughter's state, however, is transformed. The panic and terror subside and her face regains human characteristics. She begins to cry and sobs, 'Dear Grandpa! Dear Grandpa!' Then she stands and embraces her mother and the grandfather's representative. Marianne looks her in the eye and smoothes her hair. Exhausted, the daughter sinks into her mother's lap. Her mother, still rigid with fear, responds mechanically and strokes her daughter without looking up.

When the mother and daughter have recovered, I stop the work and we all take a break.

After the break, the organizer of the training group, Angelica Olvera, tells the following story, which she heard from the patient's aunt: The grandfather, the mother's father, lived in the late 1800's in a small village in the northern part of the country. When he was about 17, a young woman in the village was burnt as a witch. From the pyre, she cursed the entire village population. There was great fear that the woman's curse would bring calamity to the village, and there were rumors that this man, the grandfather, had had a love affair with the woman. In fear that they might seek to kill him as well, the grandfather left his village and went to the city. His flight was seen as confirmation that he was under the influence of the witch woman and he never again dared go back to his village.

A doctor, who was present in the group at the time, took over the patient's care and I heard from her about six months later. Her report is summarized here:

The patient is very grateful, because this constellation has fundamentally changed her life. She can sleep better and no longer has nightmares. There have been no further psychotic episodes of that magnitude and her family have ceased treating her like a crazy person. Since the constellation, her 19-year-old son, who is living in the United States, has also been doing better. At school, he was treated for attention deficit hyperactivity disorder. Since his mother's constellation, his marks at a technical college have improved dramatically. He has reported that he is able to concentrate better and is now enjoying his life and his training much more.

A year after the constellation, I encounter the patient again as a course participant. She greets me joyfully and tells me that she has started working and is currently doing a job retraining. In general, her life is in order and she feels well.

In addition to other influences, many school problems can be related to family entanglements. When children are carrying something for their parents, and perhaps even need to keep them alive, or when they are identified with someone who has been excluded from the family, they find it difficult to keep their attention and energy focussed on their work.

In countless constellations with children suffering from difficulties such as ADD and ADHD, we have seen indications of identification with an excluded family member who has died. The children find peace when the dead person is given a place in the family, and is mourned, and bid farewell.

AN ATTACHMENT TO THE DEAD

'The dead are invisible, they are not absent.' – Augustine

In constellations, the representative of a deceased family member will sometimes give the impression that the dead person is still clinging to life and the living. Often, in such cases, the deceased person has died in an accident, in childbirth, or suffered a sudden heart attack. Life was snatched unexpectedly, with no chance to say a proper good-bye to those left behind.

I remember a constellation of one patient who had suffered for years from chronic fatigue. The woman was separated from her husband and when her complaints arose she was first treated with antidepressants. At about the same time, her 18-year-old son moved to a different city near his father. When medication failed to produce positive results, the patient found some relief through a complex treatment of vitamins and supplements. Through this degree of support, she was at least able to remain active for a few hours each day.

Finally, a family constellation revealed a connection to the patient's father, who had died of a sudden heart attack three years before the onset of her troubles.

The patient was her father's favorite daughter. It appeared that she was representing his mother for him, since his mother had died when he was eight. In the constellation, the father's representative, lying on the floor, was absolutely determined not to release his daughter. Completely riveted on her, he held her so firmly that the patient's representative was not able to get free of him. He did not want to believe that he was dead or that he was hindering his daughter's life with his own longings.

It was only when a representative of his deceased mother lay next to him that he became aware of his error. He recognized what was happening and was able to say good-bye to his daughter and the living.

Within about three months, the patient was able to decrease her regime of vitamins and supplements. To her great joy, her relationship with her son relaxed as well. We might assume that he had been representing her father for her.

Often, however, it is those who are living that are hanging on to the dead, and so blocking the process of dying in the soul. Such a hindrance also causes the dead to continue to hold on to the living. In any case, the appropriate steps in a constellation are very similar. It is frequently possible to complete a proper good-bye in a constellation that for some reason was prevented in real life. This often proves to be a very moving process in which unhealthy bonds can be dissolved, allowing the dead to be dead and the living alive.

In the Face of Death and Parting

When working with patients suffering from a life threatening disease, it is sometimes appropriate to include a representative for death. At times, this figure seems to feel a deep connection to the patient and may imply an actual person who has died. Sometimes, death may appear impersonal, lofty and detached.

'WITH DEATH AT YOUR BACK YOU CAN LIVE SERENELY'
(Patient with critical dilation of the carotid artery)

According to her own report, this woman suffers from a metabolic disorder that has caused a bulge in both arteries of her neck (carotid aneurysm). She is seeking help through constellation work because she is in a very distressed state. She is currently struggling with the decision of whether or not to undergo a surgery that, according to her physicians, in her case poses a 50 percent risk of death.

As we sort out the issue, it becomes clear that I cannot offer her the kind of help she is seeking to make this decision. To emphasize this, I tell her the story of a well-known doctor. This doctor had an arrangement with 'death'. Whenever the doctor was called to the bedside of a critically ill patient, he could see death standing next to the bed. When death was at the foot of the bed, the doctor knew that the patient would recover. If, however, death was standing at the head of the bed, the patient's hours were numbered and no medical assistance would be of use. One day, the doctor was called on to visit a young girl. As he entered the room, he saw death standing at the head of the bed. He felt such pity for the girl that he turned the bed around. The girl survived, but death came in the night and took the doctor instead.

The patient seems to understand the message of this story and after weighing the situation for a while, I ask her to choose a representative for death and one for herself. She is prepared to enter into this work, and chooses a woman for herself and a man to represent death.

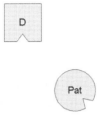

The patient's representative is trembling, sending waves through-out her entire body. Finally, she musters her courage and turns around. In the face of death, she moves a step towards him with her head high and her hands balled into fists, apparently ready for a fight.

When asked how he feels, the representative of death says, 'I am not especially interested in her. I am watching her. I am not going to do anything, but if she comes to me, then I will take her'.

Following this statement, the patient's representative takes an-other step towards the representative of death.

The patient seems disturbed by the reaction of her representative. Her representative is now standing directly in front of 'death', looking him in the eye. With his calm, imperturbable presence, her pugilistic attitude begins to falter and she gives up. She starts to cry, hammering on his chest with her fists. Slowly she drops to her knees and beats on his legs. She bends lower and hits his feet until, exhausted in her pain, she lies on the floor.

The representative of death remains calmly unimpressed as he al-lows all this to occur. When I again ask him what he senses, he says, 'it is not the time, yet'.

When the patient's representative hears these words, she slowly straightens up and looks at him. I suggest she tell him, 'now I agree'. In saying this, she gains the strength to stand up and look him in the eye again. After a while, she turns around. I gently move her back until she is standing with her back against the representative of death. He puts a hand on her shoulder.

This final image of the constellation reminds me of one of Bert Hellinger's comments: 'With death at your back, you can live serenely'. The patient's representative smiles her agreement. We end the work at this point.

About six months later, I heard from the woman who was translating in this group. She said that the patient was doing well, after an initially difficult time. She had made the decision not to have an operation. At my request, she sent me the following account of her experience.

Dear Stephan,

I can tell you that the constellation in September 2007 was a great help to me. I was very distraught with the difficult decision of whether to have an operation or not. I was afraid of dying prematurely, no matter what decision I made. Today I feel with certainty that my death will come to me when it is the right time for me.

I think that this work is the most important in my life, up to now, because I was truly at my limit. Afterwards, I first fell into a deep depression and struggled with the way my life was. I was in an existential crisis that finally led to me looking at my life through different eyes. Now, I feel fulfilled and I sense an intensity of life in me that allows me to continue on my path. I take good care of myself and I realize how important it is to accept myself and my illness with love and esteem.

Some time after the constellation, I sought the opinion of four more neurosurgeons. They all believed that an operation was not called for, since this kind of surgical intervention is only done if the aneurism enlarges, or if neurological symptoms appear that would indicate insufficient blood flow. In my case, all the indicators were stable. According to these doctors, I would have to reckon with possible consequences from an operation, such as impaired motor functions, loss of sight and memory, and it could even cost me my life.

I regard this search as my lifesaver, and today I allow myself to be more guided by my own feelings. I act when the action is in accordance with what I feel. Somehow, I feel nearer to my own soul, whereby I am more certain, more courageous and more present with myself. I have begun to realize personal and professional intentions, with an emphasis on accomplishing whatever is possible in the present. I have been to visit my mother in Yucatan for the first time in years. I had always been afraid to do so because it entails a long, difficult bus trip. We had a healing reconciliation, although my relationship to her had always been difficult. I have decided to use the time that I still have to live to serve well the people around me and myself.

I am very thankful for this help.

G.

ORGAN DONATIONS AND TRANSPLANTS

For many people with critical illnesses, the only hope of continuing to live is through an organ transplant. Advances in modern medicine demand that each of us form our own opinions and deal personally with this issue. In constellation groups dealing with illness, we continually meet people who are affected by such issues in various ways.

'DEAR MUMMY, PLEASE BLESS ME'
(Patient with liver cancer)

I ask this man of about 60, suffering from liver cancer, what his doctors have recommended for him. He says, 'that I need a liver transplant'. I ask him what he thinks, himself.

Patient: It looks like that is the thing to do.

Therapist: How are you with this idea?

Patient: I have accepted it, but I cannot actually think about that moment.

Therapist: What is your issue with me?

Patient: I want to prepare myself well for a transplant.

Therapist: Okay, what do we have to set up to achieve that?

Patient: My tumor and my mother.

Therapist: If we are to look at the cancer and a possible connection in your family, then we need the tumour. However, if this is a question of preparing for the transplant, then we don't need a representative for the tumor.

Patient: Yes, I can see that. I agree.

Therapist: So, who do we need for the constellation?

Patient: (crying) My children and the people who love me, so they can give me support.

Therapist: Children cannot do that.

Patient: Then I would ask you to work with me so I can find the strength to bear what I must bear.

In his needy state, the patient seems quite like a child. Therefore, I ask about his relationship to his mother.

Patient: She died when I was twelve.

Therapist: (after a while) If you agree, I would begin the constellation with two people, a representative for you and one for death.

Patient: I agree.

The patient chooses two men. He places his representative first and then positions the representative for death behind him, to the right. The patient's representative shudders when 'death' is placed behind him. He tries to move away by taking a step forward, being careful not to turn. When asked about this, he says, 'I don't want to see him'.

Death's representative comments, 'I am standing here quite calmly. I see him. He is not looking at me, but I am here.'

I turn to the patient. 'One thing that is difficult about a transplant is that a person who decides to proceed with it is, in a certain sense, waiting for someone else's death. He or she wishes to continue living as a result of someone else's death. In constellations, we see many cases of a bond between an organ donator and the receiver. The consequence is that the one who receives the organ must face death – their own, the donor's, and, in your case, your mother's as well. Add a representative for your mother.'

The patient chooses a woman and positions her between his representative and the representative of death. His representative shivers again. He cannot look at his mother, either, and moves a few steps away from her. When the patient sees his representative's movement, he is overcome with deep pain.

The mother's representative moves slowly towards the patient, enfolds him in her arms and holds him until he lets himself sink into her embrace. There, he eventually becomes calm.

In the meantime, the representative of death has followed the mother. He stands next to her and gazes at the patient with love and sympathy. I ask the patient if he knows who, in his family, might be represented here by 'death'. He nods and says, 'that's my elder brother. He died shortly after birth and my mother gave me his name'.

It is now clear how the patient is trapped in this situation. His mother was unable to face the death of her first child and the patient had to stand in for his deceased elder brother. With a transplant, he again could live due to another's death. It is hardly surprising that he is having difficulty with this decision.

To resolve the systemic family dynamics, I suggest that he say to his mother: 'Dear Mum, what I have carried for you, I have carried in love, but now it is over. Please bless me if I now look after myself – only myself.'

The mother's representative nods in agreement and says, 'my dear son, now I see what you have carried for me, and I will take it back now'. The patient breathes out in ease and looks over at his brother. All three representatives embrace and we end the constellation.

It is interesting to note that besides chronic rejection of a donated organ, the second most common reason for a transplant failure is 'non-compliance' with regard to taking prescribed medication to suppress the immune system (Kiss et al 2005). Whatever the reasons for such a refusal, it is very possible that here, too, the role of family entanglements is not negligible.

A colleague of mine that had referred a patient for constellation work gave me feedback about three years later about a successful transplant. The patient said that she believed that if she had not done a constellation before her transplant, she would not have been able to retain the donated liver.

The patient was born with cystic liver disease, involving a malformation of the liver. This congenital disease was inherited from her father's side of the family. It is a disease that progresses for decades to the advanced stages of cyst formation and inexorably on to death of liver failure.

The woman led a very health-conscious life in order to minimize the effects of her limited liver functions. She also received holistic treatment until her condition reached the point that a transplant was necessary.

Since the patient had already been considering the issue of organ donations and transplants for years, this was not the issue she brought to the constellation group. She formulated her concern about the difficulty she had always had in her relationship with her father, and also her mother.

In a constellation of her family of origin, the patient's representative felt drawn to her father's elder sister, who had died in an accident at the age of two. Bowing to her father's representative and to his parents, who had never got over their daughter's death, the patient was able to respectfully retreat out of the field of her father's family and take her place at the side of her mother. Here, she felt a zest for life that she had never known before.

The next case example points to the way in which carrying a difficult fate together can form a bond, but also how it may split the family when it fails.

'DEAR DADDY, I LEAVE IT WITH YOU'
(Patient with dizzy spells)

The constellation, from an advanced training group has been diagrammed and the dialogue recorded verbatim.

Patient: I have suffered from dizzy spells for three years. Sometimes, the crises are so overwhelming that I have to lie down. When I lie down, I have the feeling that I must die.

Therapist: Was there anything that happened prior to the onset of these spells?

Patient: Since I have become acquainted with family constellations, I have wondered if it could have some connection to my father's death. He died three years ago from leukaemia.

Therapist: Was he ill for a long time?

Patient: He had a low blood count for many years, and then at the end developed leukaemia.

Therapist: How many children are there in your family?

Patient: There are three girls, and I am in the middle.

Therapist: Set up a representative for your father and one for yourself.

Therapist: Where would you place your mother?

Patient: Next to my father.

Therapist: How is the father feeling?

Father's Representative: I don't want to see any of this.

Therapist: What else happened in your family of origin?

Patient: My younger sister had a daughter who was born with an insufficient passage to her gall bladder. Because of the malformation, she needed a liver transplant to survive. That was a very difficult time for all of us. In the weeks after the transplant, my father developed anaemia. My niece died when she was nine months old, as she was unable to retain the transplanted organ.

Therapist: Tell me something about your father.

Patient: He was a diplomat, a successful businessman. One of his brothers committed suicide.

Therapist: What happened in your mother's family?

Patient: That is a very complicated family. There are a lot of secrets – homosexuality, gambling addiction, incest...

Therapist: Put in a representative for your mother and also one for your sister.

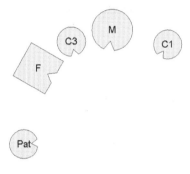

Therapist: How is the patient's representative doing?

Patient's Representative: My legs are shaking and I don't dare look at my little sister. I can't move.

Therapist: A lot is coming together here and there are many things that might have significance. However, what most strongly holds my attention is the transplant. I am wondering what happens in the soul of a family in a situation like this? We live in a time when such things are possible. We have created new options, but they might have an effect on the soul that we do not grasp straight away. What happens with a transplant? Because one person dies, another can and should perhaps live. The prerequisite for one person's life is that someone else die. That is the most relevant event in the family of origin, and the constellation shows a special connection between your younger sister and your father. I get the impression that she is your father's favorite.

The patient nods and says, 'that's true, she always has been'.

At this point I begin to suspect that the patient is carrying something for her father out of a longing to be nearer to him, since he feels some bond that has left him available only in a limited way. This would indicate that the younger sister must be representing someone for her father, perhaps his brother. To test out this hypothesis I follow the representatives' movements in relation to the transplant.

I ask the patient to add another representative for her sister's deceased daughter. When she is brought into the middle of the constellation, her legs go out from under her and she drops to the floor. Everyone in the constellation experiences shock at her appearance and the whole system seems frozen. When I ask a man to represent the donor child and lie next to the patient's deceased niece, the whole family turns away, with the exception of the patient's representative. She is very touched and kneels down next to the two dead children and takes their hands.

When the donor child is asked how he is, he answers, 'I am doing fine. I don't feel like a part of the greater system. My attention is drawn to this child here next to me. Here, I feel good'.

The patient's representative says, 'I cannot take my eyes off the donor child. Actually, I would like to go to my mother, but I can't'.

At this moment, the father's representative speaks up. 'I can't bear this burden any longer. My shoulders are so heavy. The whole thing is a tragedy and the sentence keeps going through my mind – just what have you all done, here?'

The patient answers the question. 'To finance the transplant, we

271

started a campaign to raise funds. My father was so ashamed that I took over the organisation and collected the money at my house.

Because of the complexity of the background situation, I decide to concentrate on the patient's relationship to her father. Her longing for her father and her willingness to carry something for him are obvious.

I take the patient's representative by the hand and move her a few steps away from the action of the constellation. I say to her, 'You cannot do anything here. If you want to live, you have to leave the past behind you, with love and respect for what separates this family. It is a painful process, but in doing so you are not standing in the way of a resolving movement of the soul.

The patient's representative confirms, 'yes, that's good, and basically, I know it is right'.

Now I ask the father's representative to stand in front of the patient. When asked whether he wishes to say anything to his daughter, he answers, 'it is mine and I will carry it alone'. The patient begins to weep and I have her say, 'Dear Daddy, whatever it is that you carry, I respect it and I leave it now with you.' Her father says 'thank you' and I add one sentence for him to speak. 'Now I see what you have carried for me and I will take it over'.

A year after this work, I hear from the patient that she is doing much better. She agrees to detail her memory of the experience, which I have included below.

Dear Stephan,

Last year I did a constellation with you, regarding my dizzy spells. The official diagnosis was that I had dizzy spells due to abrasions of my neck vertebrae. I would like to tell you that I am doing much better, and I have had no serious dizzy spells since the constellation.

The constellation showed the following: Everything was connected to my relationship with my father. The major connection was a liver transplant for my niece, my younger sister's first daughter. The transplant occurred 18 years ago. The high costs demanded that the whole family be involved. We decided to carry the expense together, and to collect additional funds as well. My father felt very ashamed of this, but realized there was no other way. For this reason, he asked me to organize the collection and my house was the headquarters for the whole thing. I agreed, but it was also a difficult situation for me.

The transplant operation took place, but my niece did not survive. She developed necrosis in the donated liver. We knew that the liver had come from an African child. It was all very painful.

During this time, my father became ill with anaemia, from which he never really recovered. 15 years later, the anaemia became leukemia and my father died within a month. After my father's death, I had my first dizzy spell.

The constellation showed me that I had taken on more than just taking care of the money. My father never really recovered from the death of this grandchild. In the constellation, we also had a representative for the donor child and my representative was the only one of the family who looked at this child. We could see that my representative had a caring attitude towards the dead children. My mother could not look, nor could my father.

At this point you intervened and distanced my representative from the events. That caused changes in the other representatives. Myself, I experienced it as a great relief.

Then you brought my father's representative to stand in front of me. He reached out a hand to me and I said to him, 'Dear Daddy, whatever it is that you carry, I respect it and I leave it now with you'. Much to my surprise, he spontaneously said 'thank you' and we embraced.

Since then, I have not had any dizzy spells and whenever it feels as if the symptoms are going to reappear, I visualize the image of my father and silently repeat those words. Then, the difficulty goes away. Sometimes when I go to bed, it feels as if my bed is moving slightly. If I let myself be rocked instead of fighting against the feeling, it stops again.

It has now been over a year since the constellation and I am doing well. Thank you very much. It would never have occurred to me to look at my dizzy spells in connection with this other issue. I hope this information is useful for you and your colleagues in your work, and can be of help to others.
G.

INHERITED DISEASES

From time to time, there are patients with inherited diseases in constellation groups. Their fate frequently brings them into a struggle against the parents who have passed on this health problem. The therapist can achieve a helpful effect by having patients face representatives of their parents. Facing their parents, patients can acknowledge that struggling against a mother or father burdens and weakens themselves as well as their parents. What is required is to take life, even at this high price.

IATROGENIC ILLNESS AND MEDICAL MALPRACTICE

In constellations with patients who are suffering from illness stemming from errors in medical treatment, we see that a healing movement cannot develop as long as the patient maintains a blaming attitude towards the physician. Here, too, the family systemic back-

CHAPTER 2: CASE STUDIES, FEEDBACK, AND COMMENTS

ground appears to be important. Looking at the doctor distracts from the more significant issues in one's own family patterns and blocks forward steps and resolution. What provides strength, however is to face responsibility for one's own part of what has happened.

The Unsuccessful Eye Operation

Attending a constellation group, a man of about 40 recognized that his youngest son, who was suffering from diabetes, was representing his father (the boy's grandfather) for him. He then talked about his son's eye operation, which had failed. Because of his diabetes, his son was seriously visually impaired, to the extent that only a surgical intervention could provide help. The operation on his left eye was completed without complications, but the surgeon made a mistake during the operation on his right eye and the child lost his sight in that eye.

The patient's father was also blind in his right eye. A zealous Nazi, he had volunteered for duty on the front, and was struck by a fragment of a grenade.

What became clear to the patient was that his lifelong, harsh judgement of his father had shut off his access to his father and resulted in his own child taking that role.

Patients who have suffered as a result of a doctor's error are understandably inclined to hold the physician responsible for their difficulties. Nonetheless, as we will see in the example of a disabled child, focussing on the doctor can divert attention from dealing with core issues in the family. Lawsuits and accusations create an attachment and block healing energies and useful family resources. What can provide strength is to resist the need for recompense or retribution and, despite the pain, to face one's own share of the responsibility for what has happened.

It has not been established to what extent, if at all, family entanglements can affect such trans-generational repetitions of fate. In this particular case, it is extraordinary that the client's son lost his right eye, which was also his grandfather's fate.

CONSIDERATIONS: SYMPTOMS FROM CONSTELLATIONS?

During a workshop on healing and self-healing, Dr. Serge King, a shaman from Hawaii, summarized in one sentence, his perspective on healing effects: 'Either you change the focus, or you change the frame.'

His statement was referring to the effects of inner images and beliefs and their influence on our life and health. These inner images would not be a problem if they happened to be correct, but most of our inner images are distorted, or at least incomplete.

One therapeutic goal is to correct the images that may be hindering the patient's health and life in order to expand the person's options and potential.

The following case illustrates the countering effect of a constellation and also points to the facilitator's responsibility for the images he or she helps to create through therapeutic interventions or interpretations.

'IT IS MINE, AND I WILL TAKE CARE OF IT'
(Patient with psychosomatic loss of speech)

This woman is suffering from a gradually worsening problem with hoarseness and increasingly frequent periods where she loses her speech completely. A medical examination has revealed a chronic laryngeal infection that has proved resistant to every conventional treatment. When I ask her whether she has any idea what the source of the problem might be, she says, 'there is a part of me that does not want to speak'. I then ask her to 'imagine yourself in a situation when your voice fails you, and tell me who you would want to speak to if you could speak without any difficulty.'

Patient: (responds instantly) To my son.

Therapist: What about him?

Patient: Eight years ago he was diagnosed with paranoid schizophrenia.

Therapist: Perhaps there is some connection here. Perhaps you are both entangled in the same family dynamics.

(The patient disagrees.)

Patient: No, my son's schizophrenia comes from his father's family. That showed up in a previous constellation. (*People often see primarily what they want to see.*) My son's father, my first husband, is also prepared now to work on this issue. A few weeks ago he signed up for a constellation group.

Therapist: Let's go back a step. What would you say to your son if you could speak to him without any difficulty?

Patient: I would say, 'take your medication!'

I have the feeling that this response is evading something, so I try to sense myself into the scenario of the conversation with her son. I try to feel what sentence remains unspoken that is still moving in the depths. The sentence that comes to mind is, 'Stay! – Even if I leave'. When I say this aloud the patient responds instantly.

Patient: Of course, I would rather leave than have him leave.

Therapist: You would be willing to sacrifice yourself for him, then?

Patient: Absolutely!

Therapist: If the schizophrenia is connected to something in his father's family, then it is presumptuous and contradictory for you to imagine that you could change your son's fate by sacrificing yourself. That is not a healing attitude for you, for your son, or for your first husband. If you are willing, let's set up a constellation of the situation.

The patient indicates her agreement, so I ask her for additional information.

Therapist: Have you got any other children from your first marriage, besides your son?

Patient: An elder daughter.

Therapist: Right. We will begin with three representatives – for you for your first husband and for your son.

The patient places the three representatives. The son's representative immediately begins to turn about, as if looking for something. He says he feels as though he is in the grip of a power that is stronger than him and he can only give in to it. The father's representative watches his son's movements with concern. The mother's representative turns away from her son and reports: 'Actually, I would like to leave, but I cannot.'

I ask the patient to add a representative for her son's schizophrenia. She chooses a man and places him in the middle of the system, where he immediately sinks to the floor. The son's representative stops turning and stares fixedly at the man lying on the floor.

I ask the patient to add a representative for her own complaints, her voice loss. She chooses a woman and places her behind the representative of schizophrenia on the floor. Without a glance towards the man lying in front of her, the representative of the patient's symptoms puts her hands around her own neck as if she were about to strangle herself. She begins to gulp uncontrollably and gasps to catch her breath.

Interestingly enough, the patient's representative turns to her first husband and, without any suggestion from me, she bows to him. This gesture provides great relief to the representative of the patient's symptoms and she can breathe again. She looks down at the representative of schizophrenia in front of her and lies down next to him.

The son's representative observes the two. He is just about to turn to his father when the patient's symptoms sits up and says, 'I would really like to lie here because I feel very connected, but I can't find any peace.' The son's representative says, 'she (the symptoms' representative) confuses me. I want to go to my father and I would have gone to him just now, but I can't. She is stopping me.'

The representative of the patient's symptoms remarks, 'I don't belong here. Someone else belongs here'.

The son's representative responds, 'then I will go there'. She counters, 'I cannot allow that!'

At this point, I interrupt the dialogue and ask the representative of the son's schizophrenia how he is feeling. He smiles and turns to the representative of voice loss and says, 'I keep thinking, "go ahead and say it! You know it!" I feel the strongest connection with the representative of voice loss. I want to be left in peace, but I can't settle down, either.'

I say to the patient, 'I still wonder who your son is carrying this for'. She responds, 'I already told you. For his father.' I reply, 'I am not so certain, and I would like to test something out.' I ask the patient's representative to say to her first husband, 'it is mine and I will take care of it'.

As she repeats these words, the representative of schizophrenia relaxes. The son's representative moves to his father and the representative of the patient's voice loss says, 'I could lie down there now, or even better, I could pull out.

The first husband's representative turns away, and I ask him what is happening with him. His answer: 'I don't want to look at that. I feel blamed for something that has nothing to do with me.'

I speak to the group: 'We could already see at the beginning of the constellation that the family dynamics connected to the schizophrenia are not coming from the father's family. The father's representative had no problem looking at his ill son. The one who was unable to do so was the mother. Therefore, we can assume that she or her family cannot see something or cannot accept something.'

I ask the patient, casually, 'how long have you been convinced that this comes from your first husband's family?'

Patient: For about a year, since I did a constellation for my son.

Therapist: And how long have you had the voice condition?

Patient: (thoughtfully) Since approximately that time. So, it comes from my side?

Therapist: It looks as though there is a connection.

Patient: Everybody in my family has a problem with guilt.

I do not pick up on her invitation to explore that family issue. Rather, I hold the patient to her responsibility.

Therapist: Tell your husband, 'it is mine and I will now take care of it'.

When she speaks these words, the first husband's representative turns to his son and takes him in his arms. The patient's representative kneels down by the representative of schizophrenia. She begins to weep and lays her head in his lap. He puts his arm around her and the two remain so for a bit, until the mother's representative frees herself again. They both look very content. The patient's representative turns to her first husband and then, to me. She says,

'I would like to tell my husband that I am sorry I blamed him'.

I agree, but ask the patient to take her own place in the constellation. She goes first to the representative of schizophrenia, looks him in the eye and embraces him. When she is calm again, she looks at her husband and her son and says, 'it makes me happy to see you in your father's arms'. At her words, the son's representative looks radiant. For the first time he looks like a light-hearted boy.

A year after the constellation, I met the patient at a conference. I asked her to write a few lines about her process after the constellation work.

I remember telling you that my son's schizophrenia had its roots in his father's family. The idea that my son's illness could have something to do with events in my family was deeply shocking to me. I was not at all prepared for that sort of connection and I can tell you that I felt a great resistance to that suggestion.

Nonetheless, as the constellation proceeded, I recognized that my son's representative clearly felt better as soon as I began to consider this possibility, and above all when I took the suggested step towards resolution.

Following this constellation, I was more and more able to acknowledge that a possible influence on my son's illness could be coming from my family. I was able to take over my part of the responsibility and began to do some research into my family. I discovered some new information about my mother's family. Her mother died when she was 12 years old. With the death of her mother, my mother was separated from her siblings. What is perhaps most important is that I found out that my grandfather may have been involved in a murder.

I was motivated by the constellation to encourage and support my son in having more contact with his father. They see each other regularly now and they are both enjoying it. It appears to be very good for my son and at the moment he is doing better with his illness.

It is remarkable that the patient does not mention a word about her own symptoms, for which she originally came to the constellation group.

In an advanced trainings course in medical radiaesthesia, I was often struck by the accuracy of the perceptions, but also noticed that the interpretations of those perceptions generally turned out to be wrong.

The awareness of the representatives in constellations is so impressive that it may tempt the therapist as well as the patient to make risky interpretations. What is needed here, in my opinion, is extreme circumspection and restraint on the part of the therapist. He or she also needs to observe how the patient is taking in the process of the constellation and interventions and the intrinsic images the participants take away with them after the group.

❧3❧

CONCLUSION

*'He causes his sun to rise on the evil and the good and
sends rain on the righteous and the unrighteous'*
–Matthew 5:45

I am well aware that there is a special selectivity in the choice of case examples for this book. This was, of course, heavily influenced by the extent of feedback that I had received from patients. From the perspective of systemic constellation work, there would certainly be much more to report about many other issues of health and illness.

In an effort to hold the focus on the uniqueness of each individual working process, I have intentionally held back from formulating contrasting views of frequently observed family dynamics and illnesses. The aim of this book is to raise awareness of possible applications, and primarily, the potential inherent in systemic constellation work for working with people suffering from health issues. This can only unfold by approaching each patient as a unique individual. Even when the same, or similar, family dynamics appear frequently in connection with one particular illness or pathology, the steps towards resolution remain distinctive for each patient. The art of applying this method lies in helping the patient to find a critical turning point. Just as in homeopathy, if you are not on target, a miss is as good as a mile.

For me, resolution means being able or free to take a first step. Any change demands a certain amount of flexibility. The same holds true for therapists. Therapists have to guard against their experiences hardening into rigid theories that have lost their healing potential. Experience contributes to healing power and strength when it becomes integrated into the therapist's way of being, rather than an accumulation of knowledge.

What we do see repeated in many constellations are fundamental patterns of resolution that merge and complement one another. As is clear from the case examples, many illnesses appear to be connected to the fate of excluded family members. The suffering and pain of the illness create a demand for those people to regain their rightful place in the family, or for repressed traumatic events to be recognized and given due consideration.

The prerequisite for such integration generally involves a benign process of separation and resolution with one's parents and family. The operative family conscience provides each member of the system with a definition of what is good and what is evil, thereby creating exclusions. To affirm that each person has an equal right to belong, regardless of their character or behavior, means overcoming the family conscience and moving away from those judgements and evaluations that exclude and divide.

4

OUTLOOK

'...and often with endings begin.'
–R.M. Rilke

As author, if I may wish for one thing at the end of this book, it would be that the medical profession would include a consideration of trans-generational perspectives when looking at the origins and contributing factors in illness. In my opinion, systemic constellation work with health issues has earned the right to a place of regard within the field of medicine.

In addition, I harbor the hope that the insights and understanding that emerge from systemic constellation work will proliferate and lead to a broader understanding of illness and health in our society.

We might even imagine a time when our children would be taught this wider perspective of the connections contributing to illness and health. We could hope that diet and nutrition would also recover their earlier importance in science as a support for a way of life leading to physical and mental health. Constellation work can be regarded as simply a treatment method, but in a wider sense it is a teaching of human relationships, a life philosophy, a life posture, and a way of living.

AFTERWORD

CONSTELLATIONS AND GESTALT: A CLOSER
LOOK AND OVERVIEW FOR GESTALT AND FAMILY
SYSTEMS PRACTITIONERS – GORDON WHEELER

Systemic or Family Constellations[1] is a term apparently first used by
Adler to refer to the embeddedness of the individual in immediate
social systems of belonging. As a current methodology "Constellations" is an approach developed over the past thirty or more years,
originally by Bert Hellinger, drawing on a variety of sources ranging from ancestral rituals of the Zulu people (where Hellinger spent
some years in missionary work) to Gestalt and TA, and particularly
the Gestalt-inflected family systems and "family reconstruction"
work developed by Virginia Satir and popularized at Esalen and elsewhere from the 60's through the 80's. From Satir Hellinger seems to
take particularly the ideas of "basic human validation" through the
primary family constellation triad, and of course the signature Satir
insight that the "presenting problem" is generally best regarded not

---

[1.] The terms "Family Constellations," "Orders of Love," just "Constellations" and
more recently "Systemic Constellations," also "Systems Constellations," have often been used interchangeably over the past several decades, though we can trace a
rough generational shift over this time, with the second generation of practitioners,
most of them some decades younger than Hellinger himself, may tend to use the
latter terms over the former. This particularly marks the work of the group around
Hunter Beaumont and his students and colleagues in the International Systemic
Constellations Association.

as the "real" problem, but as people's systemically determined way of dealing with the "real problem," which will likely involve a misalignment or transactional failure in the basic human validation process.

Now Hellinger certainly acknowledges Gestalt influence (personal communication), and many or most leading practitioners of his work have had extensive exposure to Gestalt training. Moreover, the whole notion that the "symptom" is or was itself, in Goodman's felicitous phrase, a "creative adjustment," is an idea that derives at least implicitly from Freud (Hellinger, like Perls, was a trained psychoanalyst), and then was given a good deal more elaboration by Anna Freud (the "mechanisms of defense," 1937) and then further by Satir (1972) as well as others. This was well before Goodman (following Rank) added his signature emphasis on the creative, life-situational problem-solving aspect of what to the Freuds was still basically a "defense" against eruptive Id-material.

But arguably this concept receives its fullest, most articulated development in Gestalt[2], where it has the status of a fundamental principle, at least from Lewin (1935) forward. After all, the idea of taking a systemic view of people's "lifespace" – that is, a perspective that treats their felt, subjective worlds as an interactive web of felt "forces" or pulls – is a whole way of thinking that comes straight from Lewin, who in this as in many other ways remains the most fruitful and influential single founder and source of a Gestalt perspective and understanding (see discussion in Wheeler, 2000). (Lewin is of course recognized as well as a or the major founder of group dynamics, organizational psychology,

---

[2] Goodman and Perls were far from the first, of course, to begin relating Gestalt ideas to clinical and "real-life" applications. Lewin's work with "lifespace" and then with living process groups, work groups, and social change processes; Koffka's work on child development, pathology, and health; Wertheimer's work with questions of values; and of course Goldstein's and other's work with brain function, brain damage, therapy and recovery, just to note a few directions, sketched and partly developed applications in these same directions.

and the broad field of social psychology as well. His signature insight in this area, "The need organizes the field," is a summation of his perspective in this area, which is a founding idea of motivational and ego psychology [see Marrow, 1969, for discussion]. But Lewin was still putting much more emphasis on "needs" and intentions that are in the subject's conscious awareness; Goodman, by contrast, is much more attuned to the more Freudian-inflected idea of pulls and drives that are out of awareness, or "unconscious." Thus both these traditions – the organizing power of conscous intention, and the often countervailing or subversive dynamic of out-of-awareness desires and pulls, are deep in our Gestalt legacy, which is hospitable to the complex dynamic of both these "organizers" of behavior and experience.

And indeed, in Gestalt, nothing is more common than the idea that some basic determinants of our behavior and experience are out of our normal awareness, and that much of intervention and restoration of capacity and health lies in bringing those connections and dynamics to light, so that our experience can become richer, more choiceful, more complex. Familiar examples would range all the way from the idea that my out-of-awareness clinched fist as I talk about, say, my older sibling, is a clue to some powerful organizing emotions in that relationship, to the common experience that some inner voice or "should" that has been directing and maybe constricting my experience and behavior, is actually linked to some important childhood figure. Once that link and "valence dynamic" (to use a Lewinesque language) is brought to awareness, with all the associated feelings and meanings and new connections that may flow from that, then I have a different picture of the attachments, "pulls," and "pushes" that have gone into the construction of what may have been a basic, out-of-awareness, and formative pattern of behavior and relationship in important parts of my life. And not just a new picture (and this is the very essence of Gestalt): once the elements are "lifted out" of their usual, firmly-integrated and embedded context and neural linkages like that, then there is the opportunity for a more supported encounter with difficult aspects of that familiar, integrated "picture," and the chance to actually experiment with new combinations of these dynamic elements and feelings, in the service of a new integration more supportive to new creative living.

Now if you're familiar with Constellations work, you may be thinking that the above description of some aspects of Gestalt work might just as well be a description of Contellations work itself; and of course I've couched it in those terms intentionallly, with emphases on aspects of both models that can easily be seen to be structurally and methodologically parallel. Still, it would seem from all these lineages, sources, and considerations that a basic harmony, or parallelism of ideas at least, between Gestalt thinking and Systemic Constellations approaches would be a natural assumption and outcome. And yet – we know that the picture of contacts and cross-currents between the two broad streams, Gestalt and Constellations, has been much muddier than that, in some quarters conflictual, even at times reactively vitriolical. Why?

I think there are two basic reasons or issues behind this widely (by no means universally) held presumption of there somehow being a fundamental incompatibility, a basic contradiction between these two models. One – the simpler and less significant issue – lies no doubt in some of the provocative public gestures, extreme positions, and authoritarian manner that Hellinger himself can sometimes seem to display. Certainly his own style of working can seem directive and "expert-based" to an authoritative (some would say authoritarian) degree; and his insistence that current generations must not form any negative judgments about their forebears can seem to go to troubling (to me) extremes, and may lend itself to being twisted into a stance of apology for family or wider-arena abuses and atrocities.

To be sure, we can readily grant, I think, that the whole business of judging/blaming one's parents and others from the past can be a trap, a dead end developmentally, and can function itself as a kind of symptom of unmourned grief and loss which goes nowhere as long as it stays frozen in an unaware, blaming, and victimized form. Still, where a parent or other caretaking person has committed terrible abuses or atrocities (toward the client or others), a doctrine that may seem to rest on "understanding all is forgiving all" strikes me as inadequate and reductive, a kind of collapse into a defensive form of relativism that is as shallow and paralyzing as the opposite extreme (ie, the kind of avoidant, self-aggrandizing judgmentalism Hellinger is manifestly intent on steering us away from). To me, it sits much better to say, more modestly, that "to understand all," and thus to begin to know more about the systemic context of evil or harmful acts, complexifies the picture, in a disturbing, challenging way, which is at least potentially healthy and life-affirming. It doesn't simplify things – or it shouldn't and needn't: rather, it shakes them up, breaking up a more familiar, perhaps simplistic (and often projective) "good/evil" dichotomy, into a perspective from which we can condemn acts and choices, without necessarily clinging to the fragile superiorty of defensive certainty that we would have acted much more courageously and nobly ourselves.

And then a new, more complex picture (of the "perpetrator," the "victim" -- who is so often also a victim him/herself, -- and their contextual relationship to each other, in a larger overall context) requires additional support to become organized in a more energizing, more freeing and life-promoting gestalt. (And here again, the idea is to achieve this without falling into the other, rather polar opposite oversimplification of "everything is relative," so we "can't form any judgments"). Plainly (again, to me) there are risks and traps here, methodologically, at both extremes: ie, the "no-judgment" extreme (except of course that harsh judgment about making any judgments!), completely relativizing our deepest ethical intuitions – and the other extreme of defensive or draining focus on judgment of others, bereft of context.

Now new systemic pictures of taking in and understanding one's own developmental context and self-story are part of the manifest goal of Constellations work – as they certainly are of Gestalt work in general. In both cases, in accordance with basic Gestalt principles of experiential organization, intervention is meant to support deconstruction of an established pattern (of understanding, or self-narrative), in favor of reintegration of a new pattern, a new gestalt "ground" more supportive of creative life and growth. Personal growth always means greater complexification of experience – which is to say, of "ground." In general this more complex picture emerges out of a clearer, better-supported focus of strengthened (more vivid), clarified and simplified elements (a familiar example is the exploration and support of embodied sensation, another common theme and tool common to both approaches). But the heightening of particular elements of experience is not just for its own sake: rather, it is always in the service of a new, more complex integration/gestalt. We heighten figural attention in order to disorganize or deconstruct a familiar ground, in the service of some new emergent organization which may include more dynamic elements, in a new configuration more open to life, learning, and creative response.

Greater complexity in turn always requires greater support, including the support of time; and it is here in particular that an intervention strategy that may look (to me) like facilitator rushing, like prescribing, and even possibly like shaming for "resistance" to a new systemic picture – all of these being behaviors I've seen at some moments in the hands of some practitioners of Systemic Constellations (and some Gestaltists, of course!).

Finally, on the related question of political activism, of energy for critical change: Here too, the business of judging or not judging the past, or one's own forebears, is a tricky felt field, not easily reduced to slogans and directive solutions (forebears such as Freud, or Perls, or certainly Jung or Heidegger for examples -- or one's own parents, for that matter, -- all of whom may or may not have been always "doing the best they could under the given circumstances" – how would I know that?!). In the same way I may look back on events and actions in my own life and feel that no, really, I actually had more available room and support to do this or that thing a little better, hold this or that commitment more fully and generously, in terms of a value system important to me and my group of ethical reference, than I in fact did do. In cases like that it is crucial to me, in my own understanding of psycho-spiritual growth, my own and others', to hold that image/memory with felt regret, not only with "self-forgiveness." This is a point I will come back to at the end of this essay.

Let's note for now the common and instructive Buddhist formulation that the two cardinal principles for right living are compassion and judgment. But – and here's the key formulation, that brings these principles right down to the level of felt living: neither of these principles is much use, really, without the other. Judgment without compassion is cold, dead, and ultimately isolates you in a small room – a frozen gestalt. On the other hand, compassion without judgment is no guide to choiceful action. In our Gestalt terms, it oversimplifies the experiential field, which doesn't serve richer living and growth.

Perhaps the most useful admonition I've had in this complex area came to me from an important spiritual teacher for me, who was given to saying to people who came to him troubled by their own judgmentalism and righteousness, something like: "that's terrible. You must never be judgmental, it will poison you. Righteousness is violent – you must give it up at once. Stop being righteous ... but (and here came the trademark twinkle) – don't give up judgment, don't give up being right!"

From all this I take: hold it lightly. Certainly the Constellations tradition, in some hands (again, like the Gestalt tradition, and many others), may fairly be taxed with sometimes not holding lightly these delicate, important, and complex tissues of people's lives, and how to address ourselves most effectively to the suffering of the world.

Now all that goes to the first and speedier problem to deal with, the personal style and sometimes rigid pronouncements and provocations by some Constellations teachers -- at least for today's generation of Gestaltists, many of us in some reaction to some of the Gestaltists we knew in an earlier generation as well (and/or to ourselves, in earlier, more righteous years...). But what about the second problem touched on above? This is the meatier question of theory, and theoretical compatibility – which goes back, in this case as always, to fundamental assumptions and principles that each of these two approaches rests on. Let's look at each of those in turn, starting with Gestalt.

GESTALT – A DEEPER LOOK

Gestalt, in the broadest and deepest formulation, is a system of thought for understanding the construction of human experience. This formulation is pithy, and may at the same time seem obvious; but it is also dense, and calls for some unpacking. What do we mean by "experience;" what goes into this "construction;" and then why is all that the most relevant and productive focus for our attention in understanding and working with people?

We begin with the most fundamental Gestalt insight, the one that all the others come from and rest on: our experience is in fact something that is constructed, not "found." It doesn't come to us whole, or even in whole chunks, from the outside; it isn't "given" in the "environmental stimuli," however those are understood. It doesn't just happen "to us." These "gestalts," or meaningful wholes of experience we're always talking about in our model (and in life), are not just "out there" in nature, all ready and pre-organized for us to take in, meaning and all. On the contrary, most of the significant "units" of perception, narration, understanding we make use of in organizing our experience and our lives are themselves the product of complex interpretive, selective, and evaluative processes.

The founding insight of our Gestalt model was and is that we actively perform and participate in these constructive processes. We don't "receive" pictures or coherent narratives of "reality;" we don't even "take in" clear usable perceptions of an object in a passive way (Lewin again: "All perception is a form of problem-solving" [Marrow 1964]). What we do do is something much more active, more personally engaged than that: we take some emergent amalgam of "what's out there" (photons, energy waves and the like, to draw on the current scientific constructs of what's physically "there"), together with what we know and expect, what we believe and want, what we feel and wish for and fear, and what the context is as we understand/construct it. Context and this constructive process are everything, in generating the "wholes of understanding" that are then emergent. (The "same" gesture by you – say, bumping against me with your body – has an entirely different import and meaning, depending on my understanding/construction of context, including centrally your motivation, as imagined by me). "Context" here includes everything we're "trying to get to," our map of ourselves and others into a social system of reference, including our culture, our personal history, and more. We take all this and synthesize it, much more rapidly than it takes to even begin to tell it here, into a "meaningful whole picture" or sequence – the best (ie, most seemingly useful) we can manage at the moment. And "meaningful" here just means "something I can use," "something I can fit in and do something with" – even if that "doing something" is just "find out more," or even "get the hell out of here fast."

All this kind of thing was the subject matter, and the rich product, of the first half century, say, of Gestalt lab and social group research, led by the founding generation, followed by Lewin, Goldstein, and their students (ultimately including the Perlses), and on to the long academic research careers of Ogden, Gibson, Lewin himself, and others in American universities. As a result, the whole broad field of psychology was revolutionized and transformed, to the point where today there really is no significant psychology in research or theory which is not fundamentally Gestalt in its assumptions and most basic models today (and this ranges over and includes contemporary behaviorist, "depth," and cognitive neuroscience branches of the field). And then of course the application of these ideas to therapy, groups, community work, organizational dynamics, coaching, and so on has been the multi-focus of the next, most recent half century or so of Gestalt therapy and other Gestalt-derived applications to human systems and problems (eg, the pioneering NTL Institute for training organizational consultants and managers, which grew directly out of Lewin's work some 60 years ago, at the same time as Goodman and Perls were developing applications of Gestalt to psychotherapy and personal growth as a life practice).

FROM GESTALT TO CONSTELLATIONS – THE HUMAN NATURE QUESTION

These insights, which underlie and have utterly transformed the field of psychology over the past century, rest of course on the foundational challenge of Darwin --as does for that matter the seminal work of Nietzsche, Freud, Husserl, James, Dewey, Kropotkin, Lewin himself, and most or all of the other pioneering forebears who are variously the "integrative" gestalt-ist, phenomenologi-cal, existentialist, developmental/behavioral and social/developmental psy-chology of our Gestalt understanding. That is, Darwin's work throws us back, and threw all the above thinkers back on the question of human nature in a radically new way. If we are adapted to some evolutionary niche, like all life forms, then what is that niche, and what is the nature of that adaptation? You can see this clear surviv-al/evolutionary flavor in Gestalt in our special "take" on the ques-tions of experience, emotion, behavior, meaning, and so forth: we speak easily and naturally of "creative adjustment," "bio/social/psy-chological" nature, "lifespace," dealing with a situation, responding to something, coping with things, integrating a "usable whole of experience," or in Goodman's intentionally homely phrase, "getting along in the world."

What is that relevant "world," for human beings, and what is our par-ticular species adaptation, our human nature and process which Ge-stalt set out to investigate in a whole new way, based in much more lifelike "situational challenge" kinds of lab methodology – with such stunning and lasting effects?

The answer, emergent now from the past twenty years to brain/mind research, anthropology and cultural studies, biology and DNA stud-ies, and evolutionary theory and research: humans are evolved, basi-cally, to deal with social complexity. This insight, which reverses and transforms a century and a half of individualistically-based evolution-ary speculation, underpins everything in our Gestalt model (and for that matter in Systemic Constellations) at the most fundamental level.

That is, our hallmark species adaptation is to be able to compre-hend, handle hold, integrate, evaluate, choose, compare, plan, and otherwise handle shifting constellations of complex social group in-teractions to a literally unimaginable degree of complex functional integration[3] (where "complex integration" the survival/adaptation strategy of our species, means the [relatively, ultimately] harmonious interaction of diverse and variable parts).

In other words, we are evolved for creative response in a variable social environment: that "variable social environment" is our econiche, the environment we are evolved to deal with. Our need for this enormous creative capacity is driven by our species need for an ability to sense, estimate, evaluate, reorganize, fit in with, influence, use, draw on, negotiate with, and strategize (both with and at times against) a social group. If you think about it, this is why you find humans all over the earth, in the most variable physical environments imaginable, while our closest relations, who share roughly 99% of our genes and a more rudimentary (yet still amazingly complex) form of our social/ organizational capacity, are restricted to just one particular physical environment: because our evolutionary "econiche" is not a physical environment, directly. Our evolutionary species niche, again, is the social group; and that niche is "portable," it travels with us.

[3.] And when we say "unimaginable," that really is a literal truth. If you take the number of individual members of what appears to be the modal, natural human social unit – which clusters around about 150, -- and then factor out the total number of possible combinations of all size and variety of sub-groups of that number, the result is a number greater than the total number of particles in the known universe. But that order of number is roughly comparable to the number of neuronal connections in the human brain. This arresting factoid gives some idea of the biological underpinnings of our capacity for integrated connectivity, which after all is our essential survival strategy, as an individually defenseless, enormously long/dependent childhood, and thus social-group-dependent animal in the open savannah.

And note that this number of possible combinations still does not take into account the fact that each human subgroup has a different "meaning," survival-wise, when organized for a different purpose, at a different moment. Lewin again (eg 1936): "The need [ie, the intent] organizes the field" [ie, the practically relevant social situation at the moment].

What this means is that our two hallmark species characteristics – seemingly limitless creative ability, and a unique species capacity for social complexity – are actually one and the same capacity. Our brains are evolved to handle, evaluate, imagine, compare, and resolve practically this endlessly shifting, urgently important social scene we find ourselves in; and the creative flexibility that has demanded of us, over the past million years in particular, has also created our unique creative gift.

We are evolved to do this by imagining and comparing "scenarios" – integrated whole pictures of a shifting social strategy to deal with an equally shifting survival situation, of maximal interdependency. To be able to do this we have evolved a frontal cortex – roughly quadrupled in size over the brief evolutionary timespan of a less than a couple of million years – which, significantly, is not connected directly to the "outside world." Rather, the frontal cortex is the brain region devoted to integrating and synthesizing signal activation from other brain centers, themselves connected to "internal" and "external" sensory/electric signals. Every moment, every selected integrated image of a felt/ perceived situation, is a new situation, phenomenologically speaking, a new "scenario" (which is a perceived situation in relation to some felt need or intention, a "dealing with" some other integrated perception).

The Gestalt research tradition has been central and key to the elaboration of this emergent picture, integrating evolutionary research with our current understanding of the brain[4]. In this picture, novelty and learning take the place of ecostability and instinct in other, more cre-

---

[4.] And note here how this emergent picture is of a brain which is inherently syntactic — because social complexity is syntactic. That is, the hallmark of social complexity is that the significance of an individual element – in this case an indivudal group member – is given not by that person's characteristics per se, but rather by the nature of the whole scenario, the particular situation and intentional activity, in which the person is being regarded at the moment. This is the definition of syntax:

atively limited animals. We are born with hardly any real "instincts" (ie, long behavioral sequences triggered in entirety by presentation of the initial stimulus event, at least in a given sort of background). Rather, we construct those sequences, those tightly integrated long chains of behavior, feeling, and evaluation, based on learned, constructed patterns that are formed, relationally, after birth. This is why it is that cultures can differ so vastly for humans, in a species that nevertheless remains fully interbreeding, essentially genetically identical across groups (allowing for mostly minor haploid variability on particular genes in isolated populations). It is also why basic cultural differences can have an almost biological force, enormously resistant to change: because many of them they are laid down as basic relational interaction patterns or templates, in the actual physical organization of the infant brain, which is born premature, unorganized, and completely dependent – and utterly adapted to respond to, encourage, and integrate the interaction with lifegiving caretakers through a long period of complete dependency. (And here we could speak of something like a proto-instinct for attachment itself). Again, basic interactional and self-organizational patternings in the brain, which take the place in humans of instincts in other species, are constructed, interactively, after birth. This construction, our basic "Gestalt act," is what we know as learning – and it is utterly socially mediated.

---

a meaningful (language) whole where the significance of individual elements cannot be understood outside a given, unique, and variable context (eg of a sentence). Thus the second great mystery of human evolution – Where did language erupt from, so discontinuously? – is also much clarified by this perspective of a brain driven by the demands of social complexity. That is, the emergence of syntactic (as opposed to just signaling) language took place in/out of a brain that was already complexly syntactic, to deal with social relations. Again, the two hallmark characteristics of our species – social complexity and creative/linguistic ability – are essentially one and the same.

The result is clusters of sequences, comprising memories, feelings, beliefs, evaluations, estimations, interpretations, needs, etc – ie, gestalts of intention – which can be very tightly organized, quite resistant to change, and very pattern-setting (or "ground") for other sequences and patterns. These sequences keep getting formed all through life: this is what we call learning – meaning a new neuronal connection which connects with and organizes other potential connections in a new way. And they can be modified and recomposed with new experience throughout life: this is what we call "plasticity." And together with the sense of what these learnings "feel like," and our reflections on them, this is what we know as experience. Experience, in our Gestalt understanding, is whole integrated, interpretive clusters of meaning (by which we mean predictive useability, potentially, in scenario planning), or "gestalts," which include sensation, emotion, action, memory, belief, estimation, evalutation, and so forth.

And it is experience in this sense – meaningful wholes of action/interpretation/ understanding/prediction/feeling – which mediates behavior. Not the "stimulus" leads to the response: rather, our experience of the stimulus, interpretation of the "stimulus" event, preselected in a context, given particular intentions, people, and conditions, yields the behavioral outcome, the resultant action (overt or "internal," as thought). This is the essence of the Gestalt revolution of the earlier, behaviorist/objectivist or materialist/reductionist understanding of behavior and where it comes from. Not simple "stimulus-response," as in most other species: rather, "stimulus (selected, interpreted)-experience-response," is our human process sequence.

Now in our Gestalt understanding (which is the essential basis for brain/mind models today), this both poses and "solves" a particular kind of problem, which is the problem posed by creativity itself – namely, our capacity to respond variably and survivably to novel situations. This problem lies in the fact that novelty, uncatalogued and unprocessed, would pretty much instantly lead to a cacophanous clog of variability, soon overwhelming even the nearly unlimited capacity of our cortex, in the face of the potentially infinite variability of the world. To be sure, we select, we attend to only parts, we use only a limited band of sensory response capability in the first place (we have no awareness of, say, gamma rays – though certainly they will affect us). How do we deal with potential overwhelm, if we don't have a pre-fixed register of instincts to limit and stabilize us?

The answer is sketched above: we rely on our capacity to create new "instinct-like" long behavioral chains, continuously and creatively, throughout life; and then we use those "template patterns" to organize other, later learning around. To use today's cybernetic imagery, we have a limited amount of "short term memory" available at any time – and we constantly have to "clear the decks" by integrating the new solution to the novel situation, into newly-created and preexisting patterns, or "automated" neural/behavioral change, in the brain.

The generation of experience – problem-solving, learning, creativity – is thus constantly being resolved, more or less, into automisms: habits new and old, which themselves contextualize other habits and automisms in memory patterns (both "conscious" and "unconscious." Behaviorists, working to accommodate these ideas, sometimes call these sequence/clusters by the useful name of "schemas" – complex integrations of behavior, thought, belief, feeling, and meaning (which again means estimation, evaluative predictability, the key to our species survival).

Living is constructive, integrative, synthetic. Novelty synthesized into habit, in the longest chains practicable under the circumstances. In the familiar example, without this constant relegating of the new into the familiar, the novel into the long habit chain, we couldn't even walk. First, fumbling steps must soon be automated into longer, smoother chains, in order to then use walking, for instrumental ends. Without this automizing step, we couldn't do anything else while walking (as indeed we mostly cannot: while learning a new skill, we can generally only perform those other skills which are fully, deeply, and very stably already integrated into habit patterns of their own. This is true of physical/mental skills, like skiing or playing the piano, obviously. And it is all the more true of those life-giving complex social skills we need for living well and growing in our special econiche, of other human beings (think of things like arguing a point without failing to listen at the same time; remembering to attend to body and emotion while focusing on a difficult patient or partner or boss, say; rapidly estimating a number of people's availability and fitness for particular roles in an urgent situation, while still focusing on the aim you're trying to accomplish or solve, which may most often itself be a complex social goal, and so on. At least major parts of complex social capacities like these have to be already automated, if we are to pay any attention at all to what's new and potentially creative in the present situation).

Living, again, is constructive, synthetic, meaning-generating -- and automism-dependent, and new-automism-generating. Both things are necessary for successful living, in the face of a variable environment: the new, and the routine as support for attending to the new. For this reason, therapy, in a Gestalt understanding, is deconstructive. All our Gestalt practices, intervention skills, and techniques, are basically in the service of taking these tightly integrated sequences of feeling, action, understanding/meaning and belief, and adding the special supports to create safety, relaxation, relief from immediate time pressure, so that we can lift out the various elements of these tightly integrated neural chains, heighten and examine them, question and set them back "in motion," bring them into contact with other elements and feelings and beliefs – all in the service of facilitating a newer, potentially better integration of elements, which then can become a new neural pattern, serving to platform new learnings, newer, hopefully richer solutions to the next novel creative challenge of living. (And "better," here, means in the direction of greater complexity, the integration of more dimensions of complex awareness – thought, feeling, intention, memory, scanning, belief, and so forth).

The more these established patterns which we are deconstructing are the residue of early learnings, socially driven, and especially the ones formed under urgent conditions of high need and low support – the more the solutions themselves, while theoretically the best possible "creative adaptation" we could achieve under those given, low-support circumstances, will tend to be rigid, not very open to new learnings and enrichment, not very complex – and in need of more of the very special supports of longer-term, deeply safe psychotherapy and other relational processes. Not for nothing did Goodman call these special learning situations, permitting of deep deconstruction of tight structures of experiential and neuronal ground, "safe emergencies."

Now, we've gone to some length here to sketch out our evolutionary heritage and nature, leading up to our gestalt-forming, integrative/evaluative human process and behavior, and needing special supports for the deconstruction of old, dysfunctional, and change-resistant "habits of ground." This is Gestalt. In the process we've sketched an animal, ourselves, that on the basis of some 200 million years of mammalian evolution for attachment and dependency, plus some 60 million years of primate evolution for social group living, perhaps 20 million years of "great ape" specialization – has progressively and irregularly grown more and more complexly integrated in social living and capacity, and more and more dependent on the complex, integrated social group.

This picture changes a number of things. It takes a good deal of the sexist perspective out of human anthropology and evolutionary theory, for one thing. No longer do we see Man-the-Hunter and Alpha-Male theories being offered in explanation of the rapid growth of the brain, and thus the establishment of our basic nature. Rather, understanding as we now do that the demands of social complexity drove the explosive growth of the brain, we know that female evolution, if anything, is at least the equal of the push for creativity in males. We also understand both the potential and the evolutionary use of our enormously long, dependent childhood: it is in this period that our brain, born severely premature and unformed, takes on organization into neural patterns and pathways; and that process is regulated, stimulated, structured, and mediated by relationship, primarily between infant and (multiple) caretaker(s) (see Hrdy, 2009). We're born to sense and deal with social relations; we live and grow through growth in our capacity to sense and manipulate social situations; we are and remain exquisitely sensitive to the complexities of our social surround at virtually every moment of life. It's how our creativity arose and works. It's how learning and memory function, through elaborate integration of mammalian emotional centers with the attentional and other memory structures and processes of the brain. And it's how and why therapy works: our deepest patterns are those holistic constructions that were supported in our early social interactions. We add support, to permit relaxation, relative deactivation, and deconstruction/reconstruction of those patterns now – in therapy, in ongoing or special relationships, and in the socially-mediated business of living.

CONSTELLATIONS - A DEEPER LOOK

We know far more than we know how to say. This is true in so many areas – physically, artistically, spiritually, and more. And it is nowhere more true than in our basic human-nature-generating situation, which is the cohesive social group.

All of us are aware of this, in many different ways. To take a familiar example, we all know the experience of walking into a room, being taken by surprise by the "atmosphere" or "vibe," – and then either just automatically "sensing what's up," or else being aware of not knowing – but knowing that something definitely is "up." "What's going on," we may say – if conditions of present estimated safety and sensitivity, and past experiences of social acceptance, permit such a direct approach. Or, we may opt to "keep our own counsel," perhaps sensing hair rising on the back of our neck (an ancient mammalian physical response, to perceived yet not-yet-known danger, or the ambiguity of sensing tension in others). We know groups. (We'd better – our species evolution as well as our personal survival pretty much depended on it). We may have learned to ignore this capacity, or to stifle it, or we may never have developed it very fully in the first place (because it was either not fostered in our original social environment, or perhaps it was actively taboo). But it is the cornerstone of our ability to, again in Goodman's phrase, "get along in the world."

When we do this, this "sensing" of the social grouping we're in, we're drawing on something that is not only evolutionarily ancient, but personally, developmentally preverbal as well. As infants and children, we "know" this social surround directly, "intuitively" as we say. Is our world relaxed or tense, stable or jumpy, "mappable" or confounding, defying attempts to make sense (in which case we may give up on the idea and feeling of being able to "make sense of our world," a potentially crippling effect). We now know, for example, that infants don't just "take in" and imitate behaviors: they imitate intent. They respond directly and complexly – as we do, and all primates and many other mammals do – to strong affect. Anger tends to spark anger – and with it, our learned "defenses" against it; sadness the same; joy, humor, sexual excitement, grief, extreme embarrassment or shame – all these states, when strong in one person, are imme-

306

diately communicated, in a direct embodied way, with or without conscious awareness of where they're "coming from," to the people around us.

We know all this and so much more. And unquestionably, we react to this "data," these felt, embodied senses of the particular social group we're in at the moment. In general, the more salient the group is to us, the more our membership "matters," the more acutely we will tend to be affected by the emotions, attachments, and complex inter-dynamics of that particular relational field. And while at times we may have that pull-back, that "what's going on here?" response mentioned above, for the most part this intuitive group-awareness, this exquisitely evolved capacity to "read" a social field, remains implicit, embodied, not clearly in verbal awareness. We read the social field – but not easily out loud, in words.

Family sculpting, certainly, in the hands of Satir and many others, arose as an attempt to put words on this embodied "reading." We live in human social systems, starting with the family (which is then "internalized," thus always with us in one way or another). We orient to these "systems," and react or respond to situations in ways that are constrained and informed by these "readings" (present or "transferred," to use the psychodynamic term, from other, perhaps earlier and more governing contexts). And with family sculpting, we try to get a fresh look, a new sense of those out-of-awareness places where we're being "pulled" by "systemic forces," so to speak, that are not in our awareness.

One limitation of this older, more static technique, a constraint on the amount of fresh information we might get out of that kind of exercise, always lay in the fact that so much of the story was conveyed in advance to the sculpture participants in narrative form. A generation or two ago, in a "pre-postmodernist" world, we had a less sharp appreciation of how much our narrative of a social system – and our own families all the more so – is already a co-construction with and in that very system and its members, already resolved into a fairly sturdy set of interpretations and meanings. We look to the sculpture to illustrate some of those meanings, and perhaps some of their implications and interactive consequences, but not so much as a source of new information, new interpretations about the constituent dynamics of that system. We're mostly looking for a more vivid illustration of the effects of known, narratized dynamics, on some system member (typically a child, who may be newly seen to be less free than we thought, to make some desired or needed move, which may only result in "systemic homeostasis" – ie, compensatory moves by other members to restore the upset balance, perhaps by pushing the child back out of the new behavioral terrain).

So what would happen if we moved to take a great deal, at least, of this pre-interpreted "story" back out of the "sculpture," before we depicted it? What if the participants, instead of "playing" a "role" to a pre-communicated story or "script," simply had nothing (or little) in the way of pre-structured story to go by? What would they use instead, as they oriented to the "sculpture" they had been inducted into? What would the induction consist in, if not a verbal relating of the pre-known story of this system? Where would any new information come from? And then would would be the import, the use of that "information?" Who would be the authority on where and how it might apply, have validity, be of use to the client?

Questions like these underlie the methodologies known broadly as Systemic Constellations. Typically, in Constellations work a client presents a system of concern, as the "theater," past or present or both, of some felt issue of concern – to him/her. But instead of telling the "story" as he/she has learned to carry it, and describing the participant/representatives in psychological and narrative detail, the focus is primarily just on the felt concern itself. Examples might be things like, "I can't seem to form a lasting relationship;" "I can't feel love for/from my partner;" "I seem to be unable to have a child, for no known medical reason;" "I can't get along with my siblings/boss/ children/ coworkers/etc;" "I can't connect with a career – can't commit – keep getting exploited/victimized," and on and on. The familiar chronic living problems of our own, our friends', our families' and our clients' lives – often problems of connection, sustaining relationship, nurturance, trust, orientation, self-sabotage, victimization, lack of direction, too little or too much feeling, and more.

Now in theory and practice, these living problems and many others may be being lived out and also may then be explored in a great range of living systems, past and present. But frequently, with problems having to do with deep relational connection and disconnection, Constellations work will tend to zero in, for a lot of evident reasons, on our early systems of belonging. One of the theory traditions Constellations work rests on, clearly, is Attachment Theory, supplemented with Satir's emphasis on "basic validation," which she (and Hellinger) see as needing to begin with a univalent flow of affirmation and validation from elder generations to younger. Where this does not happen, children will frequently adjust to the unnourishing distance by moving toward the parent – even (sometimes especially) an abusive parent, who however destructively, is still expressing and offering attachment, sometimes at a devastating price.

Added to this is the idea of "representing" absent, excluded, denigrated or otherwise marginalized members of the system: cast-off former lovers and previous spouses, the dead who have not been recognized, perpetrators or other family members held with a sense of shame and exclusion, and systemic misfits of all kinds. To the extent that these marginalized figures are not recognized and given a due, appropriate "place," psychically or psychologically in the family, then children may often take on the "role" of "representing" the marginalized figure (or legacy, or identity).

Again, these are familiar ideas from family systems work, but with greater emphasis here on the issue of a sort of "capture" of the child, in the service of a parent's or the whole system's needs for compensation, nurturance, and balance. When teachers from this tradition speak of "orders," what they mean, generally, is a reference to simple statements of fact: time, belonging, precedence, relationship, inclusion/exclusion. Thus facilitators may ask representatives, or Constellation subject/clients, to simply look at a configuration of relationships (often "disordered," in the sense that the younger generation is fixated [confluent, in a certain Gestalt language tradition] in some way on the family of origin system, and to that extent not free to move on with their own lives). Again, this is a familiar idea in Gestalt, family systems, and other experiential or structural systems of understanding.

And from there facilitators may move to asking a constellation or structural representative to make some simple affirmative statements about the structural, systemic facts: such as, "you are the parent, I am the child;" "I see your painful fate, and I leave it with you;" "I've tried to carry your burden, and I've hurt myself in the process;" "you too belong to this system, you have a place" (this to some excluded or marginalized member); or even "you are my father, this is my partner; you are not my partner," and more in that register. Awareness, affirmation of reality, bearing that with support, presence in seeing, simple experience of what then comes up – again, here we are in the realm of very familiar Gestalt moves and ideas, albeit arrived at in a different way.

When a subject or client puts him/herself forward for one of these inquiries, typically the facilitator will conduct an interview with the idea of clarifying the issue, the felt desire for change, and perhaps the imagined outcome (in the sense of how you'll feel if we get to a place of greater freedom, closer to your desired state). The difference in this method, from much other family systems work, is that biographical and psychological/interpretive material is kept to a minimum – for the simple, Gestalt-friendly reason that the story is already there, already part of the problem, already being held in some "frozen," non-helpful way by the client. That is, each of us has some narrative interpretation of events in our own lives, and to the extent that that story does not support us to move on freely and creatively, rehearsing it now with the facilitator will be more likely to forestall any new experience, than to facilitate it.

For this reason, once the distress or desire is clarified and stated clearly enough to launch an exploration, the facilitator will typically cut off the interview and ask the client to select representatives for him/herself, and a few other system members who seem relevant to the inquiry. For example, if the problem is a long series of failed relationships, then it may seem relevant to start with the client and the client's parents, to see if any new light can be shed on what system or "ground" dynamics, what frozen attachments or aversions in the past relational field, may be operating in a felt way that tends to block new movement and growth in this intimate area.

And then in a sense that's it. The client or subject takes the representatives and positions them around the available space without words (again that emphasis on how the story I already hold is a part of the problem – in a sense by definition, since if I were "holding" and living in/with this particular social field in a way that was supporting my own further creative growth, then I wouldn't be bringing the problem, the stuck area of living, in for inquiry). Areas of my life where I am freely growing, fully living well, making productive commitments and creative expansions of my experience – and this is an article of faith in Constellations as in Gestalt – will be areas that are well-supported, "internally" and "externally." In Constellations work, we would expect this to be reflected in felt systems of belonging (eg, my current experience of my family of origin system) that were arranged in configurations that supported free, choiceful, open commitments and relationships and movement going "forward" in my life (ie, moving out of that family of origin toward my own life ahead, in a free and comfortable way with a sense of a presence and an open blessing behind me), toward an open future of new engagements, new meaningful living. This is a kind of imagined ideal of a past family system, of course, but the point here is that in areas that really do feel rather like this, we will find we are free to move, live, and grow.

This kind of thinking of course parallels Gestalt perspectives on development, support, and shame. The areas of experiencing and living in which the child is developmentally supported – ie, reflected, received, "humanly validated" (in Satir's terminology), and fully contacted by caretaking others – will then generally be areas where the growing person benefits from a sort of "virtuous circle" of learning and development. That is, since that area (passionate feeling, say, or reflective intelligence, or alert attunement to others, or robust embodied self-contact, etc) is affirmed and supported/received, the growing child and youth is free to invest intention and energy there without severe nurturant cost or conflict – and thus the area enjoys all the benefits of rich contacting processes: exploration and exfoliation, rich and complex linkages with other areas of living and experiencing (and we can see this now in the living brain, through fMRI imagery), overall complexification, building of a network of skills, and of course all the rewards and further support that full exercise of a supported capacity will tend to enjoy (like growing relationships with others, expanding and well-integrated skill sets, integration with other related areas, creativity and problem solving, and so on).

These are then not the areas that we generally bring in to therapy! Rather, these are the areas where we probably respond, when asked, that that part of our lives is going well. And part of going well, of course, is that we tend to have skills and capacity to continue to organize and use ongoing support, from others and "internally," for our ongoing growth and complexification of experience in these areas. This is Gestalt.

It's also Constellations. But how does that methodology work, what is the theory of change, how does new information come into the person's experiential world, and get used for newer, more complex and creative living? This is where the more serious theoretical misgivings about Constellations on the part of some Gestaltists have tended to arise. Thus these are the more serious issues referenced at the outset of this paper.

In an earlier generation of Constellations work the evaluative criteria often did seem to come from an expert/objectivist perspective. Here again, this closely parallels some earlier work by a previous generation of Gestalt practitioners, where oftentimes we tended to see (for all the theoretical insistence on self-responsibility, authentic self-experience, and "autonomous criteria" of health) the reintroduction of the "expert model" by the back door. That is, the client was accorded the notional right to evaluate her/his own life, experience, and choices – but there was the "Gestalt expert," telling him/her in no uncertain terms whether he/she was doing it right, or falling into "resistances" such as confluence, projection, retroflection, and so on, in the old therapist/authority way that Goodman and Perls were so eager to get away from (but of course sometimes embodied).

In the same way, I've seen Constellations facilitators who seemed to be pronouncing "right answers," more than openly exploring the experiential world of the client. In Gestalt terms this is the difference between a radical experimental/experiential stance, and the collapse into the older, easier (for the facilitator, in the short term!) objectivist, right-wrong model.

But where do new information and new perspectives come from, in Constellations work, if not from the preconceived ideas of "orders" and authoritarian interpretive schemes of the facilitator? The answer is: from the lived, embodied experience of the representatives in the system being represented. That is (and to a degree you have to experience this, as a representative, to evaluate it), the information that will be fresh and useful, in an experimental, hypothetical, not objectivist sense, will be the experience the representatives are having in the living, current, here and now system they are embodying and representing at the given moment.

And here's where the disquisition above on evolutionary theory and our embodied, exquisitely sensitive embeddedness in physically present human social systems comes into play. Here's the working assumption operative in these exercises: as we stand in a social configuration evoked/arranged by a given client in a particular emotion/thought/mood space in relation to a particular felt issue, we may automatically have some access to the embodied experience of simply standing in that configuration, at those distances and angles of contact and deflection, with a group of other human animals, recruited into the same shared intentionality.

Is this data "pure," the question often arises? Isn't it "contaminated" by the personal history of whoever happens to be selected? Might people not "project" their own "stuff" and interpretations onto this situation and these roles, for all that we've tried to keep the story data to the barest minimum? Of course they may, and do. Surely if we've learned one thing in Gestalt, it's that there's no such thing as "pure data," un-contextualized, -interpreted, and –conditioned by prior experience, beliefs, imaginal/projective estimations, evaluations, intentions and needs, and so forth. The question is not, is this data "pure"? The question is, is it useful? Is it different enough, fresh enough, "in contact" enough with the present embodied social reality, to offer some new perspective, some new potentially useful insight, experimentally and hypothetically, into the felt dynamics of the client's experiential world?

This more client-centered, less expert-based approach to the information generated in Constellations exercises is exemplified, in my experience, by teachers of roughly the "second generation" after Hellinger (who is himself still active at this writing, in his later eighties). Information of this kind is generated in basically two ways: one is by standing off and simply looking at the configuration as a whole, of the picture or social tableau generated by the client's placement of the representatives around the room. Just that. Those who have experienced well-facilitated family sculptures will know something of the potential of just this much, to generate a new insight into where the client or "the system" as a whole is stuck, feels unfree to move and change.

Secondly, and often even more richly, there are the representatives themselves, giving voice to their present experience in the configuration, with the accent (again, to hold narrative closure to a minimum) on embodied experience, without yet integrating that into an overall "understanding" of the system, much less some resolution of the problem. As in contemporary Gestalt work, the intention is to support an open inquiry into the separate, "pre-interpreted" dynamics of an experiential process. The fact that no inquiry is ever totally "open," in that older, objectivist sense, doesn't change the fact that this intention also enters into the organization of the present interaction, and may well support the emergence of new perspective.

After all, this is what creative process is, in Gestalt understanding. We slow down the process, support awareness of its component parts (here the experience of simply standing in that dynamic configuration), thereby deconstruct a previous integrated whole of understanding (perhaps a narrative self-understanding), and by differentially energizing/attending to selected elements of an attentional field, we favor the emergence of a newer, more complex, possibly richer resolution of that field of understanding. We don't inquire, in a Gestalt perspective on creativity, whether that new product is in some sense utterly free of all preconceptions, all previous integrated understanding, all "transferred" or pre-organized structure (whatever that would mean). On the contrary, we assume that it is an outcome of everything we "bring to" the experience – plus something new, some new organization of the "same" elements, but differentially valorized, seen, attended to, and thereby invested with potential energy.

The process here is roughly the same. The facilitator serves in part, as in Gestalt, to propose experimental moves – not to "solve" the situation, but simply to see what difference that would make. Thus moving a representative to a different alignment in relation to the client's representative is not a "solution" to a constellation, but an experiment, for the sake of generating data. Data in the representatives themselves, and new experience for the client her/himself, who is looking on, and registering possible new images.

In the end, it is these new images that are the "product" of the constellation exercise. The process is thus very "right brain" – seeking and relying on whole pictures, as a possibly "internalized" schema of reference, which may serve to support new experience (as opposed to a new "story," a linear arrangement of narrative elements, in the way of less embodied, less holistic, therapeutic traditions – ie, not Gestalt).

My goal in laying out these reflections in this Afterword is not to persuade you of the worthwhileness of Constellations, necessarily, as a method or a tool. That would be for you to experience, and then to evaluate based on that experience as a whole. Rather, my aim here is to explore resonances between Constellations and Gestalt, which have sometimes been held as in some way conceptually opposed.

My conclusion about that question, which I offer you here, is this: If you contrast an expert-based Gestalt with an expert-based Constellations approach (and both have certainly existed and been on offer, and to some extent do still exist), then no, there is not really a difference in philosophy, just a difference in method. In either case we have a process, an organized, experienced behavioral whole – and an expert evaluating and correcting that process, and pronouncing on its rightness, or otherwise.

Likewise, if you hold up and compare a contemporary understanding of Gestalt as a system of relational coconstructionism, with a contemporary understanding of Systemic Constellations, then here too you will find extremely resonant emphases between them, in their understanding and use of awareness, intention, relationship and attachment, embodied experience, experiment, and emergent meaning in both systems.

Where you will find the sharp contrasts, I submit, is not between the one system or approach and the other – but between the older, more objectivist/reductive version of each of these two approaches, and the contemporary understanding of the same legacy and evolving tradition. As always (and as Gestalt reminds us), the "ground" of basic assumptions, intentions, and felt relationships informs and ultimately determines the "figure" of what you are seeing (in this case, the particular versions of Gestalt or of Systemic Constellations work themselves).

What Constellations in this understanding can add to some of our Gestalt approaches is then specifically an explicit exploration of ground. Figure/ground, both historically and methodologically, is a key concept and emphasis in Gestalt. And yet over the years we have often devoted much more attention to understanding "figure" (the sequence of feeling to intention to action, sequences or stages of contact, and so forth, in our conscious awareness at least as we attend to it) than to a vocabulary and tool kit for exploring process structures of ground. We know that relational ground, which is a map of our own attachment history, conditions and informs every attentional figure we form, and how we may energize and actualize those figures in living. We can see the truth of this Gestalt assumption now in contemporary cognitive neuroscience research. But where is our toolbox for understanding how relational "ground" actually operates to contextualize current process in the here and now? My own view is that Systemic Constellations, in its contemporary, non-authoritarian form, is a rich new tool for this emergent inquiry. Thus it offers itself as a vibrant dynamic element in the ongoing, emergent evolution of Gestalt theory and practice.

–Gordon Wheeler, Big Sur California, 2011

Freud, A. (1937) The ego and the mechanisms of defense. NY: International Universities Press.

Goldstein, K. (1939) The organism. Boston: American Book Company.

Hrdy, S. (2009) Mothers and others: the evolutionary origins of mutual understanding. Cambridge, MA: Harvard University Press.

Koffka, K. (1925). The growth of mind: an introduction to child psychology. NY: Harcourt Brace.

Lewin, K. (1935). A dynamic theory of personality. NY: McGraw-Hill.

Lewin, K. (1936). Principles of topological psychology. NY: McGraw-Hill.

Marrow, A. (1969). The practical theorist: the life and work of Kurt Lewin. NY: Basic Books.

Satir, V. (1972/1990). Peoplemaking. London: Souvenir Press, Ltd.

Wertheimer, M. (1935). Some probems in the theory of ethics. In Henle, M. (Ed.), Documents in Gestalt Psychology. Berkeley: University of California Press (1961).

Wheeler, G. (2000). Beyond Individualism. Hillsdale, NJ: The Analytic Press.

Appendix A

A Conversation with Stephan Hausner

This is a conversation that took place on March 6, 2010, at Esalen Institute in Big Sur, California, with Dr. Stephan Hausner. Also participating are Judith Hemming, Nancy Lunney Wheeler, Deborah Ullman, and Gordon Wheeler, in conversation sparked by the book, *Even if it Costs Me My Life,* and by a series of workshops immediately prior to the conversation, led (separately) by Judith and by Stephan at Esalen. The verbatim conversation has been edited very slightly only to take out pauses and repetitions, and here and there to add a clarifying word, that was implicitly understood in the live situation.

GORDON WHEELER: So, if I may start, the question that I think interests our readers first of all is, what is this work? What is Constellations work? What is it in a sentence? What is it in a paragraph? And then the history and the theory, all of that is very interesting. First of all, I think, the interested reader, the psychotherapeutic reader particularly, wants to know, what's going on in that room? What are you doing in there, and what are the goals?"

STEPHAN HAUSNER: I think I can only say what it is from my perspective because it is not yet even defined. Not by one Constellations association is the question answered: "What is constellation work?" Certainly it can be described. There's the method to set up a constellation, which is already explained in the book a little bit, going into how you do it. Choosing representatives, and so on. The question then becomes, what is a constellation? From my perspective, the constellation is the externalization of an internal process. Given that we do not yet know what we are setting up, what happens when we choose someone for the father and place him here? It's hard to talk about it, you know? But what we can experience is that what the representatives express very often has a deep effect on the client. He or she is deeply moved, which furthers an inner process related to what he can see and experience in the constellation process. Usually this leads to a deep emotional process. From my perspective, when I do this work, I would say, first of all, I work in a client-oriented way, and I work in a way that is question-oriented, or focused on the issue of the client.

And so, for me [what is] very important is the interview phase, leading up to articulating the point of what is to be set up. And in this phase of interview, I try to come to sort of an agreement with the client. What is an appropriate question that leads to a constellation that can show a solution for this question? That is what I am dialoguing with the client to find. From my perspective, it is the responsibility of the facilitator to find out what is an appropriate question and then to define the elements to set up, to get clarification. I remember Bert Hellinger saying that once the facilitator has a hypothesis he cannot do the work. I have found out that I cannot work without a hypothesis. I do the interview to get the hypothesis, and then I try to set it up in a way [that] it shows them whether this hypothesis can be confirmed or maybe needs to be changed, being aware that [I], as a therapist, also can have a big influence, or maybe even the main influence on the process that's going on. This is a very delicate topic, the influence of the facilitator. My role.

GORDON: Your constructs.

STEPHAN: My constructs. So this from me more or less is how a constellation starts, exploring a hypothesis, and the interesting thing is that often these hypotheses are confirmed, and very often it's the representatives themselves that bring in new aspects or show that the system that has been created around the problem so far, needs to be enlarged. I always try to start with a minimal means, in that I try to figure out which are the representatives that are definitely needed to start with. Then there are various ways to start. This gives you a little bit of an idea?

GORDON: Oh, it gives me a lot of ideas. What I'm thinking is, we're sitting here with two masters of this work, you and Judith Hemming, and of course people who are deep in the actual creation of this evolving tradition at such levels of mastery are going to start this story in the middle.

So having done that, there are so many things I want to ask you and follow up. You probably feel the same. At the same time I feel like, if I switch back to the naïve reader's chair, I didn't yet find out what Constellations are. It's a procedure or a process for looking at systems, we see that much. Where are we starting? Of course you're talking to the four of us. You know we know the work well. If you backed up and said something orienting to the new student, as you did on Wednesday night, what might you say?

STEPHAN: Well, if I were to explain it to a patient or to a student, the basic idea is the transpersonality of illness.

DEBORAH ULLMAN: Transpersonality.

STEPHAN: Illness, as not a personal, individual phenemenon. And so setting up the Constellation with respect to illness and health is a way to find out what is the function of the illness in the family system of the client. And what the illness may represent in the family system of the client, and what is excluded and needs to be included so that the illness perhaps can withdraw. So in a way, you can see illness or the creation of symptoms also as the trial to create a balance within a family system. Or, you can see it as a possible expression of an imbalance, which is being compensated.

GORDON: So, somehow the system is, I don't know if you'd say "working better." But it's that something is more stable in the system with the illness in it than without it, as the system is now?

STEPHAN: This is what you very often experience. Often I start with representatives for the patient and the illness, and sometimes the two of them have a strong connection. They feel bonded. Sometimes they do not have a strong connection. Very often when they have a strong connection, when you then enlarge the system and bring in the parents, you can see that as you bring in the parents or other family members, the connection between the illness and the patient weakens. On the other side, very often when you see there is not a strong connection, sometimes you bring the parents or other family members in, and then the connection gets even stronger. This suggests that the illness, somehow is easier for the patient than the relationships to close family.

And sometimes, even then after a while, I take the representative of the illness out to see what happens to provoke the disturbance in the system, what happens if the illness is not in the system. This often sometimes indicates the dynamic, you know? This is what we also had seen a little bit on Wednesday night, first taking the illness out and then bringing the illness back in, and then the client suddenly felt better. Even with this threatening illness.

DEBORAH: I'm just wondering if some of the unseen orders are an important thing to identify as we're framing what the assumptions are that you bring to doing the work. Does that feel important to you? In other words, there's a sense about this work that there are certain assumptions about the direction that love flows, about the balance and direction of supporting. Are these things relevant, would you say, in how you respond to an issue that a client presents?

STEPHAN: Yes. I mean, what you are referring to is what Hellinger describes as the "orders of love" in human systems. For example, the new family system takes preference over the old system – meaning that our first duty of caring goes to the next generation. So when this is not respected, very often we see that children respond with a sort of illness. So, like all types of traditional medicine is teaching, there is a relationship between order and health.

DEBORAH: When I watch you work, and I'll say when I watch *you* work in particular, I'm really struck by the power of the pace and the silence that you bring to establishing the relationship from the very beginning with a client or a patient that you're working with. I'm curious if you can tell us a little bit about the silence.

STEPHAN: Well, in fact, it's very simple. One of the principles in this work is that I only do a step when I'm absolutely sure that this step is necessary. Maybe it brings in new information or it leads toward a solution. And as long as I'm not yet sure, I just do nothing. Of course, intrinsically, I try to play with the system using the perception of how dynamics in the system are changing. For example, I imagine to bring in the grandfather, trying to sense his influence, related to the issue of the client. This goes back to my training in kinesiology, testing. With this perception I usually/often know before what happens in the system when I bring this person in.

GORDON: Because you're reading your own body, you mean?

STEPHAN: Yes, Because I'm reading my own body.

GORDON: Because that's what it looks like watching you work. You will set up just a few people and then you'll say, "The disturbance is here, not *here*." And, I'm thinking that's an intuition that is grounded on something that isn't necessarily visible to me. Now you're opening that up.

STEPHAN: Well, I was trained by my father-in-law in homeopathy, he taught us to test the disturbances in the body of the patient, and also to test the remedies to balance the energy in the body. So I can immediately feel if there is a resonance, for example, between the remedy and the body of the patient. And this sense helps me to know what path to follow when the client is talking about family members or significant events. For example, when you see in the constellation that there must be a loss in the family. And the client says, "Well, I lost my brother at the age of such and such, and my mother lost her father when she was a child." And from this kind of inner sensing or testing, I can distinguish which one is probably the important one. This is something that happens in silence because I do not want to bring in a representative that is not needed. So, going back to this what this principle means, I only do a step when it is definitely needed to get clarity or to find out something..

GORDON: I'm smiling because you asked what's going on in the silences and Stephan said, "It's very simple." *Laughter.*

It's simple -- if you had these ten years of training.

NANCY LUNNEY WHEELER: You said you're testing? I mean, what are you using to test?

STEPHAN: My body.

NANCY: Just your body?

STEPHAN: My body. My body reacts when there is a stress coming up. I feel the stress in my body. And then I also have the sense of whether this is going to be resolved by itself after a while when you give it some time, or if you need, for example, a third element.

GORDON: I'm very mindful right now that you spoke about wanting to do homeopathy, but without the remedies.

STEPHAN: Exactly. This is going back to this idea, in a way.

NANCY: So when you decide that it's in the mother's line of the family rather than the father's, what are you feeling, literally, in your body that's saying, "This is the mother, not the father."

STEPHAN: Well, you know I tune myself into the theme where the client and I made the agreement of what is the issue in this work. Then I project, somehow, or imagine the mother in relationship to this issue, and then I can feel what the reaction is. Perhaps I sense that there is a fear coming up, and this fear I can perceive. Then when I project the father, if nothing is happening in either direction, then I sense/know that the father is not important.

GORDON: So, you're talking as if there's an overt constellation going on that you are facilitating and there's a covert constellation –

STEPHAN: There are about one hundred constellations going on inside of me, checking out all possibilities.

GORDON: Now, I believe that we all have these intuitions, we all have this kind of knowledge, about the human systems we're part of, or are around us.

STEPHAN: Absolutely.

GORDON: I don't necessarily have access to that knowledge in the way that you do. People who do not approach it with that clear sense of internal kinesiology, if you could call it that, do something analogous, just as you said a moment ago: "If I don't find that, then I look for it in the constellation."

STEPHAN: A lot of facilitators do it by trial and error.

DEBORAH: That's how you work with hypotheses.

GORDON: You're doing that too?

STEPHAN: I'm doing that too. I just have, sort of, a pre-selection.

GORDON: That's what I mean about a covert stage. You're doing that internally.

STEPHAN: Yes, I'm doing it internally.

DEBORAH: I'd like to turn to Judith on this right now, because I see you do so much that also seems to emerge out of the silence. I'm just wondering if you would say you're also using your body as information or...

JUDITH HEMMING: Well, I was thinking about some of the differences between Stephan and me. And Stephan's focus is very much on illness. Because of the range of people who come work with me, I wouldn't say it particularly was. I'm probably looking at systems in a bigger way, not just thinking about the importance of connection to parents, for instance, but looking at the impact of all sorts of aspects of systems and the way other systems connect and so on. I'm not aware of using my body in the way that you describe at all. I feel as though I'm doing something that's more visual. I use the interview to see the constellation and to see where the soul energy of the person is wishing to go and what it would need in order to make that possible. So I'm assembling the elements that may be necessary in order for the movement to start again. My meter is not so much sickness and health, but stasis and movement. And that's probably because I'm not working so much with sickness. I'm working more with "stuckness."

STEPHAN: More with...?

JUDITH: Stuckness. Not being able to move. And I really find it absolutely fascinating that you are getting such clear feedback loops. I suspect that I'm much more geared to the philosophy. I carry the philosophy, the whole perceptual framework in quite an active way as something that I want to share and engage people in and educate them on. It's a journey in which I probably play a more active teaching role than you do. It's probably because I don't have the precision of that body knowledge, that I'm using some other methodology. I'm not really quite sure what more it is that may underlie some of our differences.

GORDON: Well, you know we have the popular phrase now, in American English, called "the ten thousand hours." It's the idea that that's what it takes to establish mastery, on the violin or whatever. But, of course, each of you now has ten thousand hours in constellations. And Judith, your ten thousand hours before that were in education, not in medicine.

JUDITH: Yes.

GORDON: And yours, Stephan, were in healing and medicine. So, it's making sense.

STEPHAN: I actually do not see that much of a difference because on one hand, of course, I'm focused on the illness, but on the other hand, I'm not interested in the illness. I'm also very much interested in stuckness and movement, as before every symptom there is stuckness and movement is a condition for change. This term, illness or symptom constellation, is not coming from me. I do use the symptom to start a process, but as coming from holistic medicine, I'm not really interested in symptoms. So in a way, I'm also interested in where is the energy stuck and how can it be moved? As long as there is flexibility in our body, our body is able to balance, which means, selfhealing takes place. Trauma or being overwhelmed means we are not able to move or react.

JUDITH: It does make me think about how you could teach your methodology to anyone else. It sounds really, really difficult.

STEPHAN: It is like cycling or skiing, once you got it its very simple, but the learning process itself is not easy and it takes a lot of time and training to develop security

JUDITH: This makes you something of a one-off specialist.

STEPHAN: I'm trying to find out the training concepts. I think normally I would need to integrate a way to learn this testing. There are many ways, you know? There's the kinesiology approach, or you can do it with the dowsing route. I'm sure that every good massage facilitator is doing it because it's a basic instinct that we have and we all use it.

NANCY: Well, I feel very humbled as I'm listening to this, and of course you're right, but how to disembed those things we know so that we understand them better and can communicate them is part of the reason why we're putting the book out.

DEBORAH: Yes, and I'm picking up on one piece that Judith brought up, which I have heard you speak of, and that is the image in your head of what the constellation will be. I've heard you say to an issue holder that there is one true image of the family. Timeless. Is that right?

STEPHAN: Well, true is not the word, as it is not about truth at all. Its timeless, in the sense of how you feel related. Recently I watched Marianne (Franke-Griksch) doing this work and she's not setting up anymore. She's not letting the client set up a constellation. When I saw this, I started doing the same. She just asks, "Would you ask someone to represent your father?" And this person stands up, and after a while, is trying to find his position. It works, the client does not need to set up a constellation, the field is there. But sometimes I would like to see how the client sees himself in relation to the illness or in relation to the parents or other family members: this would then be a Constellation, in our usual sense. This gives additional information, but sometimes I think it's also helpful to use this other, simpler way of doing it, just letting someone stand up and search for his own place.

GORDON: Well, we know that human groups do feel each other with great sensitivity, just like in the lobby of a theater or walking through rush hour traffic in a city; we know that human groups self-organize, on the basis of this kind of embodied knowing. So, there's a knowing that's going on there that everyone participates in, that everyone has some access to. It's happening, but it's just that we don't have a very good language for that or a very articulated theory, but we do all know it happens. We're participating in it constantly. Even in a car we can do it, in the flow of traffic, as we interpret others' intentions from subtle cues, just from their driving. Or walking down the street: I very rarely bump into anybody. So all of that is involved, even if we have trouble reducing that embodied knowing to words.

STEPHAN: But coming back to your question, I think when you ask what is a Constellation, I think this cannot be explained unless you include various levels.

On the one hand, it's the externalization of an inner process, and at the same time it's the image of a client, showing how he feels related. On the one hand you can work with how the client perceives himself in relationship to the illness or to other family members, and then there's this aspect of the representatives somehow having access to something that is there, and this brings additional information which sometimes even goes so far that they bring up information which no one in the room has ever known consciously so the client is carrying that knowledge in the body or in the aura, which is also just an expanded body.

NANCY: Often, that happens.

STEPHAN: In our research study, we have found that the quantity of truly new information coming in from the representative is not that much. We experience it as happening often, but when you do a proper genogram for example very often you can find the information also there. Still, there are these other moments where you can say there is a representative bringing in information that no one, so far, has been aware of.

GORDON: Like there's a different father or something like that?

DEBORAH: Or a child that died.

STEPHAN: But especially regarding these revelations, for me the question that is always important is, "Is this really helping?" Because the question I have is, what does the client *do* with the information that 'my grandmother maybe has lost a child' and he has no chance to get clarity about it? No one in his life can clarify it. To deal with such new information assumes a bit of security and stability within the client to deal with things that cannot be verified. Not all clients are able to do this. For me, the attitude of the facilitator here is important. There is always a solution with information or without information. The solution should not be dependent only on the information, on the constellation process, on the expressions of the representatives. So my focus is only on the range of possibilities of the client. What can he or she do? Knowing that our possibilities are limited, when I work with constellations I'm only focused on the question of what the client can do. I'm not interested in creating peace and well-organized systems --

GORDON: -- for their own sake.

STEPHAN: For their own sake, yes.

JUDITH: It makes the words *resolution* or *solution* not necessarily the most helpful ones. Because that does suggest an arc from what's wrong to what's right, and I think if you're thinking in terms of going from not being able to move to being able to move, you might be making things more difficult – and I was thinking about the last one we did this morning where I looked at somebody and I had a very clear picture of him and his family. I had a very clear picture of him in the system of his workplace organization, and of how the two suited each other and kept only a small window of opportunity open. So, if I were thinking in terms of solution or resolution, I would lose him immediately. So I was really thinking, I wonder where something could enter in, almost like a foreign body of more love that could touch him and he could carry with him, to accompany him, as he travels along, rather than being a solution to anything in itself. And I wonder if you do this too, or if it might be more difficult for you because you are dealing with more serious symptoms. I was thinking, sometimes there are very small movements that come out of those images that don't take a lot: for instance with this person, I wouldn't have wanted him to have to do anything much, all at once, given the constraints he is still under. I'm wondering if you also have this idea of steps on the way rather than complete turns.

STEPHAN: Absolutely. In my understanding "Solution" means being able to do *one next step*. Not less and not more. Sometimes you see from homeopathy that the next step is acknowledging what is, nothing more. And then, in this way, the constellation brings something to light, and then you leave the client just there.

JUDITH: So you could say that the methodology and the philosophy of constellation work is to make much more vibrantly clear what *is*, and the framework of that creates more space, more inner space in the client. After that, everything else is extra.

STEPHAN: Yes, absolutely. From my perspective, what I've seen so far is there could be a relationship between the creation of symptoms and interpretations. From my perspective, every interpretation is wrong because as soon as we say, "My mother *is*...," we only see one aspect, and we exclude a lot of other aspects. And even if we say, "My mother is a good person," we exclude a lot of other aspects. And in this way one of the effects of the constellations work is that it "relativizes" our interpretations. It always widens the space and this, in a way, gives us more possibilities.

JUDITH: I did watch you making interpretations. You do make interpretations.

STEPHAN: What do I do?

GORDON: You make interpretations. Naturally. You're a human being.

JUDITH: Last night, you were saying that she needs to turn to the father because the mother's lack of ability to feel her father entails that the client can't be "better than" the mother. Now, that's a big interpretation. There's a lot behind that, isn't there?

STEPHAN: Yes.

JUDITH: That was very helpful for her because she could see in that, both a genuine limitation in her mother, and a genuine act of love in her to hold the two things together. I thought that was a wonderful interpretation. It might've been wrong.

STEPHAN: It is!

Laughter.

STEPHAN: But it can be helpful.

JUDITH: Yes, that's right.

GORDON: By wrong, do you mean it's incomplete?

STEPHAN: Yes, I mean it's incomplete.

DEBORAH: That's what I was thinking, and that's where I see such resonance between both your ways of working. There's so much of the holding lightly to the working hypothesis so that there's room for new information to come in.

STEPHAN: From the basic attitude, you know, I think one of the criteria to do this work in a good way is to be openhearted to everybody that belongs and particularly belongs to the system of the client. And so in this way there are many more persons addressed or involved than actually set up. What you set up in the constellation is only the minimum of what you need to demonstrate something to the client, to show them something, to get them in contact with the relevant relationships. But while this whole process of constellation is going on, I try to stay much connected, for example, with the grandparents who are not set up or to the siblings who are not set up, -- especially when, like we had in this case, one sibling had died. And then after a while maybe the process indicates that it's helpful to bring this person in, in the form of a representative. But in this way, to answer your question, the constellation is much more than what you see. From the attitude of the facilitators, everybody who belongs is present. And the skill is to sense the important relationships. When you bring a representative for a structural element in – like, it can be a symptom, it can be an illness, but it can also be an emotion -- intrinsically, you sense with whom in the system this is related or in resonance. The visible constellation is the tip of the iceberg.

GORDON: I'm thinking I want to share this image, because you are describing something quite similar: I once knew a great storyteller, a great artist of storytelling. And she told stories to children. I was there one time and someone asked how she held the children so spellbound? And her answer was, "Well, you have to understand that I'm seeing the whole story but I can only tell them a few things, a few parts of that, in words. They hear the words, *but they see what I see.*"

STEPHAN: Exactly. That's a nice image

GORDON: She conceived herself as that kind of a channel. What you're saying is making me think of that.

STEPHAN: I think that one question is, of course, "What do we do when we do this work?" And the other question is, "How are we able to teach this work?" These are the basic questions. And then from the method or philosophy that is behind that, the questions of content. What is important to know?

GORDON: Also at that level of "How do we do what we do?", there can be a methodological question, -- but there also can be the question of, "How does the thing *work*? What makes it so effective for people, at times? What's going on?" And obviously there is always an element of mystery. And, there are still the elements that we can talk about.

STEPHAN: I think, for me, one of the great advantages of setting up a constellation is that there is not just the client and the therapist, there is the process of the constellation which the both can look at.

GORDON: That's where I find myself saying that you and your work, both of you, are bringing the right brain online. That's a crude way of saying it, but you're bringing your holistic, imagistic right brain online instead of it being a linear verbal skill. You're getting an all-at-once visual dimension, which for humans has an undeniable power. Verbal/narrative alone doesn't carry this power, it can only reference or evoke it, or put it in a more usable medium for communication to others.

JUDITH: I think what Stephan is talking about is about the "appropriate attitude" that can be set up when you are alongside somebody who has difficulty, and the two of you together are looking at what might help. From this stance, the connection between you and the person that wants help is not clouded by all the projections and hopes and prior experiences and angers that go on, which actually manifest as relational disturbances *in the constellation*. The constellation, almost immediately, drains those projections between you and the client out of the picture. Thus the two of you together have a chance to do something which in one-to-one psychotherapy is incredibly difficult to set up. Even if you set it up (the one-on-one therapy relationship itself), very rapidly you lose the clarity because you are doing too much inviting of yourself to look like a family member or somebody. I often think that constellation isn't very necessary and I could do a lot of the work without the constellation. However, I think the constellation keeps my relationship with the client very clear. That's one of its great functions.

GORDON: I have an image of you, Judith, because I've seen you work so much. On some occasions, the client may be just sitting there, and you are metaphorically side by side, but I have an image of you taking someone arm-in-arm and going strolling through the landscape of the constellation and just commenting on it together, like two tourists.

STEPHAN: Well that`s wonderful, I have a similar image of what the facilitator is doing, but your comment Judith brings me to another point. When I sense during the internal interview that the relationship with a client is not clear you can set up the client and the therapist.

JUDITH: I've seen you do that and it's very wonderful.

STEPHAN: This is sometimes very helpful in order to create a good therapeutic relationship. I've heard quite some facilitators say, "I cannot work with you." And the client doesn't know why. When you just ask him to set up the therapeutic relationship itself, then the client *and* the therapist can immediately see, "It's not going to work like this." Seeing what's going on, the client is not left alone with a statement or an explanation why it's not working. Client and therapist can experience/see it and sometimes can even work out, what's the problem that inhibits a good working process. So you may use the representation as a sort of supervision.

JUDITH: Yes, that's right. I think that a constellation, altogether, is a supervision for me.

STEPHAN: I totally agree. But this also means that the important movement is within the client. This is why, for me, the constellation itself has become less important because, to be honest, we do not know what's going on there. This is why my focus has shifted more and more to the client and how is the client doing with his experience, whatever it is. In fact my main focus is the body of the client, asking myself how is the client doing with what he sees, is he able to integrate or is the body reacting with stress on certain movements or statements of the representatives. The stress in the body leads me to the excluded themes or aspects, as the stress reaction is just a sign of being overwhelmed or needing some time and resources to integrate the excluded or distracted parts. So in this way I see myself doing therapy.

GORDON: But here it seems to me that it's a different conception of what knowledge or knowing is. That is, a facilitator could assume in more of what we might call a more old-fashioned attitude, that there is *a truth* about this system and that that can be revealed and we may reveal it more or less well, and that truth of the system is in some sense pre-existent. And that that's the knowing field. "The *field* knows that." Or, you could think in a more quantum mechanics sort of way that, yes, everything is in the field. The field is everything, but that by itself doesn't help you. The field "knows everything," if you will, in some potential way, but the knowledge isn't our idea of knowledge, which is something organized in a useful way. That's what knowledge is, when we use the word – something you can do something with. And here it's the question, the intention, the concern, that's perhaps co-created by the client and the therapist, that will then organize a certain *type of knowledge* that will become more salient, and that the representatives will participate in. That will all be organized by the concerns of that client at that moment, and that's why you can say it's not an ultimate or total truth. Rather, it's a truth that will be different when there's a different question. Different aspects of the system, even with the same people in it, but with different aspects of those people evoked around a different concern, would have quite a different dynamic. I'm just saying obvious things. The point is, people can really get into the question of, "But how do I know it's *really the truth*?"

STEPHAN: Yes, and this brings me to another answer to your first question of, what is a constellation. In a way, the constellation set up by a client is one reality, one image that the client has, *and* the process of the constellations, the movements of the representatives indicate that its just one reality created by the client or one reality the client is stuck within. But now the client has to recognize that there are more realities, the representatives show that the image the client has is not the only one and usually its not the one that leads forward. So today after all these years of working with constellatioins, I'm mostly interested in what sort of inner images we live, that lead to getting stuck? And how we may change these images in order that we can get more freedom, more space, more possibilities ?

GORDON: I think that a therapy patient is someone who has a story that isn't working. We all have a story. The client's story is of a person that is fixed, where he/she needs to be fluid – and the story doesn't have an obvious opening. As the therapist, you add support and start deconstructing it and it turns out that there begin to be new possibilities.

STEPHAN: Exactly. Instead of "realities" you could also talk about stories.

NANCY: Yes, but the very first question that I would want answered is still, What is "Systemic Constellations?" That's the very first question I'm asked, when I tell somebody I'm taking a workshop, or offering a class. And it's not about describing a constellation. How would you answer that question so that somebody unexposed to any of this could get an idea?

GORDON: Yes, for the BBC, say, how would you answer? Because you only get a sound bite.

JUDITH: I'm hopeless with sound bites. I think that what I can sometimes tell people is that, first of all, as Stephan says, it's a way of locating both problems and solutions as embedded in something much bigger and more connected. It's a dynamic, relational field that helps us address particular problems whether they're problems due to large systems or small systems. We're looking at how to make those dynamics visible, and how to see how a change in any particular part of the system has an effect on every other part. So we are looking at the complexity of how change is set in motion, and we're doing it at a symbolic level, in a way, that seems to help the original issue. That is something that people are very, very interested in. How can you do something in a room that affects the world outside that room? And so it has something to do with our current understanding of interconnectedness -- which is what Systemic Constellations is derived from and feeding off and able to excite.

And I also talk about the fact that, unlike a lot of other intervention methodologies, it draws on the lawfulness of systems so that we're less in a post-modern fog of ultimate choice, infinite choice: we're back in a world where everything has consequences. We've got a slightly more limited, slightly more visible, slightly more directive, more animated way of looking at complex problems. Oh my God, did I just say all that?

STEPHAN: Wonderful.

JUDITH: BBC!

Laughter.

NANCY: So, I have tried to explain what a constellation may look like and the response was, "Well, that sounds just like family sculpture." How is it different from family sculpture?

GORDON: I often say at that point that, "Well, that is one of the sources, in works of Virginia Satir." But a strong difference from the way family sculpture is often used, is that here, instead of people knowing the *story* and then moving more psychodramatically, acting that known story out, the idea here is to get *away* from the story you think you know, which we already know is not helping. To do that, there is a lot of interviewing of the representatives, and lots of use of embodied information. With that information, it's not that it's necessarily so pure and so "ultimate truth." What it is, is *relatively* more free of the preexistent story, either because the representative isn't told the story in the first place, or because the actual client isn't being asked for story comment. What's being asked for is what it felt like when he said that, or she came in, or that one left the constellation: Is it then better or worse? Simple things, not interpretive. Do you believe him – in your body, as an embodied sense of solidity? The representative is being asked for embodied information. And that gives you a fresher look with more new possibilities that were excluded by the established story.

NANCY: Okay, all of this is helpful because I'm trying to think about what someone who has had no exposure to this at all, what do they need? What questions would they be asking before they start to read about constellations themselves?

GORDON: This comes up to me, and you too, several times a week. What is this work? Because there's definitely a buzz about it, nowadays. And that *is* the kind of thing I say in response.

STEPHAN: Well, I often explain to the patients that the advantage is that the representatives do not have the same loyalties. In this way, I very simply explain to them that you can get insights about hidden dynamics in the relationship, for example, between your parents, because your father (who lost his mother) would never express that he has a longing for his mother. He wouldn't let himself say that, because he wants to be present in the family. But the dynamic is there, and this aspect is there, and in the constellation the representative probably would express it. So, you get a different image, or a more complete image, especially about all the things that are unspoken, but present and relevant.

JUDITH: It's very difficult to convey this to these people who come up and ask what's going on. Especially if they haven't got a concept of the field, if they haven't got an active connection with what an extraordinary thing a field is; because otherwise, how do you understand the difference between a representative and a Satir-type role-player? How do you make room for the idea of someone whose body is being directed? It is a very mysterious process, and we just push it aside. After your first constellation on Wednesday night, Stephan, there were people who came up said, "But how can you trust it?" What an extraordinary thing they were watching! This person (the representative) has been in some sense taken over. How do you explain it?

STEPHAN: Well, I'll address this question of "How can you trust it?" I usually just answer that this is not an important question because the client may decide whether it's relevant for him or not. So in this way I think the client orientation is very important, and a lot of problems in this work do come from an attitude that "this is the truth and you now have to deal with it." In this way it's the responsibility of the facilitator to transform the expressions of the representatives for the client so that these things that come up can develop in a helpful way within the client. This brings me to the thing that I wanted to say before. Everybody who wants to use this method needs to make decisions on what he wants to do.

GORDON: Such as?

STEPHAN: Such as: Do I use this method in therapy? Then you have to be aware that this is the tool and not the therapy. Or do you want to get insights, for example, on certain philosophical questions? When you are more interested in philosophical questions you do not need a client!

Laughter.

GORDON: Some people do need an audience though.

STEPHAN: But I think this is one of the problems in this work: that there are clients that come and ask for help for a certain question and then get a philosophical discourse, and then they feel overwhelmed by all these connections, also because the setting and the frame are not clear. I personally decided to use the tool of setting up a comnstellation in the field of therapy, psychotherapy or in the medical field, and this is why the client orientation and the issue orientation is one of the basic...

DEBORAH: -- pillars.

STEPHAN: As I said, some clients ask for therapy and they get philosophy.

GORDON: I would say, perhaps more cynically, they ask for it to be about them and it turns out to be about the therapist.

Laughter.

DEBORAH: I wonder if there's room for a question -- and this is a philosophical question I suppose -- but because I'm interested in field theory and this different way of perceiving our experience as contextual:

I'm curious to what degree you find people get scrambled because this implies a different perception of themselves in the world.

STEPHAN: I understand their confusion. I'm just not too interested.

DEBORAH: Okay, that's good. Good answer.

Laughter.

GORDON: Isn't it so, in a way, what Judith was just saying, that you can't begin to understand it if you don't have a felt sense of what a field is and what it is to participate in a field?

STEPHAN: The question I am very much interested in is if there were good results after a constellation, *why*? What are the conditions for good results? This is one of the questions I would like to talk a little bit about.

JUDITH: Have you written about it?

STEPHAN: About this? No, not yet.

JUDITH: It's incredibly important. I've got boxes of letters and e-mails from people describing good results, but I'm not sure they answer that question.

STEPHAN: I have pointed out this question in the book. And in the working process I tried to describe, and this is why I have put in certain testimonials, to see *when* it worked. But I did not make a special chapter on the conditions for its being useful. For me, one of the important conditions is the relationship between the client and the therapist. The frame where it takes place -- and the frame is created by the attitude.

JUDITH: I was noticing that you did a tremendous amount of nodding all through the work. Both last night and Wednesday night, and I wondered about the function of your nodding.

STEPHAN: Interesting.

JUDITH: And I felt that there was a hypnotic condition set in that activity. I know that people talk about my voice as being something that settles them in a very bizarre way. They could listen to me reading out the telephone directory and it probably would have quite a good effect. Hunter [Beaumont] has studied the Ericsonian principles behind Hellinger's work in terms of setting up a quality of unconscious willingness to get better. I've heard you talk about being provocative about upsetting the frame, and going to the place where there are surprises. I'd love to hear you talk more about what is going on in how you set up those conditions that make it more likely for people to not be able to escape the good effects.

STEPHAN: Well, I mean the frame is one big topic. The process of embodying is another big topic. When you talked about the nodding, I realized that I am not aware of doing it, but the effect that I would hope that it gives is security. All these things are related to each other: the frame, security, the attitude of the therapist, and then the effect on the client to integrate the experience or at least give the new story a chance. First of all, I think that in between I see a loyalty between the representatives in the constellation and the client. The representatives, when they are in contact, only bring up what the client permits, in a way.

To create conditions such that the client can open himself the most is to give him security and to create a frame where he knows he is not judged for anything he is expressing, verbally and non-verbally. So there the position, the attitude of the therapist is very important. The presence is very important. The first thing the therapist needs to have is an understanding of the problem, and taking the problem of the client seriously as it is experienced by the client. On one hand, taking the problem seriously, and regarding it as the best solution the client has. In this way, the client can feel respected with his needs and he will be cooperative, of course. With the experiences I've had in the work with illness, the bonding behavior is very important. I think even if it's just an hour, or if it's a setting of a three-day group, an attachment-oriented attitude is equally important. It means that the client can feel safe. And there, one of the conditions is one stated by a German expression, *Feinfühlichkeit.*

GORDON: Sensitivity, receptiveness.

STEPHAN: Sensitivity, empathy.

DEBORAH: I see it as kindness.

STEPHAN: A doctor in Munich, Karl Heinz Brisch, is running a clinic for psychosomatic and psychotic disturbances for children, which is connected to the university. He has created a counselling-program where he trains the parents to be empathic with their children...

GORDON: We would also call that attunement.

STEPHAN: ...which starts around the 5th or 6 months of pregnancy. The groups of 10 to 12 parents meet once a month, and then slowly the babies get born into the group. They do videotaping with the fathers and the mothers to show them how they can improve their relationship to their baby by bringing them into mind when and how they are connected in a good way. Do you know about this or maybe a similar program? It's called SAFE, (Sichere Anbindung Für Eltern)

JUDITH: Allen Shaw is very big in England, and obviously there are lots of different ways of helping parents who've lost contact, lost that attunement. They can be sat with and helped to actually notice the way that the attunement can be brought back, and a lot of it is done through videotaping. It's incredibly supportive as well. I'd say what we're doing in constellation work is restoring attachment to life through attachment to our parents. That's the essence of the work anyway.

STEPHAN: Wonderful. I totally agree.

JUDITH: In the couples work, that's really essential. It's very difficult to establish adult attachments without those very first attachments being restored.

So, I think one of the differences between you and me, and I may be wrong because I haven't seen enough of your work, is that I train people in constellations to get them more attached.

STEPHAN: You use the constellation as attachment training.

JUDITH: Yes, quite often, and certainly with couples.

STEPHAN: Well, that's one very basic aspect of this work also for me, especially in the sense of a reattachement to the source of life in our ancestors.

DEBORAH: There is also someone in this country who is developing a program in schools called "Roots of Empathy," which involves teaching small children by having mothers bring in infants and teaching the children to attune. Again, it's attunement training.

GORDON: Which they know how to do if they've been parented in that way.

STEPHAN: I mean, you have only seen me working with illness, which is a major theme because of my background in alternative medicine. But no matter in which field you work, couples therapy, the pedagogic or organizational context, I would say, the whole work is about broken connections, that might be restored and unconscious hidden loyalties, bonds, that are not helpful for personal freedom and growth.

GORDON: Definitely. I mean, earlier you said "what are the conditions of good results?" taking us back to that in these last fifteen minutes. Because it's such a visual medium, constellations, I think about how I think of therapy. That's where I've put in my "ten thousand hours" – in relational talk therapy. And where I think that the defining human transaction, and also the defining healing transaction, is "I see you're seeing me." Just "I see you," -- that's not yet a human transaction. But "I see you seeing me" is the intersubjective dimension. It may be a disturbing look. If I see you seeing me, I may have unbearable shame or something. Or fear. Or longing. All the work is there.

JUDITH: Rupert (Sheldrake) is very sold on mirror neurons. He sees it as absolutely essential because that takes it even further. I see you seeing me, and in the act of doing it, I know something about who you are.

GORDON: Yes, absolutely.

JUDITH: It's that last bit that's the really important, lasting bit because there are ways in which I could see you seeing me, but then something about the next step starts muddling us up.

GORDON: Well, I could use that mirroring to know more about that disturbed transaction, potentially for both of us. I could see you seeing me and I could know, or imagine, that you wish me harm, and then that would be a type of interaction, possibly a very pattern-setting one.

JUDITH: We saw it this morning, didn't we, with the father (in a particular constellation).

GORDON: That was so perfect that you picked me for 'purpose' because you were talking about how you couldn't have gotten him to do anything. In fact, I was actually structurally in a position for some time of trying to get that particular man whose constellation it was, to do certain things. Because we worked in the same organization, and he worked for me.

NANCY: When that client had to pick someone to be his father and himself, I wondered if he would consider picking you, Gordon, but you were writing. I wanted to go, "Look up!" You were writing as he looked at you. You didn't look up at all and so he moved on.

GORDON: That's why I was writing!

Laughter.

JUDITH: You could imagine how complicated these constellation events are with all these cross-relationships.

GORDON: I wanted him to get someone he could trust. Our relationship outside the workshop is so fraught.

DEBORAH: I think we may be winding down. We're right at two hours. Is there something else you want to make sure we put on the tape right now?

JUDITH: I want to say that I think what GestaltPress is trying to do with this book is really important, which is to take these books out of the small world of facilitators, and to get them out into the world. There are too many books that have got the same limited audience. To try and go out into a bigger world is really wonderful.

STEPHAN: I totally agree. I hope that we could answer some of your questions.

GORDON: Oh, you really have. That's why I've been pushing those questions that I've been pushing. We're trying to build that bridge, to new students and new readers. Your book, and all of your deep questions and answers in this rich conversation, will serve in that larger endeavor.

REFERENCES

The following authors have formed my understanding of illness and health in a significant way. I feel respect and gratitude to them as important teachers.

Foundational Works on Family Constellations

Hellinger, B. (2001): Love's Own Truths – Bonding and Balancing in Close Relationships. Phoenix, Arizona (Zeig, Tucker & Theisen, Inc.)

Hellinger, B. (2002): Insights – Lectures and Stories. Heidelberg (Carl-Auer-Systeme Verlag)

Hellinger, B. (2002): Der Austausch. Fortbildung für Familiensteller. Heidelberg (Carl-Auer-Systeme Verlag)

Hellinger, B. (2003): Ordnungen des Helfens. Ein Schulungsbuch. Heidelberg (Carl-Auer-Systeme Verlag)

Hellinger, B. (2006): No Waves Without the Ocean – Experiences and Thoughts. Heidelberg (Carl-Auer-Systeme Verlag)

Hellinger, B. & Ten Hövel G. (1999): Acknowledging What Is – Conversations with Bert Hellinger. Phoenix (Zeig, Tucker & Co., Inc.)

Schneider, J. R. (2007): Family Constellations – Basic Priniciples and Procedures. Heidelberg (Carl-Auer-Systeme Verlag)

Hellinger, B. with Weber, G. and Beaumont, H. (1998): Love's Hidden Symmetry – What Makes Love Work in Relationships. Phoenix (Zeig, Tucker & Co.)

Systemic Constellation Work with Ill people

Alex, Ch. (2006): Körpersymptome – was zeigen sie uns? Systemische Aufstellungspraxis (3): S.19-22

Essen, Ch. (1998): Familien-Stellen bei Angstsymptomatik und Panikattacken. In: G. Weber (Hrsg.): Praxis des Familien-Stellens. Heidelberg (Carl-Auer-Systeme), S.305-312

Eidmann, F. (1998): Erfahrungen mit der Nutzung der Konzepte Bert Hellingers als Psychotherapeutin in einer Arztpraxis mit onkologischem Schwerpunkt. In: G. Weber (Hrsg.): Praxis des Familien-Stellens. Heidelberg (Carl-Auer-Systeme), S. 288-293

Eidmann, F. (2001): Aufstellungen von Organsystemen in der Psychoonkologie - Erfahrungen und Hypothesen. In: G. Weber (Hrsg.): Derselbe Wind lässt viele Drachen steigen - Systemische Lösungen im Einklang. Heidelberg (Carl-Auer-Systeme), S. 200-216

Essl, B. (2006): Therapeutic Application of Family Constellation Work for Chronic Illness. The Knowing Field 2006 (7) pp. 5-9

Fehlinger, M. u. Gassner G. (2002): Aus der Erstarrung in die Bewegung... In: Baxa, G. L., Essen, C. u. Kreszmeier, A. H.: Verkörperungen. Systemische Aufstellung, Körperarbeit und Ritual. Heidelberg (Carl-Auer-Systeme)

Hausner, S. (2000): Coincidence or Providence. A Constellation Concerning Neurodermatitis. Systemic Solution Bulletin 2000/1. p. 37

English translation: Hausner, S. (2005): Krankheit und Seele Workshop (Live-Mitschnitt)

5. Internationaler Kongress für Systemaufstellungen. Karlsruhe (Steinhardt Film + Verlag) English translation: Hausner, S. (2007) Heilung aus Einklang Vortrag und Workshop,

6. Internationaler Kongress für Systemaufstellungen. Karlsruhe (Steinhardt Film + Verlag)

Hellinger, B. (1995): Familienstellen mit Kranken. Dokumentation eines Kurses für Kranke, begleitende Psychotherapeuten und Ärzte. Heidelberg (Carl-Auer-Systeme Verlag)

Hellinger, B. (1998): Wo Schicksal wirkt und Demut heilt. Ein Kurs für Kranke. Heidelberg (Carl-Auer-Systeme Verlag)

Hellinger, B. (1998): Schicksalsbindungen bei Krebs. Ein Kurs für Betroffene, ihre Angehörigen und Therapeuten. Heidelberg (Carl-Auer-Systeme Verlag)

REFERENCES

Hellinger, B. (2003): To the Heart of the Matter – Brief Therapies. Heidelberg (Carl-Auer-Systeme Verlag)

Hellinger, B. (2000): Wo Ohnmacht Frieden stiftet. Familienstellen mit Opfern von Trauma, Schicksal und Schuld. Heidelberg (Carl-Auer-Systeme Verlag)

Hellinger, B. (2001): Was in Familien krank macht und heilt. Ein Kurs für Betroffene. Heidelberg (Carl-Auer-Systeme Verlag)

Hellinger, B. & Kaden, M. (Hrsg) (2001): Die größere Kraft. Bewegungen der Seele bei Krebs. Heidelberg (Carl-Auer-Systeme Verlag)

Hellinger, B. & Kaden, M. (Hrsg) (2001): Liebe am Abgrund. Ein Kurs für Psychose-Patienten. Heidelberg (Carl-Auer-Systeme Verlag)

Hellinger, B. (2004): Dimensions of Illness & Health. The Knowing Field 2004 (5) p. 4

Hellinger, B. (2004): Integrating Excluded Persons and Events - Further Thoughts on Illness. The Knowing Field 2004 (5) p. 44

Hellinger, B. (2005): Der höchste Grund der Arznei ist die Liebe (Paracelsus). In: Heilkräfte – 7. Symposium der Paracelsus Akademie Villach. Villach (Verlag KI-Esoterik Geiger & Mirtitsch OEG)

Hellinger, B. (2005): Spiritual Dimensions of Illness and Health, In: Lynch, J.E. and Tucker, S. (Eds.): Messengers of Healing - The Family Constellations of Bert Hellinger Through the Eyes of a New Generation of Practitioners. pp. 269-273

Ingwersen, D. (2008): Psychomatic Symptoms in Constellation Work. The Knowing Field 2008 (11) pp.25-31

Jaruschewski, A. (2006): Symptom-Aufstellungen. Beobachtungen "aus der Werkstatt". Systemische Aufstellungspraxis 2006 (1), S. 28-32

Kutscher, I and Brugger, C. (2006): What's Out of Order Here? Illness and Family Constellations. Heidelberg (Carl-Auer-Systeme Verlag)

Kutschera, I. (2002): Das Herz. Praxis der Systemaufstellung 2002 (2) S. 36-37

Lynch, J. E. (2006): Donor Organs - A Constellation. The Knowing Field 2006 (7) p. 30

Mumbach, B. u. H. Döring-Meijer (2003): Die "früh geborenen Geschwister". Aufstellung von Zahnproblemen. In: H. Döring-Meijer (Hrsg.): Systemaufstellungen. Geheimnisse und Verstrickungen in Systemen. Paderborn (Junfermann) S. 99-106

Prekop, J. (1989) Hättest du mich festgehalten... Grundlagen und Anwendung der Festhalte-Therapie München (Kösel Verlag)

Prekop, J. u. Hellinger, B. (1998) Wenn ihr wüsstet, wie ich euch liebe. München (Kösel Verlag)

Ramos, D. u. Weber, G. (2006) Schlaflosigkeit. Eine eindrucksvolle Fallgeschichte. Praxis der Systemaufstellung 2006 (1) S. 39-41

Ruppert, F. (2002): Psychosis and Schizophrenia: Disturbed Bonding in Family Systems. The Knowing Field 2002 (3) pp. 12-19

Ruppert, F. (2003): Depressionen – Symptome, Ursachen und Verläufe aus der Sicht einer systemischen Psychotraumatologie. München: Katholische Stiftungsfachhochschule München

Ruppert, F. u. Freund, C. (2007) Hyperaktivität und ADHS. Erkenntnisse über die Ursache der Unruhe von Kindern aus zwei Aufstellungsseminaren. Praxis der Systemaufstellung 2007 (1): S. 74-82

Schäfer, T. (2004): Wenn der Körper Signale gibt. Wege aus der Krankheit durch systemische Aufstellungen. München (Knaur)

Sölter, I. (2001): Beispiel einer systemischen Lösung bei einer Tinnitus-Patientin. Praxis der Systemaufstellung 2001 (1): S. 43-45

Sparrer, I. (1999b): Systemische Strukturaufstellungen zu psychosomatischen Erkrankungen. Praxis der Systemaufstellung 1999 (2): S. 30-37.

Sparrer, I. (2002): Körperteile im systemischen Dialog. In: Baxa, G.L., Essen, C. u. Kreszmeier, A. H.: Verkörperungen. Systemische Aufstellung, Körperarbeit und Ritual. Heidelberg (Carl Auer Systeme Verlag)

Weber, G. (2007): Der Tic – Fallbeispiel einer Symptomaufstellung. Praxis der Systemaufstellung 2007 (1): S. 83-88

Walper, G. (1998): Frau hat zum wiederholten Mal Gebärmutter-Myome. Praxis der Systemaufstellung 1998 (2): S. 31-33.

Others

Bassermann, D. (1948): Am Rande des Unsagbaren. Neue Rilke-Aufsätze. Berlin (Hermann Hübener Verlag)

Bassermann, D. (1974): Rilkes Vermächtnis für unsere Zeit. Berlin (Hermann Hübener Verlag)

REFERENCES

Boszormeny-Nagy, I. and Spark, G. (1973): Invisible Loyalties - Reciprocity in Intergenerational Family Therapy Hagerstown (Harper & Row Publishers)

Butollo, W., Krüsmann, M. u. Hagl, M. (2002): Leben nach dem Trauma. Über den therapeutischen Umgang mit dem Entsetzen. München (Pfeiffer Verlag)

Campbell, J. (1972): Myths to Live By. New York (Penguin Putnam Inc.)

Dacqué, E. (1938): Das verlorene Paradies. Zur Seelengeschichte des Menschen. München und Berlin (R.Oldenburg Verlag)

DePhilipp, W. (Hrsg.) (2008): Systemaufstellungen im Einzelsetting. Heidelberg (Carl-Auer-Systeme Verlag)

Eick, K.J. (1990): Homöopathie 2000. Anger (Anger Verlag Eick)

Erickson, M. & Rossi, E. (1979): Hypnotherapy. An Exploratory Casebook. New York (Irvington Publishers, Inc.)

Franke, U. (2003): In My Mind's eye – Family Constlelatino in Individual Thearapy and Counselling. Heidelberg (Carl-Auer-Systeme Verlag)

Fritsche, H. (1954): Samuel Hahnemann. Idee und Wirklichkeit der Homöopathie. Stuttgart (Ernst Klett Verlag)

Fritsche, H. (1979): Erhöhung der Schlange. Mysterium, Menschenbild und Mirakel der Homöopathie. Stuttgart (Ulrich Burgdorf Verlag)

Gadamer, H.-G.(1994): Über die Verborgenheit der Gesundheit. Frankfurt (Suhrkamp Verlag)

Giegerich, W. (1988): Die Atombombe als seelische Wirklichkeit. Ein Versuch über den Geist des christlichen Abendlandes. Zürich (Schweizer Spiegel Verlag)

Giegerich, W. (1989): Drachenkampf oder Initiation ins Nuklearzeitalter. Zürich (Schweizer Spiegel Verlag)

Giegerich, W. (2005): Was heilt? In: Heilkräfte – 7. Symposium der Paracelsus Akademie Villach. Villach (Verlag KI-Esoterik Geiger & Mirtitsch OEG)

Grossmann, K.E. / Grossmann, K. (2003): Bindung und menschliche Entwicklung. John

Bowlby, Mary Ainsworth und die Grundlagen der Bindungstheorie. Stuttgart (Klett-Cotta)

Grossmann, K. / Grossmann, K.E. / Waters, E. (2005): Attachement from infancy to adulthood: The major longitudinal studies. New York (Guilford Press)

Gruen, A. (2002): Der Fremde in uns. München (dtv)

REFERENCES

Hahnemann, S.(1985): Organon original - Organon der Heilkunst. Berg am Starnberger See (O.-Verlag)

Hain P. (2001): Das Geheimnis therapeutischer Wirkung. Heidelberg (Carl-Auer-Systeme Verlag)

Haley, J. (1973): Uncommon Therapy – The Psychiatric Techniques of Milton H. Erikson, MD. New York (W.W. Norton & Company)

Hamer, R.G. (1987): Das ontogenetische System der Tumoren mit Krebs, Leukämie, Psychosen, Epilepsie. Köln (Amici-di-Dirk-Verlagsgesellschaft)

Hellinger, B. & Ten Hövel, G. (2005): Ein langer Weg. Gespräche über Schicksal, Versöhnung und Glück. München (Kösel Verlag)

Höppner, G. (2001): „Heilt Demut - wo Schicksal wirkt?". Eine Studie zu Effekten des Familienstellens nach Bert Hellinger. München / Wien (Profil Verlag)

Holmes, J. (1993): John Bowlby´s attachment theory. London (Routledge)

Ingwersen, F. (2002): Von der Geburt und Hinbewegung zu Systemaufstellungen In: G.L. Baxa, C. Essen u. A. H. Kreszmeier: Verkörperungen. Systemische Aufstellung, Körperarbeit und Ritual. Heidelberg (Carl Auer Systeme Verlag)

Jung, C.G. (Ed. Jaffe, A.) (1961): Memories, Dreams, Reflections. New York (Random House)

Keleman, S. (1985): Emotional Anatomy – The Structure of Experience. Berkeley (Center Press)

Kiss, A. u. Geiger I. u. Kainz M. u. Wössner, B. (2005): Transplantation und Explantation aus psychosomatischer Sicht. In: Therapeutische Rundschau 2005 (62)

Levine, P.A. (1997): Waking the Tiger – Healing Trauma. Berkeley (North Atlantic Books)

Madelung, E. And Innecken, B. (2004): Entering Inner Images – A Creative Use of Constellations in Individual Therapy, Counselling, Groups and Self-Help. Heidelberg (Carl-Auer-Systeme Verlag)

Minuchin, S., Rosman, B. L. and Baker, L. (1978): Psychosomatic Families: Anorexia Nervosa in Context, Cambridge (Harvard University Press)

Rilke, R. M. (1975): Duino Elegies and The Sonnets to Orpheus. (A. Poulin, Jr.)

Rosen, S. (1982): My voice will go with you – The teaching tales of Milton H. Erickson. New York (W. W. Norton and Company)

Satir, V. (1975): Self Esteem. Millbrae (Celestial Arts)

References

v. Schlippe, A. u. Schweizer, J. (2003): Lehrbuch der systemischen Therapie und Beratung. Göttingen (Vandenhoeck&Ruprecht)

Schrödter, W. (1959): Präsenzwirkung. Vom Wesen der Heilung durch Kontakt. Ulm/Donau (Arkana-Verlag)

Schützenberger, A. A. (1998): The AncestorSyndrome – Transgerational Psychotherapy and the Hidden Links in the Family Tree. London (Routledge)

Schusterman, D. H., (2003): Sign language of the soul: a handbook for healing. Cranston, Rhode Island (The Writers Collective)

Simon, F. B. (2001): Die andere Seite der Gesundheit. Ansätze einer systemischen Krankheits- und Therapietheorie. Heidelberg (Carl-Auer-Systeme Verlag)

Sparrer, I. (2007): Miracle, Solution and System – Solution-focused systemic structural constellations for therapy and organisational change. Cheltenham (SolutionsBooks)

St.-Just, A. (2006): Relative Balance in an Unstable World – A Search for New Models for Trauma Education and Recovery. Heidelberg (Carl-Auer-Systeme Verlag)

Stevens, J. O. (1971): Awareness: exploring, experimenting, experiencing, Moab, Utah (Real Peaople Press)

Tomatis, A. (1991): The conscious ear, Barry Town, N.Y. (Station Hill Press)

Upledger, J.E. (2002): Somato Emotional Release – Deciphering the Language of Life. Berkeley (North Atlantic Books)

Upledger, J.E. and Vredevoogd J.D. (1983) Craniosacral Therapy. Seattle (Eastland Press)

Weil, A. (1983) Health and Healing – The Philosophy of Integrative Medicine and Optimum Health. New York (Houghton-Mifflin)

Wickland, C. A. (1924): Thirty Years Among the Dead. Los Angeles (National Psychological Institute)

Zeig, J. K. (1980): A Teaching Seminar with Milton H. Erickson, M.D., New York (Brunner/Mazel, Publishers).

Selected Titles from GestaltPress

Organizational Consulting: A Gestalt Approach
  Edwin C. Nevis

Gestalt Reconsidered: A New Approach to Contact and Resistance
  Gordon Wheeler

Gestalt Therapy: Perspectives and Applications
  Edwin C. Nevis, editor

The Collective Silence: German Identity and the Legacy of Shame
  Barbara Heimannsberg Christopher J. Schmidt

Community and Confluence: Undoing the Clinch of Oppression
  Philip Lichtenberg

Encountering Bigotry: Befriending Projecting Persons in Every Day Life
  Philip Lichtenberg

Becoming a Stepfamily
  Patricia Papernow

On Intimate Ground: A Gestalt Approach to Working With Couples
  Gordon Wheeler Stephanie Backman, editors

Body Process: Working With the Body in Psychotherapy
  James I. Kepner

Here, Now, Next: Paul Goodman and the Origins of Gestalt Therapy
  Taylor Stoehr

Crazy Hope Finite Experience
  Paul Goodman, edited by Taylor Stoehr

In Search of Good Form: Gestalt Therapy With Couples and Families
  Joseph C. Zinker

The Voice of Shame: Silence and Connection in Psychotherapy
    Robert G. Lee & Gordon Wheeler, editors

Healing Tasks: Psychotherapy With Adult Survivors of
Childhood Abuse
    James I. Kepner

Adolescence: Psychotherapy and the Emergent Self
    Mark McConville

Getting Beyond Sobriety: Clinical Approaches to Long-Term Recovery
    Michael Craig Clemmens

Back to the Beanstalk: Enchantment and Reality for Couples
    Judith R. Brown

The Dreamer and the Dream: Essays and Reflections on Gestalt Therapy
    Rainette Eden Fants, edited by Arthur Roberts

A Well-Lived Life: Essays in Gestalt Therapy
    Sylvia Fleming Crocker

From the Radical Center: The Heart of Gestalt Therapy
    Irving and Miriam Polster

The Gendered Field: Gestalt Perspectives and Readings
    edited by Deborah Ullman & Gordon Wheeler (out of print)

Beyond Individualism: Toward a New Understanding of Self,
Relationship, and Experience
    Gordon Wheeler

Sketches: An Anthology of Essays, Art Poetry
    Joseph C. Zinker

The Heart of Development: Gestalt Approaches to Working With
Children, Adolescents, and Their Worlds (2 Volumes)
    Mark McConville Gordon Wheeler, editors

Body of Awareness: A Somatic Developmental Approach
to Psychotherapy
    Ruella Frank

Transforming the way we live
and work in the world

Gestalt
International
Study Center

GISC is a diverse worldwide learning community based on trust, optimism
and generosity. We study and teach skills that energize human interaction
and lead to action, change and growth, and we create powerful learning
experiences for individuals and organizations.

- **Leadership Development**
    - **Leadership in the 21st Century**
    - **Leading Nonprofit Organizations**
    - **Graduate Leadership Forum**
- **Professional Skill Development**
    - **Cape cod Training Program**
    - **Introduction to the Cape Cod Model**
    - **Executive Personality Dynamics for Coaches**
    - **Applying the Cape Cod Model to Coaching**
    - **Applying the Cape Cod Model in Organizations**
    - **Finding Your Developmental Edge**
    - **Women in the Working World**
    - **Advanced Supervision**
- **Personal Development**
    - **The Next Phase: A Program for Transition &
      Renewal**
    - **Optimism & Awareness Essential Skills for Living**
    - **Couples Workshop**
    - **Building Blocks of Creativity**
    - **Nature & Transitions**
- *Gestalt Review*

Launched in 1977, Gestalt Review focuses on the Gestalt approach at
all systems levels, ranging from the individual, through couples,
families and groups, to organizations, educational settings and the
community at large. To read sample article, or to subscribe, visit:

www.gestaltreview.com

For more information about any of GISC's
offerings to read our newsletter, visit:
www.gisc.com